THE CAMBRIDGE APOSTLES
THE EARLY YEARS

THE CAMBRIDGE APOSTLES
THE EARLY YEARS

PETER ALLEN
ASSOCIATE PROFESSOR OF ENGLISH
INNIS COLLEGE, UNIVERSITY OF TORONTO

CAMBRIDGE UNIVERSITY PRESS
CAMBRIDGE
LONDON · NEW YORK · MELBOURNE

Published by the Syndics of the Cambridge University Press
The Pitt Building, Trumpington Street, Cambridge CB2 1RP
Bentley House, 200 Euston Road, London NW1 2DB
32 East 57th Street, New York, NY 10022, USA
296 Beaconsfield Parade, Middle Park, Melbourne 3206, Australia

First published 1978

Printed in Great Britain by
Western Printing Services Ltd, Bristol

Library of Congress Cataloguing in Publication Data

Allen, Peter, 1935–

The Cambridge Apostles, the early years.

Bibliography: p.
Includes index.
1. Brookfield, William Henry, 1800–1874. 2. Cambridge. University – History. 3. Great Britain – Intellectual life – 19th century. I. Title.
LF126.B68A44 378.426'59 78-5014
ISBN 0 521 21803 9

CONTENTS

ILLUSTRATIONS

We should like to thank the following for permission to reproduce the illustrations: the Mansell Collection for Plates 1–4; Trinity College, Cambridge, for Plates 5 and 6; the Provost and Fellows of Eton College for Plate 7 (photograph by courtesy of the Courtauld Institute of Art); a Private Collection for Plate 8 (photograph by courtesy of the Courtauld Institute of Art).

PREFACE

This book deals with the origins and early history of a club at Cambridge, formally known as the Cambridge Conversazione Society, more popularly as the Cambridge Apostles. Although the Apostles are secretive about their membership and proceedings, it is well known that this student discussion group has been a training-ground for a long succession of gifted and unusual men. It is also known to have played an important part in several literary and intellectual movements, the most famous of which is the Bloomsbury Group. My subject is the group of Apostles who first established the club's influential role. This group developed in the years just before the first Reform Bill, and its central figures were Frederick Denison Maurice, Arthur Hallam and Alfred Tennyson.

The book arose from my interest in the social side of Victorian cultural history. Nearly all the artists and thinkers of the Victorian period, like those of any period, were deeply influenced by their social relations with one another. The Victorian intelligentsia consisted of several interconnected communities, one of them a numerous and powerful set of liberal intellectuals whose most notable spokesmen in the eighteen-forties and fifties included Maurice and Tennyson. In the religious controversies that rocked Victorian Britain this group appeared as the Broad Church movement, but this was only one aspect of the role they played in the cultural affairs of the time. Though they held avant-garde opinions they were well-respected members of Victorian society, and through their writings and their work in a number of professions they exerted a persistent force over public opinion. They were especially noticeable in the educational system, and here they found many new members for the group among their students. They not only taught one another: they married into one another's families and promoted one another's careers. In time, this network of personal relationships gave rise to a movement or social tradition of liberal intellectualism, extending from the group that surrounded Maurice and Tennyson to such groups as the Bloomsbury set, who were not only their cultural successors but, in several cases, their descendants.

I learned that this tradition could be traced back to two distinct intellectual coteries of the eighteen-twenties and thirties – at Oxford the so-called 'Oriel Noetics' and at Cambridge the Apostles. The Apostles especially intrigued me, for their influence can be observed in the history of the liberal intelligentsia from the eighteen-twenties down to Bloomsbury. Further investigation of the early Apostles revealed a great mass of manuscript material about them, consisting for the most part of the very interesting and amusing letters they sent one another. Since this material was so abundant and so much of it of interest to others besides specialists in the field, I decided to write a documentary account of the group. This book, then, presents a study in intellectual companionship by telling the story of the early Apostles. Quoting extensively from their correspondence and other contemporary records, it describes the group's principal figures, explains their roles and recounts the origins, development, activities and eventual fate of the group as a whole.

There have been many brief treatments of the early Apostles but only one full-length book, Frances M. Brookfield's very readable but somewhat misleading work, *The Cambridge 'Apostles'* (1906). I have been able to locate all the material used by Mrs Brookfield and much that was unavailable to her. In 1906 Mrs Brookfield had to rely on Wemyss Reid's biography of Lord Houghton; since then a much better biography has been drawn from the Houghton MSS, and they have been given to Trinity College, Cambridge. Excerpts from these papers and from other manuscripts in the Trinity College Library (notably the papers of W. H. Thompson) are published with the kind permission of the Master and Fellows of the College. Mrs Brookfield was sent transcripts of the many letters owned by Mrs Catharine Barham Johnson of Norwich (the granddaughter of both J. M. Kemble and W. B. Donne); her daughter, Miss Mary Barham Johnson, has very generously given me access to the collection itself and has helped me in many ways, especially by taking time from the edition of these letters that she is preparing to give my manuscript the benefit of her expert opinion. And Mrs Brookfield probably did not know of J. W. Blakesley's papers, now owned by his granddaughter, Mrs C. G. Chenevix-Trench, who not only went to the trouble of unearthing them for me but very kindly gave me unrestricted use of this material, almost none of which has ever been published. For permission to quote from hitherto unpublished writings by Donne, Kemble and Blakesley I am indebted to Miss Johnson and Mr Anthony Chenevix-Trench.

Other relations of the early Apostles who have been kind enough to show me family papers or to advise me about the existence and location of manuscripts are Mrs Julius Chenevix-Trench, Major Charles Chenevix-Trench, Mr F. J. A. Cruso, Mrs J. G. Dower, Mr S. H. Grylls, Miss Félicité Hardcastle, Mr M. R. Heath, Miss Elizabeth Lennard, Sir Stephen Lennard, Lord Talbot de Malahide, Mr R. L. Bayne Powell, Professor Joan Robinson, Sir Michael Venables-Llewellyn and Mrs G. M. J. L. Whitmore. For permission to quote from hitherto unpublished writings of Arthur Hallam, F. D. Maurice and W. E. Gladstone I am indebted to Sir Stephen Lennard, Professor Joan Robinson and Sir William Gladstone. Material from the Tennyson Research Centre, Lincoln, is quoted by kind permission of Lord Tennyson and the Lincolnshire Library Service.

I have had access to two partial transcripts of the Society's record books for the period of Arthur Hallam's active membership, and I have also been so fortunate as to have been given a complete list of the early membership of the Society. This list, with some emendations, appears as an appendix to this volume.

I have been greatly helped by scholars in related fields. The late T. H. Vail Motter and the late A. M. Terhune were extraordinarily generous in their advice. I am much indebted to Dr Motter's successor as the editor of Arthur Hallam's letters, Professor Jack Kolb, for his help and especially for his criticism of chapter 9. My colleagues Merrill Distad, Phyllis Grosskurth, S. P. Rosenbaum and W. D. Shaw have been especially helpful, and for their advice on a multitude of matters I am indebted to Colin Butler, Lovat Dickson, J. R. de J. Jackson, Paul Levy, Michael Millgate, Francis Mineka, Christopher Ricks, J. M. Robson, J. C. Thirlwall and Cleve Want.

I am very grateful to Dr Philip Gaskell and his assistants at Trinity College Library, Trevor Kaye and Pat Bradford, for their help, and I should like to record my gratitude to the staff of the Anderson Room, Cambridge University Library; to Mr N. C. Buck of St John's College Library; to the late A. N. L. Munby of King's College Library; to Dr J. S. Lawton of St Deinol's Library; to Mr Thompson, Chief Clerk of the Cambridge Union Debating Society; to Mr G. M. Griffiths and Mrs Kathleen Hughes of the National Library of Wales; to Mr David E. Muspratt, archivist of the Working Men's College; to the staff of the Manuscript Room, Princeton University Library; and to the staff of the Reference Department, University of Toronto Library.

The Canada Council and the University of Toronto provided financial support for my research, and I am also indebted to my Department at the University of Toronto for providing me with the services of a research assistant, Margaret Adelman, who was a great help to me. Gregory Andrachuk helped me with the Spanish sources for chapter 7; Philippa Simpson, Lorna Wreford and Alina Gildiner gave me able secretarial assistance, moral support and advice. My friend Ellen Charney and my father R. O. Allen listened patiently to me and read the manuscript in its entirety: I am deeply indebted to them for their suggestions, from which I have tried to profit. Lord Annan, whose work on the Victorian 'intellectual aristocracy' was one of my original sources of inspiration, has shown great kindness to me and helped me in many ways. My teacher, friend and colleague F. E. L. Priestley not only subjected an earlier scheme for this book to the most searching and helpful criticism but has persistently encouraged me in my work; without his help the book might never have been completed.

Innis College, Peter Allen
University of Toronto, 1977

TEXTUAL NOTE

In the transcriptions of manuscript material that appear in this book I have silently expanded conventional handwritten abbreviations (such as 'wd' for 'would' and '&' for 'and') but have used square brackets in expanding unconventional abbreviations, in interpolating words and letters missing from worn manuscripts, and in adding punctuation and comments of my own. A few distracting oddities of spelling (such as 'agreable' for 'agreeable' or 'it's' for 'its') have been silently corrected.

CHAPTER I

THE SPIRIT OF THE SOCIETY

When it began, nothing could have been more ordinary than the club known as the Cambridge Apostles. Oratory was one of the principal diversions of student life in early nineteenth-century Cambridge, and when the Cambridge Conversazione Society was founded in 1820 it was quite unremarkable among the many debating and discussion groups of the time. Little is known about its first few years, probably because there is little to know. Its earliest members were fairly nondescript students who seem to have held rather unfashionable opinions for the time and place – Tory in politics, Evangelical in religion. Their nickname, the Apostles, was earned at some unknown time in these years and for some unknown reason, perhaps because membership was limited to twelve, perhaps because the members were led by their religious views to give themselves airs as some sort of spiritual élite. Tradition has it that the nickname was a hostile one, but tradition does not say whether it was given in envy or contempt.[1]

About ten years later the Apostles were not quite so ordinary, for theirs had become the pre-eminent club of its sort at Cambridge. The Apostles of the early eighteen-thirties were exceptionally gifted and promising young men, and their political and religious views were markedly avant-garde. A mystique of superiority had grown up around the club, and its original title had fallen into disuse, except on formal occasions. Its members simply called it 'the Society' (rather as if no other might exist), and they revelled in their nickname. The term gave rise to a half-humorous rhetoric used among themselves, in which they, 'the elect' or 'the brethren', belonged to a spiritual world unknowable to non-Apostles, while the single term 'unApostolic' sufficiently described the sort of person who should never be admitted to the Society. New Apostles were made aware of the honour of their election, and great things were predicted of the Society by its members. Whether or not the earliest Cambridge Apostles were distinguished by spiritual pride, their successors certainly were.

For all their pretensions, they would not have appeared to most outsiders as anything more than a very successful (and correspondingly self-satisfied) student club of a certain type, one of the several types that existed to satisfy the current taste for rhetoric and disputation. The largest of these clubs was the Cambridge Union Debating Society, formed in 1815 from three rival debating clubs and boasting a well-stocked reading room where members could meet any day after dinner. On Tuesday evenings during term formal debates were held at the Union before audiences of up to two hundred members, and these debates were imitated in a number of smaller subsidiary debating clubs. In essay clubs like the Apostles, on the other hand, students met for informal discussion of papers given by each member in turn, and there were still other discussion clubs that were little more than casual gatherings.

William Makepeace Thackeray belonged to an essay club when he was at Cambridge, one entirely characteristic of the type. It was founded during Thackeray's second year (in October 1829), began with seven members and grew to nine, met on Friday evenings during term, and lasted for only fourteen of these meetings. Thackeray and his friends discussed all sorts of important questions:

Has woman, since the Fall, been the cause of more good or evil to mankind?

Are works of fiction prejudicial to the moral character?

Has the institution of Duelling been of benefit to mankind?

Was the Elizabethan age deservedly called the golden age of English Literature?

The quality of these papers was far from even, and the attendance of some members, including Thackeray, became erratic. Bad feeling grew within the group, and in March 1830 the meetings were adjourned, ostensibly until October but in fact for ever.[2]

Perhaps Thackeray's club was unusually short-lived; others like it survived for several years. But I know of none that even approached the Apostles' record of survival. For most of its known history the Society had fewer than twelve active members. It had little formal organization – a secretary to keep the sketchiest of records, a system of fines for non-attendance, various rules about electing new members. The scope of discussion was quite unrestricted and (unusually for such clubs) even extended to the explosive issues of religious faith and sexual mores. Yet the Society has lasted for over a hundred and fifty years, for much of that time substantially unchanged in format and purpose.[3]

Although the Society passed through many phases of opinion in its long life, for at least the first century of its existence its meetings resembled those of a small, very informal essay club of the early nineteenth century. On Saturday evenings during term the brethren gathered at the rooms of the member whose turn it was to read a paper. He was usually designated the 'moderator', but it does not appear that he had much to do in restraining disputatiousness. He merely read a short paper, and the members then discussed the subject he had raised or anything else they chose. It seems to have been the custom for each of them to speak in turn, but they could and did say whatever they wanted. Towards the end of the evening a question was formulated and written in the Society's record book; each member signed his name, as agreeing or dissenting or abstaining, and each could add a further written comment if he wished. Something of the range and character of the Society's discussions in its early years may appear from a list of the questions recorded for five consecutive meetings during 1830, when Arthur Hallam was a member:

Has the application of the system of 'The Division of Labour' since the beginning of the reign of George III been beneficial to the country? [Everyone thought it had not.]

Is the practice of Fornication justifiable on principles of expediency? [Only one Apostle thought it was, probably Arthur Buller, who was notorious for his sexual adventures.]

Is the Greek drama founded upon true principles of Art? [Seven members, including Hallam, thought it was, but one did not and one abstained.]

Is suicide under any circumstances justifiable? [Six thought it was not, three thought it was, and two, including Hallam, abstained.]

Are all mankind descended from one stock? [Four thought they were, two abstained, and three, including Hallam, thought they were not.]

In the later years of the Society it became customary to formulate the question in cryptic or facetious terms, but in other respects the meetings of Lytton Strachey's time do not seem to have differed much from those of Arthur Hallam's.[4]

The Society's remarkable longevity was partly due to a distinctive feature of its constitution. When an Apostle resigned from active membership he normally became an honorary member (in later parlance he 'took wings' and became an 'Angel'), but honorary members could attend the weekly meetings if they wished, and the Society held an annual dinner for all Apostles, young and old. From at least the late eighteen-twenties certain senior members played a supervisory, paternal role, and there seem to have been times when the survival of the Society at Cambridge was largely due to their efforts. Even more significant were those members who emerged as the Society's spiritual leaders and who, as honorary members, maintained their ascendancy over successive generations of Apostles.

The most important of these spiritual leaders was the first, Frederick Denison Maurice, who was an active member in the mid-twenties. Maurice's influence was enormous, for he and his followers transformed the Society into something quite different from the sort of essay club Thackeray belonged to. It became an instrument of education so greatly valued by those who had experienced its effect that they actively sought to transmit its principles to the Apostles who succeeded them. These principles, known as the spirit of the Society, were the key to its success, and the spiritual leaders who followed Maurice achieved their influence because they embodied this spirit and gave it new life.

The Society's spiritual leaders were not always the same as those who became its leading members because they were most assiduous in their membership. Rather, they were the few who were noteworthy as being most Apostolic. Since it would have been rather unApostolic of them to admit this, they tended to ignore the fact of their leadership and to attribute great significance to the Society itself. But the other Apostles could tell the difference between themselves and the very few who best represented all the Society stood for. 'Sidgwick says that the Society absorbed and dominated him,' wrote Leonard Woolf, 'but that is not quite the end of the story. Throughout its history, every now and again an Apostle has dominated and left his impression, within its spirit and tradition, upon the Society. Sidgwick himself was one of these, and a century ago he dominated the Society, refertilizing and revivifying its spirit and tradition. And what Sidgwick did in the fifties of last century, G. E. Moore was doing when I was elected.'[5]

The tradition that G. E. Moore and Henry Sidgwick inherited from Maurice and Maurice's immediate successor Arthur Hallam is not easily described. But Sidgwick put his finger on two of its most essential components – 'a belief that we *can* learn, and a determination that we *will* learn, from people of the most opposite opinions'. It was with considerable surprise that Sidgwick discovered these Apostolic traits in Edward Talbot, a High Churchman and Oxonian whom he met in later life. '*I* acquired these characteristics,' he noted, 'in the dear old days of the Apostles at Cambridge; I wonder where Talbot acquired them.'[6]

Sidgwick's surprise was not unjustified, for such a positive and sympathetic approach to other people's beliefs is uncommon, and the Apostles were quite right in thinking that the training the Society afforded was an unusual one. Yet its underlying principles are not difficult to understand, however elusive they may prove in practice. The most important of these principles is the recognition that ideology is a function of personal experience and that opinions are less significant in themselves than the human truth on which they rest. Any thoughtful person is aware that his opinions are not all alike in value. Some of the things we think we believe, especially when we are young, turn out to have been borrowed for the time being, while others express some of the most fundamental principles of our personalities. The problem of deciding what we really believe (and hence who we are) may be particularly acute as we emerge into adulthood, but the task is of course lifelong. It is not likely to be achieved at the level of a mere interchange of opinion with other people, for such exchanges usually demonstrate little more than their relationship to what we conceive to be our present position. A far more useful test of opinions is to explain them in terms that can be shared by someone who thinks quite differently and to accept that his opinions may be based on perceptions as valuable as our own. Not only can we learn more about ourselves from such an interchange, we learn to recognize the valid human needs that may underlie opinions we cannot share. Above all, we learn the difference between conventional or unexamined opinions and those that rest on surer ground.

The training that Apostolic discussions provided gave rise to a characteristically Apostolic view of human personality. 'I fear. . .that he will not be able to make a convert of me to a purer philosophy,' wrote one of the more sceptical of Arthur Hallam's friends, James Spedding, after talking to F. D. Maurice about Maurice's conversion to orthodox Anglicanism. 'I fancy that if I should ever perceive the *dramatic propriety* of his views – their foundation in *his* nature – it ought to satisfy me.' In this view, opinions form the superstructure of personality; they are the visible evidence of an individual's experience and, properly understood, reveal the essential principles of his character. Putting it another way, each individual creates a personal mythology of his own, a distinctive way of viewing the world that results from the interaction of personal character and the circumstances of his upbringing, including the social mythologies to which he is exposed. The Apostles of Hallam's time were of course not alone in thinking that opinion is a product of the organic development of the individual from infancy (and by analogy that the beliefs and customs of social groups derive from their distinctive patterns of history), for these were basic tenets of the Romantic movement that they so admired. They were however unusual in translating this idea into a programme for personal growth through the free interchange of opinion.[7]

Since the whole force of conventional and sectarian thinking is powerfully opposed to such thoughtful, patient exploration of why people think what they do, the Apostles felt that they were freeing themselves from the restraints of ordinary social relations, and when the time came to leave Cambridge they often had difficulty adjusting to the outside world. They did their best to prolong the special relationship they enjoyed with one another, although the circumstances of their lives often made this difficult. Quite typical of the pleasure they found in one another's company was William Johnson's delight on having the routine of an Eton schoolmaster's life interrupted by a three-day visit from a fellow-Apostle, in the eighteen-forties. They talked, according to Johnson, for '24 hours nett' and 'went through several hard subjects in the old Cambridge way, in that method of minute comparison of opinions without argument which I believe to be peculiar to the small intellectual aristocracy of Cambridge. So that those three days have lifted me more than six weeks of mere reading.'[8]

The inner world of the Society was vividly recalled in an autobiographical fragment written by Henry Sidgwick, which contains a classic and often-quoted account of the Apostolic spirit. 'I can only describe it,' Sidgwick wrote, 'as the spirit of the pursuit of truth with absolute devotion and unreserve by a group of intimate friends, who were perfectly frank with each other, and indulged in any amount of humorous sarcasm and playful banter, and yet each respects the other, and when he discourses tries to learn from him and see what he sees. Absolute candour was the only duty that the tradition of the society enforced. No consistency was demanded with opinions previously held – truth as we saw it then and there was what he had to embrace and maintain, and there were no propositions so well established that an Apostle had not the right to deny or question, if he did so sincerely and not from mere love of paradox. The gravest subjects were continually debated, but gravity of treatment, as I have said, was not imposed, though sincerity was. In fact it was rather a point of the apostolic mind to understand how much suggestion and instruction may be derived from what is in form a jest – even in dealing with the gravest matters.'

'I had at first,' Sidgwick went on to say, 'been reluctant to enter this society when I was asked to join it. I thought that a standing weekly engagement for a whole evening would interfere with my work for my two Triposes. But after I had gradually apprehended the spirit as I have described it, it came to seem to me that no part of my life at Cambridge was so real to me as the Saturday evenings on which the apostolic debates were held; and the tie of attachment to the society is much the strongest corporate bond which I have known in life. I think, then, that my admission into this society and the enthusiastic way in which I came to idealise it really determined or revealed that the deepest bent of my nature was towards the life of thought – thought exercised on the central problems of human life.'[9]

Sidgwick does not mention that the Apostolic spirit depended for its effectiveness on the most careful selection of members. The Apostles' methods of recruitment in the late eighteen-twenties have been described by J. M. Kemble, one of the leading members of the Society at that time. 'No one ever knew that he was elected,' Kemble recalled, 'till every actual member was agreed that he should be elected. Temper, moral conduct and good feeling were quite as essential as brilliant acquirements. And at one time, the "Apostles" were by no means distinguished in the University pursuits. One black ball was fatal, and no one ever knew that he was even proposed. We used to make acquaintance with the distinguished men of our time, and if upon that acquaintance, we liked them, and there was a vacancy, we elected them, and then communicated to them the fact. The election was never refused, as far as I know, by any one, when communicated.'[10]

In fact, it was the active members, those in residence at Cambridge, who decided whether a candidate should be elected, although other members might sometimes be consulted. And the Apostles certainly did not insist on 'moral conduct' in any narrow sense, or Kemble himself would not have been elected. Kemble's account may be usefully supplemented by Sir Arthur Helps' memories of the Apostles in the eighteen-thirties, which reveal the extent to which they then sought out specifically Apostolic qualities in prospective candidates:

SIR ARTHUR. The best protest I ever knew made against worldly success was by a small society of young men at college. Their numbers were very few, and their mode of election was the most remarkable I have ever known. The vacancies were exceedingly rare – perhaps one or two in the course of a year – and the utmost care and study were bestowed on choosing the new members. Sometimes, months were given to the consideration of a man's claim.

Rank neither told for a man, nor against him. The same with riches, the same with learning, and what is more strange, the same with intellectual gifts of all kinds. The same, too, with goodness; nor even were the qualities that make a man agreeable any sure recommendation of him as a candidate.

MAULEVERER. What did you go by then?

SIR ARTHUR. I really feel a difficulty in describing to you, and yet I know perfectly what it was.

A man to succeed with us must be a real man, and not a 'sham,' as Carlyle would say. . .He was not to talk the talk of any clique; he was not to believe too much in any of his adventitious advantages; neither was he to disbelieve in them – for instance, to affect to be a radical because he was a lord. I confess I have no one word which will convey all that I mean; but I may tell you that, above all things, he was to be open-minded. When we voted for a man, we generally summed up by saying, 'He has an apostolic spirit in him,' and by that we really meant a great deal.[11]

This painstaking self-perpetuation of an élite was highly effective, for the influence of the Society on most of those admitted to its magic circle is undeniable. 'No society ever existed,' claimed Kemble, 'in which more freedom of thought was found, consistent with the most perfect affection between the members; or in which a more complete tolerance of the most opposite opinions prevailed. I shall say nothing of what the actual and former members of that Society have done; but very few of the distinguished Cambridge men of our time have not been members of it; and it existed to remedy a fault of our University education. Its business was to make men study and think on all matters except Mathematics and Classics, *professionally* considered. Its metaphysical tendency has altered (first in Trinity) the system of University examination itself. The affectionate intercourse of that brotherhood, which continues to subsist in all our altered conditions, is the basis upon which some of my most valued friendships have been founded. To my *education* given in that Society, I feel that I owe every power I possess, and the rescuing myself from a ridiculous state of prejudice and prepossessions with which I came armed to Cambridge. From the "Apostles" I, at least, first learned to think as a *free man*.'[12]

The freedom encouraged by the Society has not always been admired. Another Apostle has found Henry Sidgwick's career 'somewhat depressing', for Sidgwick seemed to have been the sort of thinker 'who so clearly saw all sides that he found it difficult to take any'. And F. D. Maurice's tortuous efforts to accommodate all other forms of thought to his own were often infuriating to those not overwhelmed by the spiritual grandeur of his personality. But these extreme manifestations of the Apostolic spirit did not diminish its value for those who had come under its spell. Faith in the spirit of the Society was almost an article of religion among the Apostles. Some seem to have thought it the key to the reform of society as a whole. Others, more sober, believed it to have acted as a lasting beneficent power over themselves and their fellow-Apostles and, like Sidgwick and Kemble, have attributed the most important part of their education as young men to its influence.[13]

While some people may be irritated by the Apostles' self-congratulatory attitude and their cheerful acceptance of their status as an élite, one cannot deny that the Society has had a very remarkable effect upon some very remarkable people. If its longevity is extraordinary, its membership is even more so. F. D. Maurice, John Sterling, Arthur Hallam and Alfred Tennyson in the eighteen-twenties and thirties; Henry Maine, James FitzJames Stephen and William Harcourt in the forties; Henry Sidgwick, F. J. A. Hort, James Clerk Maxwell, Oscar Browning and G. O. Trevelyan in the fifties; A. J. Balfour, W. K. Clifford and F. W. Maitland in the sixties and seventies; and in the next three decades many names of greater or lesser fame – Walter Raleigh, Goldsworthy Dickinson, A. N. Whitehead, Roger Fry, J. M. E. McTaggart, E. M. Forster, Bertrand Russell, G. E. Moore, G. M. and R. C. Trevelyan, Maynard Keynes, Lytton Strachey and Leonard Woolf. These are merely the Apostles who tend to be remembered today for their accomplishments in one field or another. There have been many others of great renown in their time, and there are many now.

The Society's later development, however, is difficult to trace, for it is supposed to be secret. For the first three decades of its history the Society's affairs were private, but no attempt was made at secrecy, and people at Cambridge generally knew who the Apostles were. But by the eighteen-fifties the Apostles had become too popular for their own good, and they went underground. In 1855 Henry John Roby was elected and, on being asked to attend the meetings in the usual way, resigned from the Society with the excuse that he really did not have time for such things. Roby, it seems, had only been interested in the prestige of being an Apostle. According to Bertrand Russell, Roby was 'ritualistically cursed and his name was spelt thenceforth without capitals'. From that time on, Roby's letter of resignation and the curse on him – supposedly devised by the future theologian and biblical scholar F. J. A. Hort – have been more or less solemnly read to each new member, and each has been bound to secrecy. This ceremony has influenced only a few of the Apostles who have reached the memoir-writing stage of life, and a wealth of information about the Society is to be found in such sources. But an air of mystery has surrounded the Apostles ever since. The Society has become legendary: one is not supposed to know whether it still exists nor who its current members may be. Its proceedings, if any, are strictly secret, its records inaccessible to the curious outsider. One can only conclude that there is still something worth hiding and that, in one form or another, the perfectly ordinary essay club of the eighteen-twenties survives as the treasured rites of a modern set at Cambridge, itself the latest in a dynasty of such sets.[14]

It would be interesting to know whether the modern Apostles bear anything like the same relation to the University as their ancestors. In the days of Maurice and Hallam the Society resembled a cult of modernist thought, with radical notions of social change and great contempt for the old-fashioned views of the University authorities. In time, these Apostles had a decisive influence within the University and (even more) in society at large. They became a powerful coterie of considerable importance in the development of Victorian culture, allied to the Establishment, yet persistently liberal in their influence. But they began as rebellious and dissatisfied students, and the development of the Apostolic spirit had much to do with this attitude.

The Apostles were by no means alone in their dislike of the Cambridge system. The system itself contained some of its most dedicated critics, chief among them a small group of liberal dons at Trinity College, who did much to encourage reform within the University. By the early thirties two of the leading figures in this group, Julius Charles Hare and Connop Thirlwall, had established a number of links with the Apostles, and several Apostles came to join the group, as they graduated, won fellowships and succeeded to college appointments. But the liberals were always a minority in the University, and their influence was usually local or indirect. Major changes, when they came, were often the result of government intervention, for the liberals were faced by a tough, durable and powerful tradition.[15]

In the liberal view a central deficiency of the Cambridge system was its reliance on 'emulation', that is, competition among students for prizes or places in a class-list. In his memoir of John Sterling, J. C. Hare explained why such a remarkable student as Sterling might take little part and less interest in the regular course of studies at Cambridge. 'One of the mischievous consequences,' wrote Hare, in his habitually laborious way, 'from the prevalence of that hollow fallacy, that emulation is the chief spring and spur of intellectual activity, has been to narrow the range of subjects to such as afford the greatest facilities for instituting a comparison among the various competitors, that is, to such as present definite, tangible results, measurable grain by grain... [H]ence it has come to pass that almost the only study especially fostered by the University, and rewarded by its honours, except the various branches of mathematical science, is classical philology, of a somewhat meagre kind, hardly rising beyond grammatical criticism, and the minute details of archaeology.'

One result was the active disaffection of the many students ill-suited for such pursuits. 'When a race is going on,' Hare pointed out, 'they who do not join in it are mostly mere bystanders with no higher object than amusement...[T]hey lose the stimulus, so powerful with the young, of sympathy in a common pursuit: and if they follow any peculiar studies by themselves, they are thereby set in a kind of opposition to authority and established institutions, are led to look upon them with dislike, if not with disdain, and to feel an overweening confidence in their own wisdom. It is often made a matter of complaint, that men of the world, men who act a prominent part in public life, feel little affection for their University. For this there are various grounds; some of them connected with the ordinary temper of the years spent there, which is seldom reverential: but one cause assuredly is, that the University has in many cases done next to nothing for them.'[16]

The academic conditions that prevailed in early nineteenth-century Cambridge would seem rather odd to most of us. There were then three principal ways of taking a degree. One, and the most striking to our eyes, was the honorary degree, open only to noblemen and to those 'fellow-commoners' who could prove their noble descent. Fellow-commoners and noblemen formed the two highest ranks of students, as distinct from the ordinary 'pensioner' as the pensioner was from the lowly and despised 'sizar'. They had the privilege of wearing ornately decorated gowns and of dining in Hall with the Fellows and officers of the college, who generally showed them the respect due to their social rank and were not too particular about enforcing the regular chapel attendance demanded of other students. Students eligible for the honorary degree had residence requirements of only six terms, and the examinations they took were the merest of formalities.

Secondly, one could take an Ordinary or pass degree. Candidates for this degree were faced with a list of academic requirements that any normally intelligent person could master in a few weeks of cramming during the ten terms of residence required by statute. In the meantime there were various sources of amusement – the Union, the river, wine parties after Hall, prostitutes at Barnwell and Castle End, racing at Newmarket, and the traditional diversion of long walks in the dismal flatlands of Cambridgeshire. Though preparation for the final examination could be deferred, it was not unimportant, for even the 'hoi polloi', as the pass men were called, were listed in the order of their success, down to a handful (termed the 'Apostles', when there were twelve of them) listed alphabetically at the end as unworthy of ranking. If one were 'going out in the Poll' it was considered proper to be placed somewhere in the middle, so as not to rise to the miserable eminence of the top of the list (the 'Captain of the Poll'), nor to fall into the company of those at the bottom, whose level of academic achievement was unimaginably low.

Thirdly, one might stand for the Honours degree. Honours candidates tended to take their studies seriously and regarded the undergraduate population as made up of two distinct classes – 'reading' men like themselves and 'rowing' men (rowdies, not rowers, although the term later changed in its meaning and pronunciation). Honours graduates were also listed in order of their achievement, with the exception of an unfortunate few who wrote the examinations but did not come up to the necessary standards and were consequently 'gulphed', that is, listed as falling in the gap between the Captain of the Poll and the two weakest Honours graduates in mathematics and classics (respectively termed the 'Wooden Spoon' and the 'Wedge'). Few could aspire to the top positions in the Honours lists (respectively the 'Senior Wrangler' and 'Senior Classic'), but no one wished to come out at the bottom, and the scramble for places was intense. Their preparation for the examinations included some curious undergraduate arts – for example, 'pacing', or practice in writing at top speed under adverse conditions, for the examinations were always much too long for the time allowed and were written in January in the Senate House, which was unheated. To be 'frozen up' was a common enough disaster: if a student's hands eventually refused to write, no oral examination was provided, and he might well be robbed of the expected safe place in the lists. When one adds that the examiners tended to give rote memorization the first place among academic gifts, the hostility that this system might inspire in some minds is understandable.

The Apostles had a genuine regard for true academic achievement and were some of them redoubtable examination-passers. While they regarded the Honours programme as restrictive, their principal objections were not directed at the narrowness of the system so much as the narrow-minded way it was treated. Hare, Thirlwall and the most senior member of their liberal group, Adam Sedgwick, were almost unique among the dons in taking some personal interest in undergraduates other than the academically gifted or the socially distinguished. The barriers of social rank were felt at every level of Cambridge life. Even the most eminent of the younger dons, William Whewell, found it necessary to protect his dignity by being actively unpleasant to those beneath him. 'To his colleagues Whewell was overbearing, to his juniors arrogant and inaccessible,' wrote one of the Apostles, recalling Whewell's later years as Master of Trinity; 'I never heard that he spoke to an undergraduate save in official rebuke. At his formal receptions in the Lodge ("perpendiculars" as they were called) he stood up radiating repulsion.' Whewell, the son of a Lancashire carpenter, had come to the University as a sizar: although he was a close associate of Hare, Thirlwall and Sedgwick and was capable of being friendly enough in private, he grew away from the liberal group and became a staunch defender of the system to which he owed his success. His liberal friends respected Whewell, but they were insistent in pointing out the social game that he was prepared to defend in the name of education.[17]

It was this lack of concern for education in any more profound sense that most disturbed the Apostles. What they seem to have found especially annoying was that the University, after virtually ignoring the spiritual welfare of most of its students, should claim great social and moral influence over them and should demand the respect due to such claims. Among Apostolic denunciations of these pretensions, Tennyson's sonnet on 'Cambridge of 1830' best captures the indignation they felt at the disparity between appearance and reality:

Therefore your Halls, your ancient Colleges,
Your portals statued with old kings and queens,
Your gardens, myriad-volumed libraries,
Wax-lighted chapels, and rich carven screens,

Your doctors, and your proctors, and your deans,
Shall not avail you, when the Day-beam sports
New-risen o'er awakened Albion. No!
Nor yet your solemn organ-pipes that blow
Melodious thunders through your vacant courts
At noon and eve, because your manner sorts
Not with this age wherefrom ye stand apart,
Because the lips of little children preach
Against you, you that do profess to teach
And teach us nothing, feeding not the heart.

Although Tennyson was later embarrassed by this poem and dismissed it as an example of 'undergraduate irritability', it seems not unreasonable as an outburst of feeling against what he called 'a want of love in Cambridge then'.[18]

For more specific accusations against Cambridge, one has only to turn to the two journals that F. D. Maurice and other Apostles edited and helped to write during the later twenties – the *Literary Chronicle* (1828) and the *Athenaeum* (1828–9). Education was a recurrent subject of Apostolic journalism, and some of their most forceful articles were exposés of the iniquities of Cambridge. Of these the most detailed and effective is a series of open letters to C. J. Blomfield, written by Maurice's disciple, John Sterling. Blomfield, as Bishop of Chester and later of London, had attacked the projected University of London for 'commencing on a principle of excluding Christianity from its walls, and disconnecting religion, for the first time, from the cultivation of the youthful mind'. Sterling replied with a typically Apostolic distinction between beliefs and the emotional principles underlying them – in this case, between theology and religion. Theological instruction, he claimed, has nothing to do with 'the region of men's hearts'. Lectures on doctrines, 'not nourished and animated with religious feeling, are the dead dry husks, fit only for the swine to eat'. If the 'whole efficient and active system of a place of education tends to produce one state of feeling, and that essentially worldly', little is to be gained 'if some miserable rag of theology be sewed upon a garment of such different texture'. Christianity is not something that can be taught: what is needed, for the sake of Christianity, is a thorough-going reform of university education.

'If we cannot at once secure that the pupils will be Christians,' Sterling asserted, 'we may at least do (what has been carefully avoided at Oxford and Cambridge) every thing that will make them conscious of the feeling of moral dignity, and will teach them, that the exaltation of our whole being, by the attainment of truth, is not an aim which can be made subservient to the gaining a salary or a medal. We may take care that they shall feel themselves engaged in a majestic and holy office, when they are inquiring into the manner of the world's existence and of man's, instead of setting before them a piece of dead task-work, cut off from all the breathing and moving frame of universal truth, to be made the means of obtaining so much money, or of gaining a certain vain and wretched pre-eminence over others.'[19]

In the course of his attack on Blomfield Sterling descended to the details of the Cambridge system and the actual extent of the religious instruction that distinguished it from a secular university such as London. While the nominal period of residence for most undergraduates was over three years, they could escape with no more than eighteen months' actual residence during this time, and for noblemen, who (said Sterling) 'have nothing to do in after life except to legislate for the rest of the community, and who may therefore be comparatively ignorant', the requirements were even more lax. For most students the degree depended on only two examinations, the Previous Examination in their second year of residence, and the final or Senate-House examination. Neither made any pretence of demanding theological knowledge or promoting religious truth in any but the narrowest sense. The Previous Examination, for example, 'requires the students to be acquainted with the construing and parsing of some one of the Gospels, or of the Acts of the Apostles, selected and announced more than a year previously. There is similarly assigned to them beforehand, to be similarly studied, one Greek and one Latin classic, that is, perhaps a book of Livy, and one of Herodotus. The only invariable part of the examination is that which relates to Paley's "Evidences of Christianity." The young men are required to understand a portion of the New Testament, exactly in the same way as a portion of Homer or Sallust; and, as to the "Evidences of Christianity," all that is demanded of them is to give the opinion or argument of Paley upon such and such points.' Moreover, Paley's book is hardly likely to produce 'Christian feeling', for he never presents religion as 'a thing to excite emotion and love... but as a matter over which the understanding is as supreme as over the plan of a parsonage or the calculation of tithe'. Again, in the final examination 'there is no pretence of demanding theological knowledge'.[20]

Having disposed of Blomfield's suggestion that Christian instruction was a vital part of the traditional form of higher education, Sterling turned to the chapel services that most students were made to attend eight times a week. He claimed that contempt for religion was the only effect of 'this much-praying ordered by law, these statutory genuflexions', and he went on to reveal the shocking truth about student behaviour at chapel: 'one will be scribbling equations in the Prayer-book, another scratching caricatures on the wainscot, a third reading Harriet Wilson, and a fourth making bets with his neighbour for the next Newmarket Meeting. And all this time what are the words which are passing through their ears, what are the sounds which are becoming desecrated by habit? what but those which express the being and attributes of God. . .At these seats of sound learning and religious education, the students indeed kneel, – to discuss the boat-race, or the cricket-match; – and read the prayer-book, – to make it the subject of profane parodies and ribald comments.'

Not content with these revelations, Sterling then accused the college Tutors of lining their pockets while supposedly supervising the credit allowed students by local tradesmen. As for the Fellows, apparently one could not look at them 'without imagining oneself in a hospital of mental maladies'. Having been successful at his one object in life, that of winning a fellowship, the average Fellow sank into gross lethargy, according to Sterling, 'and the whist-table, the college scandal, the dull carouse of the combination-room, the getting up a petition against Roman Catholic conciliation, the forming a plan for destroying some obnoxious debating-club, supply their utmost of degrading stimulant to all that is left of his decaying sensibilities'. 'He has,' Sterling asserted (in the manner of one not unacquainted with debating clubs), 'made himself a minister of the gospel, because he would lose his fellowship if he continued to be a layman; and God is called upon to erect his tabernacle among the crumbling and weed-clad ruins of a wasted mind.'[21]

Whatever Bishop Blomfield may have thought of Sterling's views, they seem to have been generally accepted by the Apostles. Attacks on emulation as a principle of education, on the use of Paley's *Evidences of Christianity* as a set text, on compulsory chapel, on the hypocrisy and restrictiveness of the Cambridge system, are too numerous to be cited. And in this respect the Society was again led by Maurice, who continued along the lines of Sterling's arguments in a series of further articles that condemn the University as utterly failing to meet its moral and intellectual responsibilities to its students.[22]

To some considerable extent the spirit of the Apostles developed as a response to the spirit of the Cambridge system, as they saw it. In the early nineteenth century the University was rigidly hierarchical, with an exclusive ruling class devoted to an arbitrary, traditional system of rules that ensured the perpetuation of its power. The Apostles were almost entirely informal in their organization; they granted no special privileges (other than a natural deference) to honorary members of whatever social eminence; and they had no rules at all as to what a member might wish to say and another might wish to reply. The University restricted the studies of most undergraduates to classics and mathematics and directed much of its teaching towards examinations that were mainly exercises in the repetition of factual material. The Society's 'business was to make men study and think on all matters except Mathematics and Classics, *professionally* considered'; its method was to demand regular writing of essays on any subject but to offer no reward whatsoever for completing this task, although the rarely invoked penalty of expulsion followed its non-completion. The University claimed the privileges and duties of a parent but expressed its corporate affection for its children through a disciplinary code as harsh as it was ineffective. Members of the Society were one another's brothers – a tradition, not a rule, yet one rarely dishonoured. The University promoted the spiritual welfare of its students by exposing them to Paley's writings and demanding attendance at daily chapel. The Society provided an atmosphere that encouraged self-examination and spiritual development. In short, the Society strove to succeed where the University failed, and the many tributes of its members to its educational significance are evidence of its continued success throughout its known history.

Needless to say, there was rather more to the University than Maurice, Sterling and their fellow-Apostles were willing to admit as young men. But they were not mistaken in thinking themselves the natural antagonists of those who wished to defend tradition in an age of change. Certain members of the University's establishment were much inclined to see a subversive plot in the liberal tendencies of the time, and they were not entirely wrong. The time was coming when the traditional idea of England as a Christian, or rather Anglican, country would give way to religious pluralism, and university education would no longer be a privilege reserved for the male offspring of the Establishment. But the traditionalists fought hard to ensure that this revolution did not come quickly.

It was during this battle against creeping pluralism that the Apostles were first brought to public notice. In the heady days after the Reform Bill of 1832 there was much talk of opening the national universities to people of all faiths or even of none. Thomas Turton, Regius Professor of Divinity at Cambridge, was one of those who sprang to the defence of the status quo. The admission of Dissenters, he argued in a weighty pamphlet of 1834, would lead to intellectual ferment of a sort that might well unsettle the minds of the younger students. Ignoring the fact that admission to the University was in fact open to almost anyone (since the test of allegiance to the Established Church was not demanded until graduation), Turton represented the students as the docile children of the ruling classes, whom he saw as being 'yet sound at heart' in that orthodox Churchmanship still prevailed amongst them, despite the Dissenters' attempts at subversion. The proposed change, he warned, would lead to 'a flood of dangerous speculation and cold scepticism and reckless infidelity overspreading the land'. Turton was answered in an open letter by Connop Thirlwall, who repeated many of the arguments previously used by Maurice and Sterling, with some characteristically ironic additions of his own. The University could scarcely claim, he said, that it really taught Anglican theology to its students, and he suggested that compulsory chapel attendance was much less likely to edify students than to prejudice them against religion. To those alarmists who believed that the issue was, in the slogan of the day, 'compulsory religion or no religion at all', Thirlwall replied that the distinction was too subtle for his understanding. As for the lectures of the Regius Professor of Divinity himself, he assured the public that they were 'perfectly harmless' as instruments of Christian education.

Thirlwall's central point was that moral and religious values cannot be instilled into students against their will and that in this area the students must be trusted to educate themselves. The Apostles seemed to him a good example of this sort of self-education, and in the course of correcting Turton's view of the undergraduate world he described the Society to him, although he was very careful not to name it. 'Perhaps, Sir, the humility of my station gives me some advantage over you in this respect,' Thirlwall wrote, 'by enabling me to learn and observe a little more of what is really going forward in the younger and larger part of our academical world. Of their political debating societies you are no doubt well aware: but you seem to imagine that they have hitherto been perfectly exempt from the dangers of religious speculation and debate, and consequently from "the restless passions, the strife and hatred and vindictive prejudice" which in the mind of young theologians are inseparably connected with such controversies. If you are not acquainted with the fact, you may be alarmed when I inform you, that there has long existed in this place a society of young men, limited indeed in number, but continually receiving new members to supply its vacancies, and selecting them by preference from the youngest, in which all subjects of the highest interest, without any exclusion of those connected with religion, are discussed with the most perfect freedom. But if this fact is new to you, let me instantly dispel any apprehensions it may excite, by assuring you that the members of this society for the most part have been and are among the choicest ornaments of the University, that some are now among the ornaments of the Church; and that so far from having had their affections embittered, their friendships torn and lacerated, their union has been one rather of brothers than of friends. We cannot, Sir, make our young men children; and it is therefore better not to treat them as such.'[23]

Thirlwall's pamphlet infuriated the Master of Trinity College, Christopher Wordsworth, who proceeded to deprive him of his fellowship and his post as College Lecturer. But Thirlwall became a hero of the Whigs for his defence of liberalism against the University establishment, and they found him a comfortable living in Yorkshire and a few years later made him Bishop of St David's, a post he held with great distinction for the rest of his life. Wordsworth, on the other hand, had discredited himself in the eyes of many of his colleagues, but he deliberately deferred his resignation until the Whigs had lost power, so that the mastership went to the conservatively minded William Whewell.

By that time, however, a succession of Apostles had won fellowships and college appointments, and two of them – J. W. Blakesley and W. H. Thompson – were especially instrumental in perpetuating the tradition of Hare, Thirlwall and their liberal associates. On Whewell's death in 1866 Thompson became Master, presided over the College for another twenty years, and played a significant role in encouraging reform. But the real leaders of academic liberalism at that time were a later set of Apostles, chief among them Henry Sidgwick, whose resignation of his fellowship in 1869 was a key factor in bringing about the abolition of religious tests in 1871. The principal targets of the reformers' criticism then changed: the admission of women, not Dissenters, was the big issue of the later Victorian period. Sidgwick and his friends were prominent in the movement that led to the foundation of Newnham and Girton Colleges in the seventies, the opening of University examinations to women in the eighties, and the first major attempt to admit women to full membership in the nineties. In 1887 Agnata Ramsay was ranked above the Senior Classic of that year, although she was not permitted to take her degree. She was promptly married by one of Sidgwick's Apostolic friends, Henry Montagu Butler, who had himself been Senior Classic in 1855, and had now become Thompson's successor as Master of Trinity. Butler remained Master until 1918 and in the early years of this century found himself in charge of a fresh crew of rebellious young men, chief among them the Apostles of that time. And so it has gone.

From the point of view of the history of Cambridge the Society might be imagined as an officially disregarded but nonetheless useful organism evolved by the University in response to its needs, principally that of survival. In the early nineteenth century the University was on the whole resolute in ignoring modern culture, modern thought, modern social and ethical problems, and in regarding them as entirely unsuitable for undergraduate studies. The debating and discussion clubs of the time were not merely an expression of the friendships, rivalries and cliques of student life, but also a natural response to the restrictiveness of the curriculum. Some of these clubs, and the Society in particular, acted as channels through which new ideas of many sorts could reach some of the most intellectually gifted members of each student generation and hence, in time, the University itself. Though conditions altered, the function remained. Throughout its known history the Society has been persistently modernist in its influence, and since the content of modernism alters from one decade to another, the views that have predominated among the Apostles have changed accordingly, from Coleridgean in the eighteen-thirties to Marxist in the nineteen-thirties, and beyond. In theory, the spirit of the Society might be thought to favour no particular set of ideas, but in practice it has encouraged whatever ideas seem vitally important to the active members as a corrective to tradition-bound and conventional ways of thought, and this tendency may well continue to the present day.

CHAPTER 2

THE SOCIETY IN ITS FIRST YEARS

In 1863 Brazil broke off diplomatic relations with Britain, and Britain recalled her envoy, William Dougal Christie, a rather impetuous and tactless man, ill-suited for diplomacy and particularly for such a post. On Christie's return to London he retired from the service, or was asked to retire, and for a time he turned to journalism for a livelihood. Because he had been a member of the Society since the thirties he took some interest in an article in *Fraser's Magazine* for July 1864, whose author spoke scornfully of 'the club or society called "The Apostles," which boasts of having worked wonders in the domain of thought and imagination'. 'It may,' the writer admitted, 'lay claim to a man of genius or two, and several men of talent, as having belonged to the fraternity; but as regards national thought or progress, its annals might be cut out of the intellectual history of England without being missed.' Perhaps the state of Christie's fortunes made him sensitive to such slights, or perhaps he merely needed a subject for his own work. In any case, a few months later he wrote for *Macmillan's Magazine* the first published account of the Society by any of its members.[1]

It was from Christie that the outside world first learned that the Society was founded in 1820 as the 'Conversazione Society' by some students at St John's College, including George Tomlinson, later Bishop of Gibraltar. But he said no more about this early group, for the bulk of his article dealt with the careers of thirty-two Apostles who could not have been among the Society's founders. Since Christie was concerned to refute the accusation of the Society's national insignificance, he mentioned only those members with some claim to eminence and ignored more than four-fifths of the membership up to that time, including some promising younger Apostles who had as yet no established reputations. His silence about the earliest Apostles is especially conspicuous and suggests that he found them of no value for his argument.

It is not surprising that the first members of the Society yielded

Christie nothing better than a single Colonial bishop, for they were not a socially distinguished group. Another Apostle has speculated that the Society could not have been founded before 1824, for otherwise Thomas Macaulay would surely have been a member. But Christie was right and Macaulay was not a member, nor were Winthrop Praed, Derwent Coleridge, Charles Austin or any of the other bright lights of that student generation. Not that the Apostles were entirely unknown among the crowd of talented and ambitious young men who gathered at the Cambridge Union Debating Society in the early twenties, for two Apostles – John Punnett and James Furnival – often spoke at the Union and held various Union offices, including the presidency. But they were the only members of the Society to figure largely in the debates of that time, and on graduation both sank at once into obscure, if no doubt worthy, clerical careers.[2]

So many of the early Apostles became obscure clergymen that George Tomlinson's career may be thought especially notable. Yet even he was about as obscure as a bishop could be. Nor was he very different in character and attainments from the other Apostles of his time. He was industrious, but so were they, and most of them could have held his exalted post just as effectively as he did. Possibly he was more ambitious, and certainly he was luckier in his social connections. In any case, Tomlinson will suffice as a representative of the first Cambridge Apostles, perhaps as a type of the eminence they aimed at and, for whatever reason, failed to reach.

Little is known about Tomlinson's background and early education. He came up to St John's College in January 1819 and was a good enough student to win a scholarship in his third term. He joined the Union but spoke only once, on the conservative side. There seems never to have been any doubt about his future occupation: he was ordained deacon before graduating in early 1823, and soon afterwards became one of the Bishop of London's chaplains. Five years later he made his first modest step upwards by winning the post of tutor to the family of Sir Robert Peel. His connection with Peel was a long one (in fact, Tomlinson administered the last rites to Peel after his fatal accident), and it was to stand him in very good stead.

Three years later Tomlinson made his next move. He became one of the two secretaries of the Society for Promoting Christian Knowledge, and here the mettle of the man began to show, for it was from this humble post that he built the ecclesiastical empire he was to rule. Within a year, Tomlinson had been named a member of a Special

Committee of the S.P.C.K., formed to combat the frightening rise of atheism in the popular press. The committee's answer to this problem was to publish a religious weekly, the *Saturday Magazine*, and a series of 'Family Sermons', one by Tomlinson himself.

Within a few years Tomlinson had founded two other journals of deep interest to Churchmen – the *Clergy List* and the *Ecclesiastical Gazette* – and had become known as an indefatigable worker for the cause of the S.P.C.K. When in 1840 the Foreign Translation Committee decided to explore the possibility of publishing the Bible in the languages of the Near East, it was to Tomlinson they turned. He was sent out from England on a three-month expedition, during which he met the Greek Orthodox Patriarch at Constantinople and assured him that Anglican plans for invading his area of influence were undertaken with the friendliest intentions towards his Church. On his return, Tomlinson published his *Report of a Journey to the Levant*, in which he urged the extension of missionary work to the Near East and spoke particularly of widespread agitation for the establishment of an Anglican bishopric for the whole Mediterranean area. The idea seems to have been a popular one with the S.P.C.K. and acceptable to the government, for in the following year (1842) the new see, based at Malta but named for Gibraltar, was created, and the Prime Minister appointed its first incumbent. The first Bishop of Gibraltar was of course Tomlinson; the Prime Minister, Sir Robert Peel.

A later Apostle, George Venables, has provided a useful glimpse of Tomlinson's work at Malta. According to Venables, Tomlinson was 'a zealous Protestant bishop, whose services were in no degree required by the English residents, while his presence and his title were in the highest degree offensive to the Roman Catholic population'. The Maltese resented Tomlinson's arrival on the scene, and not only the Maltese, for he encountered great difficulty in establishing his authority over some of the existing Anglican churches in Italy. But Tomlinson's energy and self-confidence made him more than a match for his enemies. He travelled widely in his enormous diocese, set up several new churches under his direct control, promoted translation of the Bible into such languages as Arabic, Coptic, Maltese and Armenian, conducted services for the men and officers of the Mediterranean fleet and went as Chaplain General to the Crimea, where he consecrated the cemetery at Scutari and won the Crimea Medal for his contribution to the war effort. After these accomplishments, however, his energy seems to have flagged. Little is heard of him in his later years: when he died in 1863 nobody, except his family and his old comrades at the S.P.C.K., much cared or noticed.[3]

The one occasion on which Tomlinson is known to have had anything to do with the later Apostles provides a good example of his cultural distance from them. In 1847 Henry Lushington was appointed Chief Secretary to the Government of Malta, and for the next eight years he played an important part in Maltese politics. Lushington was a central figure among the Apostles in the period immediately after Arthur Hallam's reign over the Society. A consumptive tendency had barred him from the brilliant legal and political career which might otherwise have been his, but the post at Malta provided some scope for his abilities and a climate then thought suitable for his condition. The political climate was less attractive, for the island was in the midst of a constitutional battle between the ruling British Protestants and the Roman Catholic populace. They formed two equally illiberal, bigoted and violent factions, quite deaf to a voice of reason and calm moderation such as Lushington's. Tomlinson's Protestant ardour made the situation even worse, and it is evident that Lushington viewed 'our apostolical bishop' (as he called him) with some distaste. The two men were separated as much by temper as by political and religious conviction. An unbridgeable gulf lay between the energetic sectarianism of Tomlinson and the 'fine Athenian spirit' ascribed to Lushington by his Apostolic contemporaries.[4]

Nor would Tomlinson's friends have been much more attractive to Lushington's. The early Apostles were nearly all Johnians or small-college men. Before 1823 the Society had in effect moved to Trinity, by far the more fashionable of the two big colleges, and in the next thirty years nearly all the members were Trinity men. Unlike Lushington and his friends, few of the early Apostles came from well-established families. The later Society had several members whose families were not well-to-do or well-connected, but these were generally men of extraordinary academic talent, whereas the early group had no very outstanding scholars. The personal ability or social position of the typical later Apostle generally won him eminence in later life, where he might appear as a prominent figure in any of several professions. The typical early Apostle was ordained within months of his graduation and spent years in humble curacies before obtaining a rural living, to which he clung until he died. Attained or potential social eminence seems to have become a considerable factor in the election of members: one may doubt that many of the early Apostles would have been elected to the Society, had they been students in the early thirties rather than the early twenties.

On the other hand, they might not have wanted to join, for they might well have been offended by the freedom of speech and catholicity of interest of the later Society. The young Gladstone, who heard of the Society through his friend Arthur Hallam, thought the religious overtones of the Society's nickname to be 'somewhat inappropriate and extraordinary'. 'It is said originally to have been an association for supporting missions,' he reported to his father, rather dubiously, and he added, 'It must have undergone a pretty complete metamorphosis, in order to arrive at its present state.' Although this rumour about its origin seems unlikely, one may guess that few members of the early Society would have been happy among the Apostles of the early thirties, who were regarded most distrustfully by the more conventionally pious of their fellow-students. ('The brethren here flourish,' one of the later Apostles wrote, 'to the great disgust of Christ's little flock etc. who have got up a new Hugh of Lincoln story against us, and swear we crucify a child every Saturday Evening, by way of beginning the Night's Amusement.') One cannot be certain of the religious beliefs held by the early Apostles while they were students, but their later careers and the publications of those who published anything both suggest that staunch, orthodox Churchmanship was the key-note of the early group.[5]

By the middle of the century the term 'Churchmanship' would require further definition in terms of the distinct parties that then divided the Church, but in the twenties it was still possible to hold opinions which would later be regarded as contradictory, and in particular to combine old-fashioned High Church opinions with distinctively Evangelical interests. Henry Thompson, third among the Society's founders, was a rigid Tory and a traditional Churchman, who found nothing of particular interest in the Tractarian movement of the thirties, since, he primly said, 'their views, in the main, are the views that have ever been entertained by all well-read Churchmen'. But Thompson was a friend of Hannah More and wrote an excellent biography of her, which praises her work and that of the Clapham sect while claiming that the views of this group owed nothing to Calvinism. The work and opinions of other Apostles, including Tomlinson, suggest an equally distinctive, if not easily definable, figure – a zealous, socially concerned, hard-working, traditional Anglican whom one may term an Evangelical only if one distinguishes the type from the later, more narrowly partisan figure caricatured in Dickens' Mr Honeythunder and Trollope's Mr Slope.[6]

There is much evidence that the later Apostles contemptuously rejected the traditional Anglican views that seem to have predominated in the Society's first years. For them William Paley's *Evidences of Christianity* was an especially objectionable symbol of outmoded orthodoxy, since it was a set text for the Cambridge examinations. One can imagine the amused scorn with which they would have greeted the view of Paley and the eighteenth-century Establishment that appears in Henry Thompson's *Life of Hannah More.* According to Thompson the Establishment had heroically championed Christianity itself against the insidious influence of the French. 'In the universities of our land,' he proclaimed, 'fenced by the cautious appointments of elder wisdom from the intrusion of heresy and schism, the pure deposit of the Christian record was religiously guarded by profound and varied learning. In the Church, deriving its supplies from those untainted springs, the same holy truths were preserved under the same tutelage. Accordingly, the press, the lecture-room, and the pulpit, became every where vocal with the evidences of Christianity, which, but for this aggression on revelation, would never have been called into publick notice. The simple were confirmed; the thoughtless were instructed; the freethinking coxcomb found out that Christianity had learning on its side...A more enlightened and a more zealous Christianity immediately succeeded. Nor did that generation alone reap the benefit of those Christian efforts which the assaults of the French revolutionists called forth. Works which will enlighten the Church to the end of time, the evidential writings of Paley and Porteus, to mention no others, were providentially raised from the chaos of French atheism.'[7]

But it would be unfair to leave Henry Thompson without mentioning that, whatever the insularity of his mind and starchiness of his prose, he was a good scholar and, in a limited sphere, an effective teacher. The early Apostles were not without talent, and one can see signs of the future in some of them. John Stock, for example, who was elected in 1821 and who probably brought F. D. Maurice into the Society, remained an active member until 1826 and seems to have accepted with some enthusiasm the distinctly non-Evangelical phase into which the Society passed. Stock later gained moderate eminence in the legal world; his publications were few but varied, for they include a volume of poetry and a treatise on the law of lunacy.

Another exception to the general rule was the Apostle whose election immediately preceded Maurice's – Erasmus Alvey Darwin, the elder brother of Charles. Erasmus Darwin was an active member of the Society for a very short time (a few months in 1823), and there is no evidence that his membership had any lasting effect on him, for his close friends in later life were not Apostles, and he does not seem to have attended the annual dinners. But in his personality and interests he resembles a recurrent Apostolic type: the sickly, gifted, charming man whose sweetness of disposition almost compensates for his failure to fulfil his early promise and whose ailments almost justify the dilettantism that replaces his intended career. Erasmus Darwin, following in his father's footsteps rather more willingly than Charles, completed his medical training but never practised as a doctor. For the rest of his long life – and he survived to seventy-six – he lived in London, an invalid, almost a recluse, with wide intellectual interests and a small circle of people who found him delightful company. The Carlyles were among his visitors, and Jane 'discerned him to be' a 'perfect gentleman' – an approving judgement that annoyed Mrs R. B. Litchfield (née Darwin) as too obvious to need discovery. But one feels that the phrase borrowed by Mrs Litchfield to praise her uncle – 'an amateur at living' – would not win him the approval of someone like George Tomlinson or Henry Thompson.[8]

The names of Stock, Darwin and a few other early Apostles might suggest that the Society was already drifting into a new phase when F. D. Maurice was elected in November 1823, the thirtieth election in the Society's short history. But the character of this phase was not determined by Maurice, for during the period of his active membership he was no more than the leader of a small clique within the Society. The Society was then composed of a number of cliques, for it had become a club for the outstanding members of the various parties represented at the Cambridge Union. Maurice may have had little to do with this development, since he was not an especially notable figure in the student world of his time. The Society's increasing reputation among the young men of the Union was more likely due to the election of Benjamin Hall Kennedy in 1824. Kennedy was known to everyone at Cambridge and was pre-eminent at the Union as the leader of its largest faction. Kennedy's personality and career made him a symbolic figure for many of those who knew him. He may fairly be taken as the primary example of what was happening to the Society in the mid-twenties.

Kennedy was a man who won high distinction in the academic circles of his time, and academic success was the key-note of his life. He was the eldest of four brothers, all of them Cambridge men. One after another, all four won the Porson prize for Greek verse, and the elder three graduated as Senior Classic. Their father, Rann Kennedy, was a popular Birmingham clergyman, well-known in Whiggish circles. He was also a teacher, and he carefully prepared young Benjamin for Shrewsbury School, which under the headmastership of Dr Samuel Butler was the foremost classical school in England. Erasmus and Charles Darwin were at Shrewsbury with Kennedy, and Charles hated the place. 'I learnt absolutely nothing except by amusing myself by reading and experimenting in chemistry,' he recalled. 'Dr Butler somehow found this out, and publicly sneered at me before the whole school for such a gross waste of time.' Kennedy's career at Shrewsbury was just the reverse: within a year and a half of entering at the age of fourteen, he stood at the top of the school and was Dr Butler's favourite. Competition for the Porson prize was not then restricted to Cambridge undergraduates; Kennedy managed to win it before leaving Shrewsbury and would have won other prizes, had the University authorities not hastily closed the loophole that allowed a mere schoolboy to compete with his elders. Kennedy had to wait until he became an undergraduate himself before going on to win numerous prizes (including the Porson, twice more), in the course of establishing himself as the most proficient classical student of his time.[9]

As one might expect, Kennedy's reputation preceded him to Cambridge, and on going up to St John's in 1823 he found himself courted by some of the more prominent students. In a letter written to his old Headmaster early in his first term he sent his thanks for a letter of moral exhortation from Butler and mentioned that he had met Praed, Townshend and Ord ('the leading members of the Union Debating Society') but that through Butler's 'kind advice' he had 'been enabled to resist the temptation' to join the Union. As for political matters, he assured Butler, 'my feelings on the subject are neither strong nor warm, and my opinions are not such as can injure me. I never make them the theme of conversation.'[10]

By the beginning of his second term Kennedy had become less cautious. He not only joined the Union but took part in a political debate the same evening, and in that year (1824) he went on to become one of the most prominent debaters at the Union, appearing as a speaker at twelve of its nineteen meetings, invariably on the liberal or

Whig side. Despite an early setback at the hands of the Trinity men, who seem to have resented his success, he was twice elected to Union posts, including the presidency.[11]

But Kennedy's enthusiasm for the Union waned as he approached his final examinations. On graduating as Senior Classic in 1827 he turned his attention to the more practical matter of getting on in the world and applied to Dr Butler for a teaching position at Shrewsbury. As he frankly told Butler, he had been unable to win a fellowship at St John's that year. Moreover, he found Cambridge an expensive place to live, and he wished to free himself 'from the oppression of a numerous acquaintance' there. In the same year, at the age of twenty-three, he applied for the headmastership of Rugby, but the post went to Thomas Arnold. After a year at Shrewsbury the fellowship at St John's came his way, and he returned to Cambridge for a time, to tutor undergraduates and prepare himself for the next step towards academic eminence. He was ordained, as was expected of someone with such ambitions, taught for six years at Harrow, then in 1836 succeeded Butler as Headmaster of Shrewsbury, a post he held with great distinction for thirty-three years. But in the end Kennedy returned to Cambridge, where he was Regius Professor of Greek for another twenty-two years, from 1867 to his death in 1889.[12]

Kennedy enjoyed being an Apostle and in later life recalled his years of active membership (1824–7) with great pleasure. But there is no sign that he was much influenced by the Society, and although F. D. Maurice's son recorded that his father regarded the eminent Dr Kennedy 'with the greatest respect', one cannot help suspecting that Maurice, and the Apostles most influenced by him, must have found Kennedy rather unApostolic. His pupils at Shrewsbury have left many accounts of Kennedy, the shrewdest and funniest of which is Samuel Butler's fictional account of his old Headmaster – Dr Skinner of Roughborough in *The Way of All Flesh*. The evidence of other, less satirically inclined pupils suggests that Butler's is a somewhat unsympathetic but not unfair portrait. Dr Skinner appears as a devoted but narrow-minded pedagogue, amusingly unconscious of his own eccentricity and pomposity and perfectly comfortable in fulfilling the reputation he had won so early in life. Butler's tone of mocking admiration suggests the resentment he harboured from his years at Shrewsbury, where, as the great Dr Butler's very unpromising grandson, he had not won Dr Kennedy's approval:

[Dr Skinner] had been a burning and shining light in every position he had filled from his boyhood upwards. He was a very great genius. Everyone knew this; they said, indeed, that he was one of the few people to whom the word genius could be applied without exaggeration. Had he not taken I don't know how many University Scholarships in his freshman year? Had he not been afterwards Senior Wrangler, First Chancellor's Medallist, and I do not know how many more things besides? And then, he was such a wonderful speaker; at the Union Debating Club he had been without a rival, and had, of course, been president. . .It is hardly necessary to say he was on the Liberal side in politics.

. . . . . .

Dr Skinner's pupils distinguished themselves at whichever University they went to. He moulded their minds after the model of his own, and stamped an impression on them which was indelible in after-life; whatever else a Roughborough man might be, he was sure to make everyone feel that he was a God-fearing earnest Christian and a Liberal, if not a Radical, in politics. Some boys, of course, were incapable of appreciating the beauty and loftiness of Dr Skinner's nature. Some such boys alas! there will be in every school; upon them Dr Skinner's hand was very properly a heavy one. His hand was against them, and theirs against him during the whole time of the connection between them. They not only disliked him, but they hated all that he more especially embodied, and throughout their lives disliked all that reminded them of him. Such boys, however, were in a minority, the spirit of the place being decidedly Skinnerian.[13]

Some of Butler's reasons for not publishing *The Way of All Flesh* during his lifetime will be obvious. In the biography of his grandfather that he published in the eighteen-nineties he suppressed his satirical instincts and contented himself with noting that Kennedy chose to cling to Dr Butler's 'emulative system' and regarded it as the key to academic success. As one of those rejected by the system, Samuel Butler was not fond of it, and the Apostles of Hallam's time would have sympathized with him. Kennedy was a remarkable exponent of the traditional system; year after year he turned out proficient prize-winners and examination-passers in classics. But one may doubt that this talent, and his complacent profession of political liberalism and Christian orthodoxy, would win him the esteem of the later Apostles.[14]

If it is difficult to imagine the young Kennedy aspiring to an Apostolic ideal of character, it is probably because no such ideal existed in his time. For the Apostles of the mid-twenties it appears that the talents that went to make a successful Union debater were quite enough to qualify a man for election to the Society. The Society had undergone a great change from its earliest years, when few of the Apostles were well-known speakers at the Union and those who did speak held strongly conservative views. The Union's records show that the change began abruptly in late 1824 (about the time Kennedy was elected), when five Apostles appeared together on the liberal side in one debate. In the next few years Apostolic names became increasingly prominent among the liberal and radical contingents at the Union. By 1827 all three Union offices were held by Apostles, and Apostolic domination of the debates was complete. At one point in that year a debate occurred in which every speaker was an Apostle, although it was saved from tedium by the fact that one of them was then passing through a conservative phase and spoke against the others.[15]

The change within the Society is equally evident from what is known of the Apostles elected after Maurice. At the time of his election the membership was undergoing rapid change, and within a year (again, about the time Kennedy was elected) it had almost entirely renewed itself. Including Maurice, some twenty new members were elected between the end of 1823 and the end of 1826. While it is not easy to generalize about this group of Apostles, one fact is evident – for most of them the Church was no longer the first nor the inevitable choice of profession. Unlike George Tomlinson's friends, they tended towards secular careers and in later life were often eminent in their professions. Many of them read for the bar and then branched from law into politics or the civil service or journalism. Maurice himself became a law student, as did at least six of the seven Apostles elected immediately after him, and four of these eventually rose to hold high legal offices. This group of twenty Apostles includes three Members of Parliament, two fairly eminent journalists, a Chief Poor Law Commissioner, a Fellow of the Royal College of Surgeons, several scholars of some repute, and John Sterling, who is uncategorizable, having been successively law student, journalist, political activist, West Indian planter, clergyman and writer. Including Maurice and Sterling, five of the twenty became clergymen, but all were liberal in politics and theology, and two of these clerical Apostles were outstanding academics, who had to be in orders for the sake of their professional careers. Apostolic names increasingly appeared high on the graduating class-lists of the mid-twenties, and the Society could boast of two Senior Classics in four years.

Some rather curious people became Apostles at this time, among them several whom W. D. Christie may well have known about and deliberately ignored in his public defence of the Society. One was

William Smith O'Brien, an Irish politician with an unremitting dedication to the absurd. O'Brien, a member of an aristocratic Irish family, was first elected to Parliament in the Tory interest two years after his graduation in 1826. He distinguished himself as an M.P. by asserting extreme and seemingly inconsistent political views and by fighting a duel with one of Daniel O'Connell's followers. In 1831 he lost his seat and for some reason came back to Cambridge, where he was elected President of the Union, although he took no part in its debates. In 1835 he was returned to Parliament as M.P. for Limerick, and in the following years he became increasingly prominent as an Irish patriot. By the early forties he had come to agree with O'Connell in seeking independence for Ireland, but his contribution to the cause was, to say the least, quixotic. In 1846 he was subjected to a month's imprisonment in a cellar of Parliament, for having persistently defied the Speaker's orders. In 1848 he made his last speech in Parliament, during which he admitted to being a traitor, 'if it is treason [he said, to the accompaniment of jeers] to profess disloyalty to this house and to the government of Ireland by the Parliament of Great Britain'. When the government began legal proceedings against him and his followers, O'Brien tried to start an Irish insurrection. The main event was the so-called 'battle of Widow McCormack's cabbage patch', a brief exchange of words and bullets with the local police, which ended with eighteen rebels, and no policemen, being killed. O'Brien was arrested, found guilty of treason and sentenced to be hanged and quartered. Not drawn, just hanged and quartered: the practice of extracting a traitor's entrails after half-hanging him had been abolished, but the rest of the gruesome ritual had survived as the mandatory sentence for treason. So far from being daunted by this fate, O'Brien made repeated attempts to be subjected to it, and an Act of Parliament had to be passed to save him from himself by commuting the sentence to transportation for life. Although O'Brien indulged in a number of further shenanigans, he was eventually allowed to return to political retirement in Ireland, where his death in 1864 was celebrated with an elaborate funeral and a near-riot.[16]

It is probably inappropriate to use O'Brien as a representative of the Society of the mid-twenties, since he seems to have been a member for a very short time. But he exemplifies, in an extreme form, the intense, enthusiastic political commitment then shared by many members of the Union and most of the Apostles. Inevitably, the Society came to reflect the character, the balance of opinions, and the factions of the

Union. The majority, in the Union and in the Society, are probably best represented by Kennedy rather than O'Brien. In his taste for disputation, his political partisanship and his ability to blend liberal rhetoric with conventional social values, Kennedy was entirely typical. Other members of the Union may not have matched Kennedy in his complacency, and he himself should not be judged entirely by the opinions of his middle age, but it seems likely that most Union members held similar political views. While the Tories ruled an unreformed Parliament and Catholic Emancipation was the issue of the day, liberal attitudes came easily to young men at Cambridge. But, as one of them wrote in retrospect, this liberalism was largely that of 'the so-called Whigs, who except for two or three popular crotchets to which they had incautiously pledged themselves during their long exclusion from the responsibilities of office, were little other than rather free spoken Tories, who claimed the privilege of speaking evil of dignities to which they were at heart as devotedly attached as their rivals'.[17]

While a rather superficial liberalism, generally but not always professing adherence to the Whig party, predominated in the Union, two distinct minority parties were frequently heard from. A small group of determined, if usually not very talented, speakers defended the Tory cause. A slightly larger and much more significant group expounded the Philosophic Radicalism of Bentham and his followers. Some of the most outstanding speakers of the time were Benthamites, or were then passing through a Benthamite phase in their development, and at first sight, before one notices the voting patterns at debates, they seem the dominant group. But neither the Tories nor the Benthamites could command the support of the house. Undiluted Toryism, undiluted Radicalism and even too distinct Whiggism were not acceptable to the majority of Union members, who preferred vaguely liberal ideas to party dogma. Perhaps a list of some of the questions that came before the house in the mid-twenties, and the votes cast on them, will best illustrate the opinions that prevailed. (It should be noted that such qualifications as 'previous to the year 1800' were merely evasions of a standing rule against discussions of recent political events; soon after the Union was formed in 1815 the popularity of its debates on current affairs brought it under the suspicion of the University authorities, who suspended all debating from 1817 to 1821 and allowed it to resume under the restriction of this rule.):

Is an Elective Monarchy a beneficial form of Government? [No, 121–54]

Is the Conduct of Mr Burke as it regarded the French Revolution consistent and justifiable? [Yes, 94–50]

Was the condition of the Slaves in the West Indies, previous to the year 1800, such as to entitle the Planters to the support of Parliament? [No, 78–55]

Is the Constitution of England, or that of America, to be considered more favourable to the Liberties of the Subject? [The English, 109–37]

Are any dangerous results to be apprehended from the general diffusion of knowledge among the lower orders of Society? [No, 94–7]

Was Parliamentary Reform upon the principle that *Elections* should be *annual*, that the *Vote* should be by *Ballot*, and that the *right of voting* should be enjoyed by *every man who could read*, desirable in the year 1805? [No, 46–9]

Ought the Catholic Claims to have been granted previous to the year 1806? [Yes, 52–40]

Is the law of Primogeniture entitled to support? [Yes, 51–25]

Would it not be desirable, for the happiness and prosperity of this Country, that all Revolutionists, Republicans, and Radical Reformers, should migrate from this land, and colonize in some other quarter of the Globe? [No, 56–53]

Is an Hereditary Aristocracy beneficial to Society? [Yes, 39–20][18]

Although it is often hard to tell what such votes mean, the general drift of opinion can be gathered from this sample of Union debates. Within the Society itself, so far as is known, Whiggish liberals like Kennedy were very much in the majority. But the other parties were represented, for two Apostles – George Patton and James Farish – appear to have been Tories, and two others – John Wilson and John Sterling – to have been Radicals, with some leanings towards Benthamism. In time, Sterling became F. D. Maurice's most devoted disciple and did even more than Maurice himself to transmit his ideas and his concept of the Society to the next generation of Apostles. But when Sterling was elected to the Society in late 1825, all this was to come, and there is no sign that he was chosen for any other reasons than those usual at that time, that is, his concern for party politics and his eloquence as a debater. In one of their rare points of agreement, Sterling's biographers, J. C. Hare and Thomas Carlyle, both deplore the state of his mind as an undergraduate. 'In later years,' says Hare, 'speaking of the crude opinions on morals and politics and taste, which he held when he first went to College, he told me that, while a boy, he read through the whole Edinburgh Review from its beginning; a diet than which hardly any could yield less wholesome food for a young mind, and which could scarcely fail to puff it up with the wind of self-conceit.' Carlyle, less wordily than Hare but no less disapprovingly, says that the life of Sterling's circle at Cambridge 'seems to have been an ardently speculating and talking one; by no means excessively restrained within limits'.[19]

Of all the schemes that might be hatched by such a varied lot of speculators and talkers, perhaps the least likely to succeed was the scheme they tried. In November 1825 appeared the first number of the *Metropolitan Quarterly Magazine*, a substantial journal which, from its title and its use of the Temple Bar as frontispiece, might appear to be an attempt by London journalists to rival the famous quarterlies of the period. In the leading article the supposed editor, one Ralph Rennett, announced the new journal's aim. He asserted, in 'defiance of the general diffusion of steam and education', that the age was an age of folly. The corrective he proposed was one of universal satire and the inculcation of proper literary values. Unfortunately, the remaining contents of the first number suggested all too clearly that the writers were young, inexperienced, uneven in talent and uncertain in purpose. Not surprisingly, the *Metropolitan Quarterly* lasted for just four numbers.

The editors of this short-lived journal were F. D. Maurice and his friend and fellow-Apostle Charles Whitmore. 'Ralph Rennett' was on that occasion John Stock, and the contributors include nearly every Apostle known to have been a member of the Society during the year of the quarterly's run. Maurice and others wrote reviews and lengthy articles on the tendencies of the age. Kennedy wrote some dreadful verse and a defence of the public-school and university system against the republican and subversive attacks of the *Westminster Review.* Whitmore seems to have scribbled incessantly, and many Apostles tried their hand, with no great success, at whatever was needed to fill up space. No doubt the demands of the journal were oppressive – each number ran to about 250 pages – and it appears that contributions to it may have partly replaced the usual Apostolic essays, for the number of essays written for the Society drops sharply at this time. The results of all this effort, however, are not especially instructive or entertaining, except for a few exercises in parody and light verse – forms of writing more suited to undergraduate abilities than the weighty political and literary judgements that make up most of the journal.[20]

But the *Metropolitan Quarterly* is not entirely uninteresting. The Apostles recruited a few other contributors, mostly Cambridge men, and one of these was Samuel Taylor Coleridge's second son, Derwent, who with Praed, Macaulay and others had recently taken part in a similar but more distinguished student venture – *Knight's Quarterly Magazine* (1823–4). Derwent Coleridge's contributions to the *Metropolitan Quarterly* consist of two excellent critical essays on Wordsworth and Shelley, in which he attempts to explain the work of these poets to a somewhat hostile public. Derwent Coleridge was not himself an Apostle, but he may have been a considerable influence on F. D. Maurice. Maurice was acquainted with S. T. Coleridge's writings before he came up to Cambridge, and in the course of his stay there he had become an ardent anti-Benthamite and a proponent of Coleridge and the writers associated with him. Maurice's contributions to the *Metropolitan Quarterly* foreshadow this development in his thinking, which was to lead to the formation of a distinct group within the Society. The 'mystics', as the group was nicknamed, comprised those who followed Maurice in holding that social regeneration would come not through political change but through the spiritual influence of modern literature, specifically the writings of Coleridge, Wordsworth, Shelley and Keats. Under the leadership of Maurice and John Sterling the mystics became a predominant influence in the Society and the basis for the Apostolic cult that developed around the figures of Arthur Hallam and Alfred Tennyson. But this was a later development: no single set of values or attitudes appears from a reading of the *Metropolitan Quarterly*. The only major point of agreement is one that might have been expected from an assortment of young speculators and talkers of the Cambridge variety – a brash assertion of their own importance and their superiority to popular and conventional notions.[21]

Not much is known about what went on within the Society until about 1828, but it would appear that the formation of the mystic clique was a gradual one. At the beginning of 1827 only three active members remained of the group that had begun the *Metropolitan Quarterly* – Maurice, Sterling and Edward Romilly – and these senior Apostles probably had a good deal of influence over the elections of this time. Edward Romilly, a son of the famous liberal reformer Sir Samuel Romilly, was a product of King Edward's Grammar School at Bury St Edmunds, then a highly regarded school among people with avant-garde leanings. A succession of Burians became Apostles in the mid-twenties, among them John Mitchell Kemble (the eldest son of the actor Charles Kemble) and his close friend William Bodham Donne. Kemble, Donne and two other of the Society's new recruits – Richard Chenevix Trench and Joseph Williams Blakesley – became closely associated with Maurice and Sterling, and these six Apostles formed the nucleus of the mystic group. But it should not be thought that the members of this little group were in agreement with one another from the first or that they were all disciples of Maurice in the way Sterling was. Taken as a whole, the Society continued to be a somewhat random assortment of Union debaters and their friends, and the cause of the mystics slowly developed in the midst of a club centring on the Union and its affairs.[22]

When Kemble, Donne and Trench came up to Cambridge in the Michaelmas term of 1825, all the officers of the Union and several of its best-known speakers were Apostles. In the course of that academic year Kemble, Trench and two second-year men, Charles Buller and Spencer Walpole, established themselves as important debaters, and at the beginning of the next year they were joined by a startlingly gifted freshman, Thomas Sunderland. The prominence of these men at the Union was probably one reason that they were among those chosen by the Apostles as places in the Society fell vacant towards the beginning of 1827, and their membership in the Society helps to explain why Apostolic involvement with the Union seems to have reached its height in that year.[23]

The various factions of the Union continued to be represented in the Society. Spencer Walpole was a strong Tory, not only then but throughout his long career in politics (one with a somewhat inglorious culmination, for it was he who has gone down in history as the Home Secretary who was supposedly reduced to tears by the Hyde-Park rioters). Charles Buller was as strong a Radical and equally devoted to party politics. Although he had been tutored by Thomas Carlyle before coming up to Cambridge, Buller was an ardent Utilitarian, who began his political career soon after graduating and rose to a position of some eminence before his early death. Buller remained a favourite among the later Apostles. He had, among other valuable qualities, the endearing characteristic of never appearing to take himself seriously, and this, while it greatly annoyed his fellow-politicians, gave him a perspective on his own opinions that the Society found congenial.[24]

Gradually such traditional political factions as Tory and Radical became secondary, within the Society itself, to the ideological factions of mystic and Benthamite. But the rivalry was largely a friendly one, and at least two of the new recruits of this period became accepted members of the later Apostolic inner circle, although tainted by Benthamite opinions. Arthur Buller, Charles' younger brother, was a handsome, flippant fellow whose lively personality and numerous sexual exploits made him the affectionately regarded clown of the group. The Apostles' letters abound with stories about Arthur Buller and humorous deprecation of his behaviour. 'The Bullers have returned from Germany,' says one such letter, 'and I am sorry to say that I have heard of no improvement in Arthur's morals. I did not expect that he [would] get nearer to virtue than the contempt of half-crown copulation but I did hope he would reach this point.'[25]

A more important acquisition for the Society was James Spedding, a schoolfellow of Kemble and Donne at Bury St Edmunds and later a central figure in the group that surrounded Arthur Hallam. He regarded the mystic cause, as he regarded most things, with amused cynicism, but good feeling was always more important to the Apostles than ideological differences, and in character few men could have come closer to the Apostolic ideal than the amiable and witty Spedding. In the later Society such differences of opinion were a matter for joking, as one can gather from a letter written by Blakesley to a fellow-mystic in 1830, when both Sterling and Donne were on the point of marriage. 'What a quantity of truth will be propagated,' said Blakesley, 'if all the wise and good follow the example of these two. They were both mystics. – Thank God, the Bullers, Spedding and the rest of the Utilitarian party remain in single blessedness.' 'The wise and good' is Apostolic slang for the Apostles themselves, including the Utilitarians, and Blakesley was far from serious.[26]

It is obvious that to be Apostolic did not preclude holding distinct political and social opinions. Nonetheless most of the Apostles of the early thirties were in substantial agreement with one another, and the views that prevailed amongst them were directly inherited from the mystic clique. The main reason for this was the mystics' success at promoting their views in the *Literary Chronicle* and the *Athenaeum*, the two journals that Maurice and Sterling edited in the late twenties. But the relative unanimity of the group also resulted from the negative influence of a very strange Apostle, Thomas Sunderland, who did his best to cause conflict within the Society. Largely because of Sunderland, the Apostolic spirit became more fully defined as demanding that one should not put forth one's personal views in such a way as to disrupt friendships or inhibit one's own development.

Sunderland also played his part in the development of the Apostles' view of the Union. Up to 1830 Apostles continued to figure largely at the Union, but by the end of that year they had almost entirely deserted it. Evidently they had come to regard it as unApostolic, and they maintained this attitude until the late eighteen-forties. It had become important to select members on the basis of their potential ability to sympathize with one another, and to avoid the factionalism that prevailed at the Union and that had reached an extreme in the person of Sunderland.

Thus the Apostles' involvement with journalism and the Union, during the late eighteen-twenties, played a large part in the development of a predominant form of thought and a single concept of the Apostolic spirit. Although F. D. Maurice later came to think of both debating societies and periodicals as forms of madness akin to the party feeling he loathed, both were essential to the Society's development. Yet Maurice's association of madness and debating has a curious and specific relevance, though he could not have known it, for the most outstanding debater of them all, Thomas Sunderland, was indeed on the edge of madness.[27]

CHAPTER 3

THOMAS SUNDERLAND AND THE CAMBRIDGE UNION

Like so many of the Apostles of the late eighteen-twenties, Thomas Sunderland was the product of an established family and a good public school. He was the eldest son of a provincial clergyman – a pluralist and squarson in the fashion of the time, who held at the same time four ecclesiastical posts in different parts of England and lived comfortably on the family estate at Ulverston, Lancashire. An early friend of Sunderland's recalled that even as a young man he showed remarkable powers of conversation, 'coupled however with some degree of originality of thought and tenacity of opinion' and coupled also with a delight in argument for its own sake. Sunderland went to Rugby at the same time as Charles Whitmore, but this point of contact with one of the Apostles is not needed to explain his election to the Society, for his dominance at the Cambridge Union might well have been enough. He came up to Cambridge in 1826, joined the Union at once and spoke at the second meeting of the term. It must have been an extraordinary performance: the conservative side, on which he was the last of four speakers, won overwhelming support for a change, and Sunderland had the unusual honour of opening the following week's debate and, moreover, of proposing and opening a debate on his own motion just two weeks later. But this was only the beginning, for he was to make over thirty-five speeches at the Union before he suddenly disappeared in mid-1831. The opinions he expressed were always extreme, yet wholly changed their character during his second year at Cambridge. He 'made his *début* as a Jacobite,' recalled one observer, then 'afterwards turned into something like a Jacobin'. But, whether Tory or Radical, Sunderland held the house spellbound with the brilliance and fluency of his oratory.[1]

Sunderland was elected to the Society at the end of his first term, in December 1826, and it appears that he quickly established himself as a disruptive force. During 1827 John Sterling and Edward Romilly went down, with the result that the active members were nearly all recently elected men. Early in the following year the most recently elected of all, J. W. Blakesley, had become sufficiently upset by Sunderland's behaviour to seek advice. In the absence of senior members at Cambridge, he wrote to Sterling. 'My dear Blaksley [*sic*],' Sterling replied, 'I am extremely sorry to see from your note that you are not satisfied with your position in the apostles as regards the *μεγα θηριον* [great beast] Sunderland. I do not believe that his manner towards you indicates anything else but his general cold superciliousness. I am very anxious that you should not desert the camp – especially as the numbers are just now so diminished – and I have been consoling myself with the idea that you would be one of the firmest supports of a society which I am sure has produced more pleasure and advantage to myself and others than any thing I can remember. Pray do not blench when the storm blows high – but you may throw over Jonah as soon as you please. Seriously if Sunderland runs restive and attempts to overmaster the other members I think he ought to be immediately expelled, or the society be dissolved and reconstructed without him.'[2]

But the principles of free thought and speech within the Society prevailed, and the other Apostles did nothing more about Sunderland than keep a distrustful eye on him. 'Sunderland, quis credit, is turning Transcendentalist again,' Kemble told Donne in 1829: 'he has already mounted up through presentations, sensations, conceptions and notions and cognitions within sight of the Deity, and thinks Christianity a very fair style of thing, and the Trinity a tolerably passable notion, there are therefore you see hopes of him still.'[3]

Although Kemble had himself experienced a recent change in his religious views his tone was far from friendly. Sunderland's intellectual vagaries met with distrust rather than sympathy because he cultivated an inhumanly distant, self-consciously amoral manner. The horrified fascination he inspired in the Apostles is perfectly captured in a character sketch of Sunderland written by Tennyson:

A CHARACTER

With a half-glance upon the sky
At night he said, 'The wanderings
Of this most intricate Universe
Teach me the nothingness of things.'
Yet could not all creation pierce
Beyond the bottom of his eye.

. . . . . .

He spake of virtue: not the gods
More purely, when they wished to charm
Pallas and Juno sitting by:
And with a sweeping of the arm,
And a lack-lustre dead-blue eye,
Devolved his rounded periods.

Most delicately hour by hour
He canvassed human mysteries,
And trod on silk, as if the winds
Blew his own praises in his eyes,
And stood aloof from other minds
In impotence of fancied power.

With lips depressed as he were meek,
Himself unto himself he sold:
Upon himself himself did feed:
Quiet, dispassionate, and cold,
And other than his form of creed,
With chiselled features clear and sleek.

Most disturbing of all was Sunderland's systematic violation of the spirit of the Society: it was this that caused Sterling to think of him as the beast of the Apocalypse and Trench to call him the Judas of the Apostles.[4]

The undergraduate experiences of another Apostle, Richard Monckton Milnes, help to explain the role played in the Society by Sunderland and throw a good deal of light on the Apostles' relation to the Union at the time that Sunderland was pre-eminent among its debaters. Milnes was an attractive if apparently insubstantial person – a vain, charming, lightheaded dilettante, somewhat eccentric and disarmingly unaware that anyone might find him ridiculous. When he became an Apostle in 1829, Blakesley (by then a senior member) thought him no great gain to the Society. The judgement may have been reasonable in the circumstances, but this somewhat unpromising recruit proved to have more value than first appeared. Milnes was a compulsive collector of new experiences, people, mementoes, records. To this Boswellian tendency in him we owe the first biography of John Keats; the same tendency gave him in time an important role in the Society's history, and it led him, on hearing of Sunderland's death in 1867, to unravel the mystery of what had happened to him after his sudden disappearance in 1831.

None of this could have been apparent in 1827, when Milnes was eighteen and first came up to Cambridge – a somewhat effeminate, playful, rather pretty youth, so filled with a sense of his own importance that one could hardly dislike him for it. Milnes at once set out to explore the undergraduate world, with the aim of moving in all the best circles as soon as possible. Having entered Trinity as a fellow-commoner, he was careful to cultivate friendships among the dons and young aristocrats whose company he gained by his privileged status. But he was even more interested in the Union. His father had been a Tory M.P. who, years before, had quixotically deserted a brilliant political career when it had scarcely begun. Richard Milnes longed for the glory his father had forsaken, and planned a quick launching of his career as politician and orator.

In those days the Union held its weekly meetings in a room later described by Milnes as a 'low, ill-ventilated, ill-lit apartment, at the back of the Red Lion Inn – cavernous, tavernous – something between a commercial room and a district branch meeting-house'. A typical evening is brought vividly before our eyes by a contemporary observer, although his account lacks one essential point – that the behaviour of the young men of the Union often owed as much to drink as to political enthusiasm:

Suppose this to be Tuesday, the –th day of —, and behold the 'Union' in all its glory. A long, low room, with three or four rows of benches down the sides, and the President's chair at one end, exhibits a muster of perhaps two hundred members. Tables with candles stand in the centre, and the orators are generally congregated near them. After some minutes spent in private business, the President announces, that 'the question for this evening's discussion is, – ought the claims of the Roman Catholics to have been granted previous to the year 1808? The opener is at liberty to begin.['] (*Order*, *order!*) My friend Williams rises, with his eyes upon the ground, and his hands upon the ballotting-box. (*Hear*, *hear*, *hear!*) – 'Mr President, I should not have proposed this question to the society, had I thought that it was commonly discussed elsewhere on the proper grounds. This question is, in fact, a contest between the people and the aristocratic monopolies, which scarcely even pretend to represent the people,' etc. etc., and so on for half an hour. Then rose Mr Billingsgate, a soft-voiced young gentleman of large fortune, and a fellow-commoner; yet, though a fool, a favourite with the society. 'I protest, Sir, against the use of such expressions as those which have been expressed by the honourable gentleman. They are decidedly unconstitutional; I say, Sir, they are decidedly unconstitutional. I maintain, Sir, that the House of Commons does fully and fairly represent the people. By the people, I do not mean the rabble, but persons of birth, influence, fashion and fortune. The glorious constitution, Sir, is composed of three powers, all exactly equal to each other, and yet no two of them superior to the third. I consider that the speech of the honourable gentleman was decidedly unconstitutional, and in favour of the bloody papists, and ought to have been interrupted from the chair.' (*Hear, hear, hear, and loud laughter.*) Then am I seen to rise, or some moderate, well-informed, and eloquent member, and the assembly is stilled into silent expectation. The discussion is restored to its proper path, the opposing arguments are admirably balanced, and the whole question is settled in one rolling accumulated peroration.

An evening of this kind seldom terminates without a supper party.[5]

Milnes' first evening at the Union was just such an occasion. Sunderland had spoken the week before and kept his peace this time; an ambitious freshman, J. C. Symons, undertook to open the debate, in which a lone Tory faced eight supporters of Catholic Emancipation, two of them Apostles and another a noted writer of prize poems, T. E. Hankinson. The next day Milnes wrote home and reported the event: 'I went last night to the Union for the first time to hear the Catholic claims debated. It was opened by a freshman, who made a complete failure of the attempt, but some of the speaking afterwards was very tolerable. Charles Kemble's son was energetic and fluent and a Mr Sterling told us we were going to have a revolution and "he did not care if his hand should be the first to lead the way" – but perhaps the best, was a Mr Hankinson, who wrote a poem last year on the Druids, which Grandmama admired, whose whole speech was one continued strain of sarcasm and irony, so well managed that an Honorable Gentleman rose and begged to know "which way the Honorable Member intended to vote[.]" At the very fullest there were about 200 in the room and on the whole there was a great deal more declamation than argument.'[6]

Milnes lost no time in plunging into the debates. Indeed, with that chameleon-like quality that always distinguished him, he entered so thoroughly into the Whiggish spirit of the Union as to disguise his Tory background and opinions. Not content with eminence at the Union, he joined a number of private debating clubs and towards the end of his first term at Cambridge managed to attend three debates on the same day.

By the beginning of his second year Milnes had become almost too well known at the Union. Although he told his parents that he might have been elected President that term and had stepped aside only because his opponent was a third-year man who would not have another chance to run, one may doubt that the other members took him as seriously as he took himself. However, there was the new lot of freshmen to impress, among them one or two promising young noblemen and Arthur Hallam, who as the son of the famous historian Henry Hallam was almost equally interesting to Milnes. Moreover, Arthur Hallam had something of a reputation of his own, from his days at Eton with W. E. Gladstone and Milnes' cousin, J. M. Gaskell. Although Milnes at first found Hallam 'reserved, deep, and quiet', he had no trouble in striking up a friendship with him and introducing him to one of the private debating clubs he belonged to. Within a few months he regarded Hallam as one of his two closest friends and (he admitted to his parents) 'the only man here of my own standing, before whom I bow in conscious inferiority in every thing'.[7]

It was this sort of temporary victory of good sense over vanity that won 'Dicky' Milnes the amused affection of his friends. In fact, Hallam's mind, with its extraordinary range of talents, independence of judgement and absolute commitment to the pursuit of truth, was not on the same plane as Milnes'. The difference between the two young men is evident even from their first reactions to the Union. Milnes saw the Union simply as a curiosity and as another place to make his mark. After a few weeks at Cambridge and a single evening's debate, Hallam drew up an assessment of the Union's moral and intellectual significance, for the benefit of his equally serious-minded friend, Gladstone of Christchurch College, Oxford. 'Now for the Union,' Hallam wrote. 'Its influence, as might be expected, is very much felt here, extending even among reading men, who have actually no share in it, but are modified in one way or another by its spirit. That spirit I consider as bad. You will take this of course as a Freshman's judgement, who as yet is not competent to say *much* from experience: but what I have seen I dislike. The ascendant politics are *Utilitarian*, seasoned with a plentiful seasoning of heterogeneous Metaphysics. Indeed the latter study is so much the rage, that scarcely any here at all above the herd do not dabble in Transcendentalism, and such like. Their Poetic creed has undergone many revolutions, I understand: but at the present day *Shelley* is the idol before which we are to be short by the knees. For my own part, I am sorry my taste is so stubborn, but I cannot bring myself to think *Percy Bysshe* a fine poet.'[8]

By the end of his first year, however, when he was elected to the Apostles, Hallam had become 'a furious Shelleyist'. That summer he arranged for the publication of Shelley's 'Adonais' in England and gave out copies to friends and whatever converts he could make to the new cause. In the following November he, Milnes and Sunderland took part in a memorable debate – the Cambridge–Oxford debate on the relative poetic merits of Shelley and Byron. On this occasion Gladstone voted with the Cambridge men in favour of Shelley, spent the rest of the evening and part of the next two days talking to Hallam and Milnes, yet on their departure confessed himself unsure of 'the Cambridge philosophy' to which his old friend had become a convert.[9]

The Apostles' ambivalent attitude to the Union and to debating helps to explain the involvement of Milnes and Hallam with a figure like Sunderland and their conversion to a distinct way of thought in which Shelley was a central figure. On the one hand, the Apostles were increasingly repelled by the factionalism ruling the Union and carried by Sunderland into the Society itself. On the other, they were increasingly attracted to the ideas of F. D. Maurice and the mystic clique, and by the summer of 1828 the mystics had gained an important means of expression for their ideas, first in the *Literary Chronicle*, then in the *Athenaeum*, with which the *Chronicle* was merged. Whatever their reservations about public debating, Maurice and his followers could not ignore such a useful vehicle for telling their own generation about their avant-garde views on the social function of modern literature, and they went out of their way to encourage debates on suitably Apostolic subjects. But the vehicle was a difficult one to manage and in the end proved altogether too much for them.

The first such Apostolic debate on the subject of poetry seems to have occurred at the Union in May 1827, when John Sterling proposed, opened and (despite the opposition of Charles Buller) carried a motion attacking 'the Character and tendency of Lord Byron's Poetry'. Disapproval of Byron was as much an article of faith with the mystics as was enthusiasm for the other great Romantic poets. 'I rejoice to h[ear] you are studying Wordsworth,' Richard Trench wrote to Milnes in the Long Vacation of 1828; 'he brings the mind to a sound and healthy tone; do you not find him and Byron as the opposite scales of a balance – as the one rises, the other must necessarily sink[?]'[10]

During Milnes' first year the Apostles had arranged two further debates on general literary matters, but their first attempt to debate their specific doctrines came the next year, in November 1828, when J. M. Kemble proposed the question, 'Is Mr Wordsworth or Lord Byron the greater Poet?' The attempt, however, came to nothing, for the Union's official record tells us, 'No discussion took place on this question as the President deemed it necessary to dissolve the Meeting in consequence of the turbulent state of the Society.' The minutes of the meeting reveal the difficulty: in the discussion of private business which preceded the evening's debate and which normally ended at a fixed time, the Treasurer had been accused of irregular behaviour and had attempted to resign. Feelings ran so high that no one would listen to Kemble when the President asked him to stand up and begin the debate. Kemble walked out in a fury, and the President thought a hasty adjournment the best course of action. The following week he faced a written protest against this decision, but he refused to entertain it on the very reasonable grounds 'that the names attached to the protest had previously been signed to another protest; from which they had been cut off and tacked on to the one now brought before the Society'.[11]

Cambridge in the later eighteen-twenties was hardly a place for rational discussion of any contemporary issue, much less that of modern poetry. Towards the end of 1828, student clubs, each with its distinctive dress, were (according to Milnes) 'all the rage here', and his aristocratic friends looked 'like livery servants in their different costumes'. Of these cliques the most prominent was a group of ardent supporters of George IV, calling themselves the Brunswick Club and headed by Lord Norreys and by one of the Duke of Wellington's sons. This High Tory faction was to play an active part in the Apostles' next attempt at a debate on poetry. Earlier that year, J. C. Symons (the unlucky freshman of Milnes' first visit to the Union) had proposed a motion favouring legislative action against cruelty to animals. Symons, it appears, was an admirer of that extraordinary politician, Richard 'Humanity' Martin, an Irish M.P., once a friend of George IV but estranged from him over the affair of Queen Caroline, more persistently a friend to animals, having brought in several laws on the subject and having helped to found the R.S.P.C.A. in 1824. Symons' motion won the support of Kemble but was attacked by Sunderland and four other Apostolic speakers, and rejected by the house. Nonetheless, R. C. Trench revived the subject some months later, though the motion as he proposed it took a somewhat ludicrous form.[12]

'We had a capital debate last night,' Milnes told his family, 'on the subject "Will Mr Coleridge's poem of the Ancient Mariner or Mr Martin's acts, be most effectual in preventing Cruelty to Animals."? It was opened with some very deep poetical criticism by a friend of Coleridge's [R. J. Tennant, an Apostle] – then a great unpoetical

Kingsman [L. S. Orde, of Queens' College, not King's] tried to turn the poem into ridicule and I answered him. Sunderland followed me with the most absurd strain of hyperbolical radicalism ending "To give the people an opportunity for developing their poetic sympathies, we must give them a liberal education – to give them this we must overthrow an aristocratical government" – Then Mr Symons – "he knew Mr Martin well – he would not compare his senatorial abilities with the silly production before them – he knew Mr M was actuated by the best of motives, – Mr M had been much hurt by the aspersions cast upon him in that society" etc.etc.etc. – much better however than I ever heard him before. – then a clever utilitarian speech [by Joseph Carne of Trinity] and lastly, a most eloquent commentary on the poem itself from a very superior man [J. W. Blakesley], which so won on the hearts of the House that when he read the last verse, the cheering was tremendous. Coleridge however would not have carried it had it not been for the Brunswickers, who arrived in full Orange badges to vote against Martin.' But it was a close thing, for the Union record reads, 'Votes *for Mr Martin*, 45; *for Mr Coleridge*, 47.'[13]

A few weeks later the Brunswickers appeared in force at a debate and managed to reduce the Union to an unprecedented level of disorder. 'The Catholic question was discussed at the Union last Tuesday,' Milnes reported in another letter home, ' – the debate had been adjourned from the previous week, when Norreys made a very good speech on the Brunswick side and FitzRoy also spoke – last Tuesday a clergyman, a great friend of mine [W. G. Cookesley, one of the four Apostles who spoke against the Brunswickers], answered him most beautifully, and cut him up very serenely – I had intended to have spoken, but the tumult grew so great about 10 o'clock, that it was impossible to make a word heard – and the room was so full that there was a division into the yard – this was a most noisy proceeding – all kinds of cheers and groans mingled together – on one side, Norreys screaming out "three cheers for the Church and State" and Savile – "3 cheers for Lord Eldon" – on the other FitzRoy bawling "three for the Pope" and little Wentworth squealing "3 for Ireland" – all which were reciprocally answered by groans and hisses. The tellers at last appeared at the windows and announced that the votes were a majority of 10 against the Catholics, but the yell of the victory of the Brunswickers had not subsided, when one of the tellers came forward and said that owing to the confusion, a mistake had been made and the votes were 46 in favour of the Catholics – the change of countenance was ludicrous. . .I had no idea that the majority would be so small, but the canvassing on that side had been most vigorous.' In fact, the confusion was even greater and the majority even less, for the official record shows that the final vote was 143–114 in favour of emancipation.[14]

While debate raged at the Union, Milnes was taking steps towards joining that most select of Cambridge sets, the Society itself. By the summer following his first year he was in friendly correspondence with Trench. Early in his second year he told his parents, 'I see a good deal of Kemble – not a moment is lost in his society, I feel quite attracted to him.' During this year he became friends with Hallam, some time before Hallam formed a more lasting and important friendship, that with Alfred Tennyson. At the end of the academic year (in May 1829) Hallam became an Apostle; Tennyson and Milnes were elected the following October. Milnes was proposed for membership by Arthur Buller, with whom he may have had a more than friendly relationship. A note from Buller to Milnes survives from their undergraduate days: beginning 'My Dearest Richard' and ending 'Yours lovingly', it consists of homosexual ribaldry and contains a pretty explicit invitation.[15]

During 1829 Milnes also became increasingly Apostolic in the more usual, ante-Stracheyan sense (for in those days homosexuality was not itself regarded as being particularly Apostolic); that is, he was increasingly drawn to the mystic clique and their way of thought. He read the Romantic poets, became preoccupied with metaphysical questions and, when he was set a Latin declamation, chose as his subject 'The Truth of the Essential Dualism of Heraclitus', much to the amusement of his Lecturer in classics, J. C. Hare. '[A]s this subject penetrates to the very foundations of Coleridgian philosophy,' Milnes confided to his family, 'it will give me some hard Fagging.' However, he found time to write some reviews and poems for the *Athenaeum* and to spend some time in London with Sterling, Kemble 'and all the Athenaeum men'.[16]

As John Stuart Mill records in his *Autobiography*, Maurice and Sterling had by that time become prominent in the London Debating Society as 'Coleridgians', a distinct group on the liberal side, yet equally opposed to Benthamite and Tory thinking. In the mental crisis from which he was then slowly recovering, Mill had found much solace in Wordsworth's poetry and, like the Apostles, had learned to dislike Byron's influence. But his friend J. A. Roebuck, a more rigid Benthamite, had (Mill says) 'a strong relish and admiration of Byron, whose writings he regarded as the poetry of human life, while Wordsworth's, according to him, was that of flowers and butterflies'. 'We agreed to have the fight out at our Debating Society,' Mill goes on, 'where we accordingly discussed for two evenings the comparative merits of Byron and Wordsworth, propounding and illustrating by long recitations our respective theories of poetry: Sterling also, in a brilliant speech, putting forward his particular theory.' Milnes was present on the second evening and told his parents that the 'London Union does not seem half so good as ours – Stirling [*sic*] spoke splendidly and Mill made an essay on Wordsworth's poetry for 2 hours and ¾s, which delighted me – but all the rest was meagre in the extreme'.[17]

With Maurice and Sterling to inspire them in the *Athenaeum* and at the London Debating Society, the Apostles continued to pursue their cause at the Cambridge Union, but not very successfully. In May 1829 five Apostles – Milnes, Sunderland, Blakesley, Tennant and Richard Barnes – told the house the right answer to the question, 'Has the spirit of Mr Shelley's poetry been beneficial to mankind?' but attendance was poor and the response negative (30–19). In November of the same year Milnes, Hallam and Blakesley tried again, on the question, 'Is Wordsworth or Lord Byron the greater Poet?' and were rebuffed by a vote of 50 to 23. J. C. Hare thought the vote for Wordsworth too large, for in his view there were not twenty-three men in the room worthy of being true Wordsworthians, but this opinion was little consolation for the Apostles. Later that month, however, they discussed within the Society itself the problem of whether Shelley's poems have 'an immoral tendency' and agreed (8–3) they had not.[18]

During this term Gladstone had formed an essay club at Oxford in direct imitation of the Apostles, and between the two groups the idea arose of sending a Cambridge delegation to the Oxford Union to join in debate on the relative merits of Shelley and Byron. On 26 November 1829 the Apostles' three best public debaters – Milnes, Hallam and Sunderland – left Cambridge on the Pluck coach and that evening spoke at the Oxford Union, drawing an audience of well over a hundred, double the usual attendance there.

Some of the participants in this historic debate rather considerably embroidered their later accounts of it. In later life Milnes – then Lord Houghton – was not sure that he had not obtained permission to leave Trinity during term time by letting the Master, Christopher Wordsworth, think that the three undergraduates meant to defend his brother William's poetry, not that of the infamous Shelley. In 1866 Henry

Manning – then Archbishop of Westminster – paid exaggerated tribute to the Cambridge men in the *Pall Mall Gazette*: 'We Oxford men were precise, orderly, and morbidly afraid of excess in word or manner. The Cambridge oratory came in like a flood into a mill-pond. Both Monckton Milnes and Arthur Hallam took us aback by the boldness and freedom of their manner. But I remember the effect of Sunderland's declamation and action to this day. It had never been seen or heard before among us: we cowered like birds and ran like sheep.'[19]

Sir Francis Doyle, who had proposed the motion and opened it in favour of Shelley, provides another and soberer account: the three Cambridge men all spoke very well, but the decisive speech was that of Manning, whose argument, says Doyle, 'amounted just to this: Byron is a great poet, we have all of us read Byron; but. . .if Shelley had been a great poet, we should have read him also; but we none of us have done so. Therefore Shelley is not a great poet – *à fortiori* he is not so great a poet as Byron.' The argument struck home, for the final vote was 90 to 33 in favour of Lord Byron. 'Both parties cheered loudly,' according to one participant, 'as both were quite satisfied with the result.'[20]

At about this time in his undergraduate career Milnes, whose susceptible nature was plain to anyone who knew him, found himself courted by Sunderland, who evidently nursed plans for weakening the Society by electing members unsuited to its friendly atmosphere. A note to Milnes, undated but probably written in the Christmas vacation of 1829, refers to A. W. Kinglake, later well known as the historian of the Crimean War but never known as a sociable person:

My dear Milnes

I called on you today to talk to you about securing Mr Kinglake's election to the apostles –

I still think the best plan will be to say nothing about the matter to the other men till a day or two before our first meeting. Then I will ask them *separately* and as they will not have time to concert a rebellion en masse, I have no doubt we shall succeed perfectly. But if we fail in doing the thing good-naturedly, why we must e'en *drive* them into it. Therefore pray don't say anything about the matter at present.

. . . . . .

We really must introduce some one among them, who is not so vulgarly gregarious as the larger portion of our worthy brother-apostles.

Ever yours faithfully

T. Sunderland[21]

Kinglake was not elected, but Sunderland did not stop trying to change the character of the Society. A letter from Kemble to Trench recounted the final attempt he made before going down after his graduation in 1830. Kemble mentioned that Charles Buller had become an M.P. and, as might be expected of him, had retained his sense of humour and his independence as a Radical thinker. 'You will see him make a figure some of these fine days, depend upon it,' concluded Kemble, before turning disapprovingly to Buller's fellow-Radical, Sunderland: 'Not so [Sunderland], except, indeed, it be in the pillory, for distributing of seditious pamphlets. [Sunderland], who, like Caliban to this Stephano, would kiss his foot and worship him, raves about a certain piece of clockwork, called the "Rational Intuition," which his dam's god Setebos has just discovered, and with which he means to prove God Almighty a liar on the very first opportunity. There are wagers, however, that [Sunderland] will never be let through the gate of heaven to try the experiment. Conceive this precious associate of ours. . .trying to introduce into the Apostles the preposterous custom of making three balls instead of one necessary for the exclusion of a member. As might be very well expected, this was rejected.'[22]

'So [Sunderland] has tried to betray the Apostles,' replied Trench. 'A Judas! His measure was precisely the one which might have been expected from [Sunderland], whose entire conduct showed that he could not, or would not, understand the principles on which the Society was based. I rejoice to hear the Society flourishes, and now that you have cleansed it of that perilous stuff it should flourish more.'[23]

'Sunderland has gone to the Isle of Man,' Milnes informed his father early in 1830, 'to live there some time in perfect solitude "to expatriate himself as much as he can," he says, "from human feelings, and to be able to cut his father's throat, if necessary in the good cause".' 'I should be very sorry to lose sight of him,' Milnes reflected, 'though he is a man whom I could never make a friend of. He yearns after power and certainly, if talent can force a way to eminence, his will do it – his self-conceit and contempt of all others except the oligarchy of his momentary admiration, will stand in his way, but even this may be of use in imparting to him a dignity and high tone of conscious power, which is so good a substitute for rank and circumstance[.]' Nonetheless, Milnes had made plans to travel in Germany with Sunderland. 'Sunderland is a professedly cold-hearted, ambitious man,' he admitted to his parents, 'and a person you are obliged to be much on your guard against but I think we should get along pretty well together – that is, if I let him have his own way in everything'.[24]

The Apostles' reaction against the party politics, factionalism and flamboyant speechifying of the Union had had its effect on Milnes. In a letter written to his parents on the day Sunderland went down he protested against being asked to identify his politics and claimed that he had arrived at certain political principles that were too general to be classified in party terms or even 'to be applied with any accuracy to business of the day'. Using Sunderland as a negative example, Milnes strongly disagreed with his father's view that he should cultivate his natural powers of rhetoric: 'My poetical taste – my line of reading – every thing would incline me to be rhetorical and to shine in such sentences, as this one, by which Sunderland charmed part of the Union last night – speaking of bringing government into contempt – he said, "And Sir does not every petition of the people, implying a deficiency in the Government, bring the Government into contempt – does not the signature of the pale and emaciated mechanic – the signature of the starving labourer, with his children shrieking for bread around him – no, not *his* signature – *for he has not strength to hold a pen* – does not that bring the Government into contempt?" – Is this the Rhetoric you would have me aim at?' And this letter ends with a renunciation of Milnes' former ambitions at the Union, one which suggests how much he had learned from two and a half years at Cambridge and some months of membership in the Society: 'I remember you once told me to lead the Union, this I could not do – if I staid here a century – and for this reason – a leader there must be a violent politician – and a party politician, or he must have a private party – I shall never be the one or have the other.'[25]

During 1830 the political excitement rising through the country seems to have infected the Union and to have led its members on to further excesses of the sort the Apostles deplored. In the Michaelmas term L. S. Orde and Joseph Carne ran for the presidency, and the contest was staged as a show-piece of mock-Parliamentary behaviour. The voters were canvassed, and the candidates went so far as to hire vehicles to take them up to the poll. Moreover, the Union took the deliberately provocative step of formally abandoning the standing rule against discussion of recent political events, and some members confidently predicted that their debates would be put down by the University authorities. The predictions were wrong, but the Apostles, led by Blakesley, formed a new debating society, the Fifty, 'for the purpose of debating in a more gentlemanly manner'. The new club inspired much comment and some feeble satiric verse about the 'holy "Quinquagint," Formed at th' "Apostle's" godly hint':

> Here B[lakesley] sits enthroned in state,
> While Apostolic brethren prate;
> And H[allam] spouts from out the pages
> Of his own father's 'Middle Ages.'

Two rules of the Fifty were particular sources of amusement – one which restricted the club to a membership of sixty-five, and one forbidding members from applauding or showing other signs of approval or disapproval. The latter rule made for dull debates, and Blakesley had an austere manner that did not help: 'by all accounts,' wrote a friend of Milnes, 'the president looks like a fog and speaks like an east wind'. Nonetheless, Blakesley seems to have kept the club alive for several years and to have introduced suitably Apostolic subjects, for in 1835 Tennyson's poetry was discussed there.[26]

After the formation of the Fifty in November 1830, the Apostles rarely spoke at the Union. But in the spring of 1831 the pressing question of Parliamentary Reform was twice debated by the house, and Sunderland, who seems to have been staying in London at this time, appeared for these occasions. It may well have been his presence that induced Blakesley and Hallam to return to the Union and speak on the other side. They and several other Apostles were opposed to the Reform Bill as it was then proposed, with the strange result that Blakesley (a man of liberal principles throughout his life) was later asked to stand for Parliament as the Tory candidate for the town of Cambridge.[27]

Sunderland, as one might expect, looked forward eagerly to the new age that then seemed to be approaching. But his last-known letter to Milnes, written in London in July 1831 while debate on the Reform Bill raged in Parliament, struck an ominous note. 'If they throw out the bill,' he wrote, 'we shall all of us have something to smile at at any rate. How d—d absurd does this revolution, which I have been sighing for these three years and do still sigh for, appear as it approaches. . .You may depend upon it the end of these things is not distant. When the guillotine shall be in full play down by poet's corner, I should like to see you and Orde (I don't mean on the guillotine but as spectators) and all the other scoffers who used to deride my anticipations regarding the revolution.'[28]

It seems to have been during this summer, while he was travelling on the Continent, that Sunderland's mind gave way. Significantly enough, his madness took the form of a belief that he had been denied the highest kind of political eminence. After his death in 1867, Milnes learned the details from a letter written by Sunderland's younger brother, a naval officer, whose flat prose aptly closes the story of that remarkable rhetorician, Thomas Sunderland:

I think about 1830 (I was at Sea at the time) his Father and he were travelling in Switzerland together, when he suddenly showed symptoms of derangement by pitching a boatman overboard on the Lake of Geneva, who he fancied was placed as a Spy on his actions and in the pay of the English Government; his first delusion being that he was a legitimate son of the Duke of York; consequently after the death of the Princess Charlotte heir to the Throne. This seemed to occupy all his thoughts for many years; and I think to the last never entirely left him. This aberration of intellect of course unfitted him for any profession; he had intended to try the Law; a few years after poor fellow he got intemperate habits so firmly fixed, that he never could shake them off and which naturally encreased his mental infirmity. Thus was a most brilliant intellect utterly shattered; for some years he lived in the Isle of Man, and then led a nomad life; having no settled residence about fourteen years ago he came to Ulverstone [*sic*], making that his head quarters, and travelling here and there, as fancy dictated: he was fond of astronomy, read a great deal, and wrote essays on many subjects, chiefly National Government, most of them shewing great talent, but all more or less mixed with wildness.[29]

At the beginning of 1830 J. W. Blakesley found himself the lone survivor at Cambridge of the original group of mystics. 'You ought to come home,' he wrote to Trench, then on a tour of Spain. 'The salt of the earth is too scanty to allow of its being as yet scattered over the face of it. We have a handful of men in Cambridge who will continue the race of the Maurices and Sterlings, and cherish an untiring faith in the undefeated energies of man. The majority of the Apostolics are decidedly of the proper way of thinking, and the society is in a flourishing state.'[30]

The Society was passing into a new era, one of self-conscious recognition of the Apostolic spirit and 'the proper way of thinking'. The choice of new members became an infrequent and painstaking process, conducted for some years under Blakesley's paternal eye. The mystics had won control of the Society, and the story of the Cambridge Apostles is henceforth the story of the Apostolic inner circle formed by F. D. Maurice and his followers.

CHAPTER 4

MAURICE: THE MAKING OF A VICTORIAN PROPHET

For the Apostles of Arthur Hallam's time F. D. Maurice was a mysterious, awesome figure. The most striking testimony to his reputation among them is that of Hallam himself, on learning that his old friend Gladstone had met Maurice at Oxford. 'I have today seen Rogers, who tells me amongst other things that you know Maurice,' Hallam wrote to Gladstone, in some excitement. 'I know nothing better suited to a letter of somewhat a serious kind than an exhortation to cultivate an acquaintance, which, from all I have heard, must be invaluable. I do not myself know Maurice, but I know well many whom he has known, and whom he has moulded like a second Nature, and these too men eminent for intellectual power, to whom the presence of a commandin[g] spirit would in all other cases be a signal rath[er] for rivalry than reverential acknowledgement. [The] effect which he has produced on the minds of man[y] at Cambridge by the single creation of that society, the Apostles, (for the spirit though not the form *was* created by him) is far greater than I can dare to calculate, and will be felt both directly and indirectly in the age that is before us.'[1]

It may be hard to imagine Maurice, whatever his abilities, having a force equal to that of Nature herself over such a staunchly conservative Apostle as Spencer Walpole or such a staunchly radical one as Charles Buller, to mention two typical figures in the Society of the mid-twenties. But there can be no doubt of his power over some of the Apostles of his time and especially over John Sterling, who described himself as little more than 'a patch of sand to receive and retain the impression of his footstep'. This near-idolatry spread among the Apostles who immediately succeeded Maurice and Sterling in the Society, and in some of their earliest letters we find them eagerly comparing notes on Maurice. W. B. Donne and J. W. Blakesley were among those who felt the effect of Sterling's discipleship. 'Do you know Maurice [?]' Donne wrote to Blakesley. 'Sterling has raised my curiosity to see him by declaring that "he qu[ite] worships him." What an Apollo he must be to have the adoration of such [a] Hercules.' 'I do know Maurice,' Blakesley replied, 'but have seen as yet very little of him. My adoration is at least equal to Sterling's. He is a complete divinity.'[2]

For later Apostles the period of Maurice and Sterling's active leadership became in retrospect a primary, heroic age which their successors could only hope to emulate, never surpass. 'The days in which the giants walked on the earth' became an Apostolic phrase thenceforth, though it came in time to include the period of Hallam and Tennyson. As late as 1837 Richard Monckton Milnes called Maurice the Apostles' 'caposetta', and while Maurice himself would have disliked the term and always denied that he was the leader of any sect whatever, he remained a prominent member of the Society throughout his life. As his theological writings began to appear in the eighteen-thirties he won new disciples among the Apostles of that time and further established his reputation among his contemporaries in the Society, even those who could not agree with his religious opinions. For some years his only direct contact with the Society seems to have been the annual dinners, which Maurice, an intensely serious man, apparently attended as a matter of duty rather than pleasure. With the emergence of a social movement centring on his leadership and thought (the so-called Christian Socialist movement of 1848–54) Maurice renewed his personal influence, for several members of the movement were drawn from the Society, and when the movement culminated in the foundation of the Working Men's College Maurice's work was imitated in Cambridge by the creation of a similar school under largely Apostolic leadership. At about this time, after a slack period, the Society took on new life at Cambridge and began to attract some outstanding undergraduates, among them F. J. A. Hort, who at first was hesitant about becoming an Apostle and only accepted membership after Maurice assured him of the Society's serious purpose, notwithstanding the flippancy assumed by many of its members. In 1866 Maurice himself returned to Cambridge as Professor of Moral Philosophy. Forty years had passed since his own undergraduate days, the Apostles of the eighteen-sixties had deserted the Coleridgean philosophy that Maurice had helped to establish, and the most eminent among them, Henry Sidgwick, felt a considerable antipathy towards Maurice's theology. Yet he cultivated Maurice's friendship and drew him into the discussions of the Grote Club, a group of senior Apostles and their friends that had been created in imitation of the Society.[3]

But Maurice's reputation was not merely derived from his personal contact with other Apostles. His real importance is that he was the key figure in establishing the principles that became known as the spirit of the Society, and these principles had an even wider influence than he himself had. As Charles Buller's radical opinions softened in the later thirties. W. B. Donne remarked that Buller had 'stood honourably aloof from the party he nominally belongs to, for some time. Is that not owing to his being like Master Slender a gentleman born, and above all to his apostleship[?]' Donne may well be right about the Society's effect on Buller, and if so there may be more truth than first appears in Arthur Hallam's enthusiastic description of Maurice as a moulder of minds. It seems that even as a young man Maurice had the most extraordinary understanding of the intellectual and emotional needs of other young men, for his example served to create a tradition that retained its effectiveness for generation after generation of students. While it survived, the University and society itself underwent such drastic changes that Maurice seemed the relict of another era to Sidgwick, who himself seemed an historical curiosity to the Apostles of the early twentieth century. One wonders if Maurice would have been pleased by some of the later manifestations of the Apostolic spirit. What he would have thought of Lytton Strachey is past imagining. But a spirit may inhabit all sorts of bodies and take forms its originator never thought of.[4]

It is not even certain that Maurice would have approved of the more immediate effects of his influence, that is, the emergence of a distinct set of friends, much aware of themselves as a group and self-consciously Apostolic in their outlook. The small, painfully select club of the eighteen-thirties developed around Hallam, not Maurice, and it was as Arthur Hallam's Round Table that this group was remembered in later years. Maurice was almost obsessive in his hatred of parties or anything resembling them and might well have disowned this group, or at least disapproved of its sense of exclusiveness, had he known it better. Although the group itself recognized him as its spiritual founder and leader, Maurice seems to have been largely unaware of his own influence, and certainly he never sought it.[5]

What gave Maurice his power over the Cambridge Apostles? Few records of his undergraduate life have survived, and these give almost no clues to his role in the Society during his three years of active membership. But there is much information about the period immediately after this, when he emerged as the main exponent of Apostolic thought.

And still more may be known about the formative phase of his life. Maurice's upbringing was extraordinary: it gave him at an early age a profound depth of spiritual understanding, and it fixed him in his lifelong dedication to the cause of religious tolerance. The story of Maurice's family background and early life reveals the forces that underlay his thought and personality as a spiritual leader, not only of the Apostles but of the age itself. And it provides valuable insight into the intellectual and religious atmosphere of the time – an atmosphere so uncongenial to the spirit of the Apostles that the Society sometimes seemed to them an oasis in a desert of intolerance and unreason.

Maurice's early years were dominated by conflict among the members of his family. At the most obvious level, this was a theological conflict between the Unitarianism of his father and the Calvinism of his elder sisters, but at a deeper level the issue was one of religious education. His father was non-doctrinaire in his beliefs, perfectly tolerant towards all forms of religious thought, and not the least concerned to promote anything more specific than tolerance in other people. His sisters were precisely the reverse and believed that the inculcation of dogma was the moral duty of all true believers. Because Maurice could not accept either of these views and yet respected the motives behind them, he was forced to seek a form of religious education that would reconcile the two. One might say that the spirit of the Society took its form from the fact that, while Maurice believed deeply in the loving God of his father and shared his sisters' anxious concern for personal salvation, he rejected both attitudes to other people's beliefs.

His father Michael Maurice, the son of an orthodox Nonconformist clergyman, had been educated at Leeds Grammar School and at two of the academies that then provided Dissenters with an alternative to Oxford and Cambridge. These academies were especially noteworthy for their tolerant attitude towards differences of religious opinion and for their uncompromising support of political liberalism. Of the three clergymen who ran the Hoxton Academy during the seventeen-eighties, when Michael Maurice was a student there, one was an Arian in theology, one a Socinian and one a Calvinist. But all three were prominent among those who regarded themselves as the 'friends of civil and religious liberty'. Maurice was also one of the first students at Hackney College, which became notorious as a nursery of radicalism, a school for sympathizers with Tom Paine and others who upheld the principles of the French Revolution.[6]

It would not be unfair to say that the religious liberalism taught at these institutions was often little more than a by-product of political sectarianism. The young men were exposed to a variety of religious beliefs and encouraged to choose for themselves, but this experience was intended to teach them not to take any form of faith very seriously, especially any that might interfere with the liberal political opinions they were expected to hold. Students at these academies might read what they liked, discuss what they liked, think what they liked, but the usual effect of this freedom was to produce a single kind of liberal mind.

Michael Maurice became a typical liberal of this sort. He was converted, while still a student, to Unitarianism, but to that nebulous form of Unitarianism whose central dogma is the avoidance of dogma. It was later said of him 'that it could not be inferred from Mr Maurice's preaching, unless it were negatively, what were his distinctive views', and at one time he carried his sympathy with orthodox views to the point of preaching in the afternoon only, to ensure that the congregation of his chapel might also attend the local church. His dislike of dogmatic religionists was intense, and it led to one of the few conspicuous events of his life. While still a young man he opposed Thomas Belsham, eminent as the leader of the doctrinaire Unitarians, in an election held to pick the afternoon preacher at the Gravel Pit Chapel in Hackney. To Belsham's disgust and everyone's surprise, Maurice was elected by a single vote and became the colleague of the illustrious Joseph Priestley, then the morning preacher at that chapel.[7]

But Michael Maurice was not a man suited by nature for prominent office. Before joining Priestley at Hackney he had had a humbler post at a chapel in Great Yarmouth, where in his spare time he taught classics to the five daughters of an influential local merchant, William Hurry. Maurice had fallen in love with one of these girls, and after two years at Hackney he left, married his former student and settled down to a quiet life as a clergyman, part-time farmer and tutor to the children of Nonconformist families like his own. His wife, Priscilla Hurry, was essential to his modest success: while devoted to him, she was distinctly his superior in intellect and firmness of character, and her family connections provided him with the patronage he needed. Within a few years of their marriage her brother gave them a house large enough to contain their growing family and a thriving boarding school.[8]

As a teacher, as a father, as a clergyman, Michael Maurice's principles were those of the political and religious liberalism in which he had been brought up. The God he worshipped was the fulfilment of his own assured faith in the virtues of reason and benevolence. 'I believed God to be a merciful God,' wrote his daughter Anne, recalling the beliefs of her childhood; 'too kind to punish for a long continuance any whom he had endowed with life, and ready to accept the prayers and good works of any of his creatures; and on this indulgent Deity I relied to save me. The thought of his justice never once entered my head, at least so as to excite the least uncomfortable feeling. I thought Christ was a great teacher; a very good man whom God enabled to perform various miracles, and that he had set us a perfect example, which we were to follow as far as we could, and trust to the mercy of God to forgive us what we could not attain: yet, I often felt a wish to know that God certainly did forgive us, and wished to have some token that I might be *sure*, he had forgiven *me*.'[9]

His daughter's uncertainty would probably have been seen by Michael Maurice as a natural part of the religious education he gave his children and the several students who lived in the Maurice household. From their earliest years his children were exposed to the views of all faiths and of none, and Maurice taught them and his students from books chosen with no concern for the religious bias of the authors. He encouraged the discussion of religious controversies in the certainty that such discussion would make apparent the folly of controversy and the virtue of his own sympathy for other religious beliefs. And public benevolence was as obligatory as rational faith for the Maurice children, who were all involved, as soon as possible, in the many charitable schemes he instituted or supported and the various worthy societies to which he belonged – societies for peace, against slavery, for national education, against the Test Laws, for the 'improvement. . .of the Gipsies', against the employment of 'Climbing Boys in chimneys', and so on. There were times in his life when the effectiveness of his liberal values seemed doubtful to Michael Maurice. 'When will men differ without being angry with each other?' he wrote in despair to a Unitarian friend: 'When will they discuss without becoming furious?' But he could never have imagined, in the early years of his marriage, that the principles of his teaching would defeat themselves and produce in his own family the intemperate zealots he deplored.[10]

Michael Maurice and liberals like him could never quite understand that some of the people who held other religious views – the Calvinists in particular – could not accept him in the way he accepted them. Their God was not one who forgave as a matter of course, and the Calvinists' insistence on man's innate sinfulness, on the need for redemption through Christ, on the great gulf fixed between the saved and the damned, meant that there were strict limits to their tolerance of Unitarians.

The Maurice children began to learn this at a very early age. Maurice's sympathy for his religious opponents had brought him students from varying religious backgrounds, among them the three sons of Joseph Hardcastle, a close associate of the great Evangelical reformers and a pillar of the Missionary Society. Hardcastle's religious views may be deduced from an anecdote told of his reaction to being caught in a display of affection for his little daughter: he felt obliged to offer an apology by saying that 'although we know that ever since the fall the seeds of native evil have been deeply rooted in every human heart, he confessed that he had not yet discovered its development in that dear child!' While Hardcastle respected Maurice as a teacher, he was worried about the spiritual welfare of his boys in the Maurice household. With good reason, from his point of view, for at about this time (1806) the Maurices adopted their niece, Anne Hurry, a girl who was renowned for her beauty and cleverness, and at least two of the Hardcastle brothers fell in love with her. Toleration of one's heretical neighbours was one thing, wanting to marry one of them another, and the young Hardcastles were withdrawn from the school.[11]

Soon afterwards, the Maurice children had another practical lesson in religious sectarianism. Their father needed a governess to teach Anne Hurry, her brother Edmund (whom the family had also adopted), and the three oldest Maurice girls – Elizabeth, Mary and Anne. Rather typically, he chose a governess from an Anglican background. He had previously taught his daughters himself, and the intellectual freedom of the education he had given them had made the Misses Maurice formidable children. They were then between eleven and seven years old, and the governess, Esther Parker, was eighteen, but she discovered in them an intellectual curiosity that she was hard pressed to satisfy and a flair for theological argument that she could not withstand. When her pupils questioned her orthodox views, she found herself unable to justify them, and gradually she forsook them. Her conversion to Unitarianism must have helped to encourage the Maurice girls' zeal for spreading the doctrines of their sect. By the time they were adolescents the elder two, Elizabeth and Mary, had become militant Unitarians, and in their impatience with their father's refusal to take a party line in religious matters they must have longed for a chance to go beyond him.[12]

Their opportunity came when Anne Hurry's brother Edmund

suddenly died. According to the *Monthly Repository*, he 'was pursuing the study of medicine, when a rapid consumption, which he bore with singular patience and Christian resignation, removed him from earth to heaven'. Edmund's equanimity in the face of his early death – he was only eighteen – was partly due to his conversion to orthodox belief. When he discovered he was going to die, the comforts of a rational, Unitarian faith proved unsatisfactory to him in comparison with those afforded by the concept of a personal Redeemer, and he persuaded both himself and his sister Anne of this before his death in October 1814.[13]

Anne Hurry's rejection of Unitarianism brought her not only a Redeemer but a husband. The governess, Esther Parker, bore the news of her conversion to the Hardcastle family in London and touched off a flurry of events. One story has two Hardcastle brothers rushing off to the Maurice home near Bristol to fling themselves, simultaneously, at Anne's feet. Another has one Hardcastle nobly repressing his love and arranging a carriage for the other, so that he might lose no time in dashing off for his father's blessing and Anne's consent. In any case, just eleven weeks after Edmund Hurry's death Anne Hurry married Alfred Hardcastle and by her marriage became a favoured member of a powerful, rich and socially prominent family.[14]

It is hard to know whether Edmund's death or Anne's marriage had the greater effect on the Maurice sisters, but each in her different way was greatly influenced by these events. Mary went to stay with Anne Hardcastle in her new home and became more assertively Unitarian in a Calvinistic environment. Elizabeth paid a visit to an Anglican family and became uncertain of Unitarianism. Anne Maurice, who was a cripple and confined to her home, found that her habitual study of theology was leading her in new paths. Their governess had by this time left her post with the Maurice family, but she was bombarded with anxious letters from Anne. 'Oh! my dear E[sther],' wrote Anne, about the time of Anne Hurry's marriage, 'if you still doubt concerning the comforting doctrine of the atonement, read Paul's Epistle to the Hebrews regularly, chapter by chapter, without going to consult your favourite books, but in hearty prayer to God, to give his Holy Spirit to direct you to see the truth. Then tell me how you can explain it without believing that through the blood of Christ we must look for the forgiveness of our sins? — has become so orthodox, you would hardly suppose it; but he believes that Christ is God, and that there is a devil, and many other doctrines of the same kind: my faith does not extend so far.'[15]

Indeed, Anne did not feel certain of the deity of Christ for another ten months. In the meantime her sister Elizabeth came home, the two girls discovered that their opinions were changing, and they decided that, however incomplete their conversion to orthodoxy, the time had come for drastic action.[16]

In July 1815 Elizabeth and Anne, then nineteen and fifteen years old, informed their father that they would no longer attend his Unitarian chapel. Michael Maurice was overwhelmed by the news, but his principles of education forbade him to command the girls' obedience. Their sister Mary at first took their father's part in the family arguments that followed, but a further calamity won her over as well. In the following September Anne Hardcastle gave birth to a child and one week later died, urging Mary to forsake her heretical opinions before it was too late.[17]

Elizabeth, Mary and Anne became as militant in their new beliefs as the elder two had been in their old. However, the object of their zeal varied: all were strongly Calvinistic, but Elizabeth joined the Church of England, the other two became Baptists, and quarrels among the sisters were frequent. On only one point were they in full agreement. Having nothing but contempt for their father's indulgent, relaxed attitude towards the propagation of his faith, they planned a concerted frontal attack upon the heathen. The energetic campaign they mounted soon claimed its victims. The hapless ex-governess underwent a second conversion and returned, rather uncertainly, to her original beliefs. Mrs Maurice was even more thoroughly unsettled: about two years after the girls' conversion she admitted to her husband that she too had changed her opinion, in her case to the conviction that she was eternally damned.[18]

Frederick Maurice, the only boy in the family, was nine years old at the time of his sisters' break with Unitarianism – a brilliant boy and, not surprisingly, a desperately confused one. His father made efforts to prevent the older children from influencing Frederick and took his education into his own hands. It is unlikely that the boy was attracted by his sisters' unamiable spirit; at the same time he came to realize that his father's point of view was based on a fundamental incoherence of thought. 'My Father was strong in his own belief; has [*sic*] some difficulty in conceiving how any other was possible,' Maurice wrote in old age. 'And yet he was even passionately zealous for a union of all persons holding different opinions and was angry with his own sect, and with all others if they were inclined to stand apart. His dislike of orthodoxy was chiefly from the divisions which he supposed it created between those who ought to be agreed. This I was obliged to understand in very early years. It gave rise to a number of perplexities and contradictions in my mind as I grew up. But whatever I have learnt or hoped for has been connected with the question how such an agreement is possible without destroying diversities, without establishing a mere dead uniformity either of denial or of profession.'[19]

If such a spiritual union was impossible within his family, Frederick at least had a centre of stability in his unquestioning love for his mother and his younger sister Emma, neither of whom had the aggressive qualities of his elder sisters. But his mother's mental balance had been undermined in the religious controversies that swept the household. She had come to accept as certain the Calvinistic doctrine of the elect, but she was overcome by depression in her equal certainty that she herself was not of its number. Emma was perhaps even more important than his mother to Frederick, and he was deeply influenced by her personality and religious development. Emma was an unusual child, with a lively and affectionate nature and extraordinary qualities of courage and unselfishness. For most of her life she was an invalid: when very young she had suffered from what was diagnosed as water on the brain and had been cured of it, despite the attentions of the local surgeon, who put burning caustic on her head 'to produce severe counter irritation and absorb the water'. Emma was disfigured for life and in pain much of the time, but these and many other trials she bore with remarkable patience and cheerfulness.[20]

When the governess, Esther Parker, left the family, Emma passed under her sister Anne's care, and Anne, then in the throes of religious conversion, found herself with the interesting prospect of having in her charge an impressionable young mind and, in her view, an unregenerate soul. Their father had demanded from the older girls a promise that they would not try to convert the other children, and for a while he restricted the books that could be used for their education. But Anne found it easy to evade her promise by reading certain passages of the Bible with a peculiar emphasis and by asking the seven-year-old Emma such questions as 'Do you feel yourself more a sinner than you used to do?' During a good part of this year (1815) Emma was seriously ill. Anne watched closely over her spiritual welfare and took notes of her development. 'It is interesting to watch the growth of grace in Emma's mind,' she wrote. 'I delight to mark her progress in the ways of God; yet, though I endeavour to promote it by every means in my power, there is much depravity to combat.' The battle for Emma's soul was intensified when Anne Hardcastle died. She had been loved by everyone, and Emma was greatly moved, for we learn that her death 'was the first means of impressing this young disciple, who was then only between seven and eight years of age, with the necessity of seeking salvation through the blood of the Lamb.'[21]

Emma, always a tractable child, learned her lesson well. At the age of nine she confessed herself a '*vile* sinner', at ten she felt she was saved, and thereafter she showed deep concern for the spiritual state of the other children, especially her brother. While Elizabeth, Mary and Anne had promised their father not to proselytize Frederick and the younger girls (there were eventually five younger girls), Emma was under no such compulsion. Passages from a letter she wrote at the age of twelve to a younger sister may be taken as typical of one aspect of her influence. 'You will perceive that I have enclosed "Baxter's Call," ' Emma wrote, 'a book which has been the means of the conversion of many. Oh! that it may be of yours! You, my dear [Priscilla], I trust, have been and still are, alarmed about your eternal welfare. . .You are to-day ten years old; now if you were to begin from this day, and never do another wrong thing, all the sins of ten years would still remain, and you would be sent to hell for these alone.'[22]

It is fair to add that Emma was equally insistent on God's mercy. Like her sister Anne she kept a diary to record her own sinfulness (Anne's diary was called 'The Unveiling of an Evil Heart'), but she did not think herself damned, as her mother did. Though the motives of her elder sisters might be suspect, Emma herself was sincere and unselfish in her concern for the souls of Frederick and the other members of the family, and her influence, as an instrument of her sisters' programme of religious education, was great. The younger girls found it impossible to resist, and Frederick was greatly swayed by it.[23]

Nor could he ignore his elder sisters, who were entirely successful in their efforts to disrupt their father's work as a Unitarian minister. Anne Maurice would not attend her father's chapel, but when she could not get to the Baptist chapel in Bristol, she would go to the Quaker meeting-house, the only place of worship in their little village, and when she was not too ill 'she would visit the poor and endeavour to win them to the Saviour'. Michael Maurice made a show of resistance and brought over at least one convert from orthodoxy, but he had lost the respect of his own family and many other people. In 1821 his wife finally asked if she too might be excused from attending his chapel, his sixteen-year-old son Frederick had plainly forsaken his earlier desire to become a clergyman, and Michael Maurice himself was left the only professing Unitarian in a family of eleven. After 1825, when the family moved to another area, he never took another post as a Unitarian clergyman.[24]

The religious convulsions of the family continued, and several of the younger children grew up to resemble their elder sisters, each of whom seemed to have cast herself in the central role of a religious drama of her own composition. Mary fell in love with a Roman Catholic, allowed herself to accept his proposal of marriage, and then in a public agony of conscience renounced him. Elizabeth became a hopeless epileptic but did not release the young clergyman to whom she was engaged. He eventually made a dash for his freedom (and was unfrocked), and Elizabeth spent much of the rest of her life praying for his soul. Anne died young of tuberculosis, and greeted the event with ecstasy. Emma survived to the age of twenty-three, to see her brother at last come round to her beliefs. All the members of the family, except the father, eventually joined the Church of England, and even he, at the age of ninety, in the year before his death and while his wife was on her deathbed, confessed that he had finally come to accept an orthodox faith. On Easter Sunday 1854 Frederick Maurice (then a well-known, even notorious, Anglican clergyman) administered Holy Communion to his parents and his surviving sisters, and the Maurice family was at last, after forty years, united in its religious beliefs.[25]

Considering that for much of his early life F. D. Maurice was surrounded by as many as nine females in various stages of religious hysteria and physical debility, for several of whom he nonetheless had more respect than he had for his father, it is surprising that he retained his own mental balance as well as he did. He grew up to be an introverted, uncertain, painfully shy young man, with an ingrained habit of criticizing his own motives and a tendency to periods of extreme depression. Maurice's obsessive earnestness and the extraordinarily complex web of religious theory that he wove around his every action were to earn him the dislike of many of his contemporaries, but the intensity of his search for truth, his utter selflessness and the brilliance and subtlety of his intellect all served to lend him a power of spiritual leadership that impressed even those who disagreed with his ideas or who had no sympathy for his 'virtually morbid' humility and lifelong 'paroxysms of self-distrust'.[26]

From his earliest years Maurice had a curiously specialized mind, oblivious to many of the usual interests of childhood and preoccupied with moral and social problems. These concerns were of course intensified by the religious dissension within his family and by his own uncertainty about his relation to its various factions. During this time, and particularly after his decision to give up his plan of becoming a clergyman, he seems to have been deeply unsettled. From the Calvinism of his sisters he had learned that it was his personal salvation or damnation that was at stake, but their concept of salvation could not satisfy him for long, since it involved a denial of God's love for people who did not believe as they did. Maurice's real allegiance was to the merciful, all-forgiving God of his father's religion, yet his father could not recognize the enormous importance of personal belief or sympathize with the emotional forces underlying his daughters' feverish pursuit of religious certainty. Moreover, personal salvation for Maurice meant somehow finding compensation for the loss of his own family as a family, somehow healing the wounds of the religious warfare that had dominated his early life. 'The very word Unity,' Maurice wrote in old age, 'has been haunting me from my cradle.' The unity he now sought was one beyond his father's Unitarianism, with its negative acquiescence to everyone's right to think what he liked, beyond his sisters' ecstatic union with a jealous God, with its corollary of the eternal damnation of others.[27]

Little is known about the period of his life between sixteen and twenty. He had decided on a legal and political career, for the family remained united in its political liberalism, and Frederick, like the others, was a strong supporter of the social and political causes then thought progressive. He had encountered in Thomas Erskine's liberal theology a counteracting force to his sister's Calvinism, he had learned something of modern German thought from Madame de Stael's *De l'Allemagne*, and he had read Coleridge. He decided to enter university: Cambridge was chosen, mainly because at that university one did not have to profess oneself an Anglican until graduation. It does not appear that Maurice had any high expectations of the education Cambridge offered, and he may never have intended to graduate. His primary motive seems to have been to escape the restrictive atmosphere of his family, and it may be of this period that he was speaking when he later recalled being 'ashamed of my birth – partly because I should have liked it to be more creditable in the eyes of the world[,] partly because I disliked the Unitarian sect'.[28]

But in going to Cambridge Maurice was far from escaping his past, for his closest associate during his first few terms was an Apostle, John Stock, who had first-hand knowledge of the religious warfare conducted by Maurice's elder sisters. Stock's father was a doctor, a prominent citizen of Bristol and at one time a well-known Unitarian. When Mary and Anne Maurice adopted the Baptist faith they became ardent disciples of a Bristol clergyman named Vernon, 'a most heavenly minded man', who was on the point of dying, piously, of heart disease. With their usual gift for stirring up trouble, the girls asked Dr Stock to attend Mr Vernon and to see how a Christian could die. Stock was converted to orthodoxy by the experience, and angry accusations and counter-accusations were flung back and forth in an outburst of pamphlets on the case. Dr Stock's son would know only too well what Frederick Maurice's background was.[29]

It was probably Stock who introduced Maurice to the Cambridge Apostles, for he had been a member of the Society since 1821. Maurice must have made a favourable impression, for he was elected on 22 November 1823 – that is, in his first term and within one month of his arrival at Cambridge.

Stock was not the only Apostle to have links with Maurice's background, for at least three of the founding members of the Society were closely associated with the Bristol wing of the Evangelical movement. Stock may well have owed his election to the fact that his father was well known in Bristol as a convert from Unitarianism, and it is even possible that Maurice himself was elected under the misapprehension that he held the sort of religious views favoured among the earliest Apostles.[30]

Conjecture aside, there is no doubt of the important role played by Evangelical and Dissenting orthodoxy in Maurice's early life, and it seems likely that one common characteristic of this form of religion left its mark, not only on him, but on the Society. The letters exchanged by the Apostles of the late twenties and early thirties bear more than a hint of what might be termed the 'confessional group' – the sort of group in which a few believers meet to profess their faith, admit their sins and examine the state of their spiritual welfare. Groups of this sort are of course not restricted to Evangelicals and Dissenters, and indeed the Maurice family itself can be seen as an extreme example of the confessional group – extreme in its hysteria and in the fact that communication within the group took the form of long confessional and accusatory letters written to members of the same household. Among the Apostles the letters are the normal, friendly ones that one would expect such young men to exchange, and the sins they discuss are intellectual rather than failures of faith, yet the accents of the confessional group are unmistakable. 'You excite,' says one such letter, 'not my envy, but my admiration and applause, by that delightful hectoring which you bestow upon that mind of yours, not less from within than without: Do not fear that you are not fulfilling the very highest duty which you can, as frail mortality[,] aspire to pay; the cultivation of our own powers, in order that we may use our encreased Capacities for the advancement of Human Happiness, and the Development of our own mind that we may be the better able to direct and guide those that have wanted the "vital impulse" into the way of improvement, are all the Repayment we can make to the Being, be he whom he may, from whom we first received them.'[31]

This somewhat self-righteous attitude derived in part from the Apostles' belief in their own social importance as an intellectual élite. But it derived more fundamentally from a belief in the necessity of patient, laborious soul-searching. This belief remained basic to the Society throughout its known history, a fact that gives further significance to Maurice's early experiences of religious conflict within his own family. In learning to reject his father's superficial liberalism he had learned to seek salvation by discovering the roots of personal belief through painstaking self-analysis. His family's failure to agree had made the pursuit of spiritual union with others an unchanging concern. As he wrote towards the end of his life, 'whatever I have learnt or hoped for has been connected with the question how such an agreement is possible without destroying diversities, without establishing a mere dead uniformity either of denial or of profession'. He came to think that every form of human belief might be seen to contain elements of truth that might be discovered by close analysis of the form and by an attempt to sympathize with those who held to it. Perhaps these ideas were not consciously formulated until after his undergraduate days, but they grew naturally from his early experiences and from the habit of soul-searching, which was an outstanding characteristic of Maurice's mind before he reached Cambridge. It seems reasonable to conclude that this process of painfully honest self-scrutiny was shared with his undergraduate friends (as it was with later friends), and that the spiritual maturity forced on Maurice in early life largely explains his power as a leader of other students and had much to do with the gradual conversion of a rather ordinary essay society into an instrument for the spiritual regeneration of its members.

It would be difficult to exaggerate the importance of this tradition in contributing to the continued effectiveness of the Society. This aspect of the Apostolic spirit encouraged the choice of new members on the basis of their potential for spiritual growth. Once elected, a new member found himself a part of an intimate, exclusive group which invited, expected, but did not normally compel him to confess his deepest thoughts and to share with others the experience of self-examination. For a sensitive, developing young mind, this experience could doubtless have an important educational effect. It could also encourage a tendency to narcissistic élitism, which perhaps reached its extreme in Lytton Strachey. The freedom and intensity of relations among the Apostles could breed contempt for the relations usually found among non-Apostles, and the Society sometimes developed what looked to outsiders like a fixation on the enormous importance of the difference between inside and outside. Strachey himself perfected the art of unapproachability, and he decisively influenced his generation of Apostles, and through them the Bloomsbury set, for whom exclusiveness became a part of the sustaining atmosphere they breathed. But this vice of the Apostolic mind is of long standing and might be almost as well exemplified in the lofty sense of superiority that marked George Venables' personality or in the surprise with which Henry Sidgwick recorded the discovery of Apostolic traits in a High Churchman and Oxonian.[32]

Not only might the Society help unfit its members for more ordinary human relations, but it sometimes encouraged them to be so addicted to self-scrutiny as to be wholly indecisive. On the other hand, it is pleasant to know that 'the method' (as Strachey and Leonard Woolf called it, in the mistaken notion they had invented it) had its limits, even for Apostles, and that not all members of the Society were its proponents or its victims. When 'the method' was applied to Saxon Sydney-Turner by Strachey and Woolf, they 'successfully uncovered the soul of Saxon but. . .disastrously confirmed him in the determination to stifle it in an infinite series of veils'. It seems doubtful that Sydney-Turner himself would describe this act of psychological self-defence as disastrous.[33]

It is useful to keep in mind such recalcitrant Apostles as Sydney-Turner when one is tempted to draw a straight line from Maurice to James Strachey, an Apostle who was one of the four psychoanalysts in the Bloomsbury Group. There are interesting parallels between the methods of Freud and his successors and those of the confessional group or the barely secularized version of it practised by the Apostles. But

Maurice's election had nothing like the effect of immediately converting the Society to some form of group psychotherapy, and soul-searching was not the main concern of most Apostles, then and later, although it remained an essential aspect of the Apostolic spirit. Indeed, Maurice's election seems to have coincided with a move away from exclusiveness and introversion, for the Society soon came to resemble not so much a meeting of the faithful as a miniature version of the Cambridge Union. Nor, at this stage in his life, was there much to distinguish Maurice himself from the other young men who gathered at the Union. Maurice's development in these early years was a gradual and complex process, a series of assumed and abandoned positions in a painful search for the meaning of his life.

CHAPTER 5

MAURICE: THE RISE OF APOSTOLIC THEOLOGY

Once Frederick Maurice had forsaken the idea of becoming a Unitarian clergyman, his next ambition was to become a left-wing politician, a radical reformer like Sir Francis Burdett, whom he and his elder sisters idolized. Although religious discord ruled his family, and his father had been discredited in his eyes, the family's political faith remained intact – the one remaining sign of unity but sufficient reason to prepare himself for a career in law and politics. Thus Maurice might desert the Unitarian sect to begin his studies at Cambridge, a stronghold of the Establishment, and yet, in his own eyes, not betray his principles or go over to the enemy. This solution was, however, unsatisfactory, for he became increasingly dissatisfied with the political liberalism of the time. Liberals, in those hectic years before the passing of the Reform Bill, naturally enough were concerned with purely political measures, and Maurice's instinctive desire for a religious or metaphysical approach made his alliance with them an uneasy one. 'I did not. . .at Cambridge or London, wear the proper Liberal livery,' he later claimed, 'though on practical questions I shouted with them.'[1]

Nonetheless, he began conventionally enough. One would expect a young man with political ambitions to be drawn to the Cambridge Union, that nursery of future orators and legislators, and indeed Maurice became a member at the earliest opportunity in his first year. But apparently he was not anxious to make his mark as a debater, for he waited two terms before making his maiden speech. In May 1824 he proposed and opened a debate on the question, 'Was the conduct of the Whigs during the last Century, such as to entitle them to the support of Parliament and to the gratitude of future times?' The phrase 'during the last Century' was the sort of ritual bow that had to be made to the standing rule against discussing contemporary politics; Maurice's motion was in fact an open appeal to the party feelings of the time. It seems that he had not as yet discarded 'the proper Liberal livery', and it is interesting to note that such overt partisanship did not win the support of the house, which rejected the motion by a vote of 37 to 23.[2]

In later life Maurice guiltily recalled his susceptibility to party feeling and student factionalism at this time, and in particular an occasion on which he allowed the traditional college rivalry between Trinity and St John's to overrule his better judgement. In the election of Union officers for the Michaelmas term of 1824 he helped elect a fellow-student of Trinity as Secretary, although the other candidate, Kennedy of St John's, was a far more outstanding member of the Union. Ironically, Kennedy soon afterwards became an Apostle and a personal friend, a fact which may help explain why Maurice was especially ashamed of his part in this incident.[3]

Maurice's brief involvement in the party politics of the Cambridge Union was doubtless a step towards his subsequent and lifelong hatred of parties and party feelings of any sort. In time, his views were to influence the Society, and it would become characteristically Apostolic to hold oneself superior to parties and to reject the Union and all it represented. But Maurice himself did not entirely forsake public debating for some years, and the Society was slow to follow his lead.

Little is known about the Society during Maurice's undergraduate years, but clearly he was prominent within it. By his own account, he 'defended Coleridge's metaphysics and Wordsworth's poetry against the Utilitarian teaching' of other Apostles, Benthamism being 'the prevalent faith' among 'the younger and cleverer undergraduates of the day'. His closest friends within the Society, after John Stock, were Charles Whitmore and John Sterling. Sterling, who was elected two years later than Maurice (in November 1825), became Maurice's most devoted admirer. He spoke of himself as one who spent his time 'in picking up pebbles beside the ocean of Maurice's genius', and he made it his business to promote the teachings of his new prophet whenever possible.[4]

Maurice found the academic system at Cambridge no more satisfactory than the Union in providing him with a direction in life. Distrust of the supposed narrowness and rigidity of the Cambridge system was commonplace among Dissenters, and Maurice seems to have found it a pleasant surprise to be able to tell his family, after the first few weeks, that there seemed to be little substance to this view. 'Nothing at Cambridge is so earnestly recommended as the perusal of general literature,' he claimed, giving as an example his Lecturer in classics, J. C. Hare, who took a genuine interest in his students' intellectual welfare and suggested a wide range of books for them to read. According to Maurice, no respect was given to the 'regular northern plodder who, without any feeling or taste, comes up to the University perhaps from a school where he had been all his life cooking for a senior wrangler'. But this early impression of Cambridge did not survive Maurice's stay there. In his third year he admitted to an ever-increasing dislike of the system and spoke with apparent approval of a recent attack on the University – an article by Macaulay that praised the newly founded London University as a useful corrective to the narrow perspective of the older universities. Nonetheless, Maurice pursued his studies with considerable success. After two years at Trinity he migrated to Trinity Hall, to read for the Civil Law Classes of 1826–7, in which he took a first. But his religious uncertainty cost him his LL.B. and the possibility of a fellowship, for he was reluctant to take the necessary test of allegiance to the Church of England.[5]

Maurice left Cambridge for London in early 1827, ostensibly to continue his legal studies. But he and Sterling, who joined him in London in the course of the year, seem to have spent most of their time in consorting with other rising young men and in conducting an ideological battle on several fronts. One was the London Debating Society, where their Coleridgean views set them off from the Benthamite and Tory factions that made up most of the membership. Journalism, however, was their principal means of expressing their message for the age.

In later years Maurice came to equate periodicals and debating societies as sources of the madness of factionalism and party feeling. Yet he never could renounce journalism altogether, since it was, for better or worse, one of the most potent forms of instruction the age afforded, and Maurice wished above all to instruct, to impart his vision of unity to others. Throughout his life he involved himself in one journalistic venture after another. The first of these, the *Metropolitan Quarterly Magazine*, had no specific editorial policy other than that of general satire, but after Maurice and Sterling had left Cambridge, a clearer programme emerged.

Maurice wrote two lengthy articles for the *Westminster Review* and, for the recently founded *Athenaeum*, a series of 'Sketches of Contemporary Authors' that constitutes the fullest expression we have of his personal beliefs at this stage of his development. Sterling also wrote for the *Athenaeum* and in May 1828 joined Maurice and others in buying the *Literary Chronicle and Weekly Review*. Two months later, when the *Athenaeum* came up for sale, they acquired it and merged it with the *Literary Chronicle*. For about a year Maurice seems to have been the principal editor and, although circulation was poor and became even worse, the *Athenaeum* had enthusiastic support from many of the Apostles and some help from such sympathizers as J. C. Hare. The *Athenaeum* under Maurice and Sterling quickly became a major rallying-point for the Apostolic group that was evolving under their leadership, the group described by one of its members as 'Maurice and that gallant band of Platonico-Wordsworthian-Coleridgean-anti-Utilitarians'. But the editors found their work onerous ('it does the mind harm to be over-milked in support of a weekly journal,' Sterling complained), the journal was unpopular, and Maurice became increasingly preoccupied with family problems and with his growing conviction that he should return to university and enter the Church. What with 'mismanaging proprietors and an indifferent public', the task proved too much. By May 1829 Maurice had withdrawn as editor. Sterling continued for some months, but by September, according to J. W. Blakesley, the *Athenaeum* was 'conducted by a man of the name of Atkinson of whom I know nothing, except that he lives in the temple and has a horrid utilitarian engine in his room which does every thing at once, – for instance, roast a saddle of mutton, make chocolate and black shoes – perhaps also write articles for the Athen[aeum]'. And Blakesley added that he expected 'but few emanations of the divine idea' from such a man. Not long after, Atkinson reportedly attempted to sell the proprietorship and back stock of the *Athenaeum* to the editor who had preceded Maurice, but he refused, although the asking price was only £100, and Atkinson finally disposed of it to Charles Dilke, in whose hands the journal flourished.[6]

Despite the difficulties encountered by Maurice and Sterling, the *Athenaeum* served as a useful platform from which to expound their unpopular ideas. At this point in the Society's history these ideas were well on their way to becoming Apostolic theology, for the Society was rapidly turning into a cult of true believers who looked to Maurice and Sterling for inspiration. There probably never was a time when all the active members of the Society subscribed to a single set of beliefs, and even those who agreed to the main tenets of the Apostolic faith disagreed with one another in various important ways. Nonetheless, one can see in the *Athenaeum*, and especially in Maurice's articles, certain basic ideas which, without being so definite as a binding creed, were sufficiently distinctive to be termed 'the Cambridge philosophy' by an outside observer like the young Gladstone.[7]

In his 'Sketches of Contemporary Authors' Maurice makes clear that his quarrel with Benthamism was based on an objection to materialistic thought of any kind. The great Whig critic Francis Jeffrey is one of the several writers whom he damns because their philosophy is 'of the stamp which brings everything from without, and sees in the human mind nothing more precious or powerful than an empty receptacle for those dead forms which are borne in upon it by the external world'. Shelley's professed atheism, Maurice claims, is more truly religious than the essential atheism of such men, for Shelley 'was, in spirit and habit of feeling, the most strongly opposed of all men to that philosophy, if philosophy it may be called, which spends itself among physical causes, and can find satisfaction in mere phenomena. He uniformly referred, for the reason and the truth of things, to invisible principles within us or without, of which natural appearances are merely the clothing and the shadow.'[8]

But mere transcendentalism is not enough, for Maurice praises even more highly the writer who recognizes that the spiritual order underlying the world and the human mind is divinely created and who believes that God can be known from man's innate religious sense. Southey's great virtue, Maurice says, was such a recognition – 'a strong sense of the presence and goodness of God, whose existence he seems to have found manifested, not amid the dissections of the anatomist, nor in the crucible of the chemist, nor in anything appertainable to the order of this visible world, but as a life and power in the depths of his own heart. He saw the Deity in every thing around him, because he felt his spirit eternally within him.'[9]

In Maurice's introduction to this series of articles one can sense the significance for the Apostles of this belief in an innate divine principle that may be discovered within oneself. Here Maurice suggests that the study of contemporary writers, 'as well as every other species of human research', has as its primary purpose the pursuit of self-knowledge, for an understanding of the way the divine principle affects the individual must precede knowledge of its operations in the world at large. Knowledge of those around us becomes most important 'after the secrets of our own being have become manifest to our eyes'.[10]

The practical significance of this emphasis on self-knowledge is spelled out in Maurice's essay on Wordsworth. Wordsworth's writings, he says, 'afford an admirable illustration of the mode in which it is really useful and wise to combat the evil cause of privileged monopolies and unchristian sectarianism. It is the effect of almost all his works to make men look within for those things in which they agree, instead of looking without for those in which they differ.' The general tendency of social thought, according to Maurice, is in the other direction, towards an emphasis upon the superficial and merely phenomenal and hence towards the divisive forces of egotism, sectarian feeling and lack of concern for social ills. 'We do not trouble ourselves about the poor, for thanks to the vagrant act and the standing army they are kept pretty much out of our way...[W]e shut our ears to the gasping of decrepit children in the stifling atmosphere of cotton mills, and turn away with carelessness from the flood of debasement and misery which rolls along our streets, and overflows into our prisons.' Wordsworth's vision of God's 'vast and glorious unity of design and feeling' is thus of immediate social significance in promoting the state of mind, the sense of spiritual reality, that is the key to social awareness.[11]

Materialistic thought, on the other hand, promotes a lack of concern for one's fellow men. Maurice accuses Jeffrey and his kind of being dead to human feeling and of having no sympathy with schemes of social regeneration. The professed reformism of such materialists is, like their philosophy, a matter of mere surface. Believing that circumstances or phenomena can alone explain human behaviour, they can do no more than tinker with the machinery of society. This peremptory dismissal of much of the liberalism of his day seems to be based on a rigid application of a Coleridgean distinction between reason and understanding, or rather an expansion of this idea into a scheme of polar opposites. On one side we have the real or noumenal world of divine truth, perceived by the faculty of reason and leading us, if so perceived, to a knowledge of our true selves, to an extension of human sympathy, to a belief in social regeneration by promoting such growth of insight in others. On the other side we have the apparent or phenomenal world of ordinary appearances, perceived through the faculty of understanding and restricting us, if we perceive no more, to assertion of our egotistic selves, to selfishness and lack of concern for others, and hence to delusive schemes of reform through the manipulation of social circumstances.

This way of thinking explains Maurice's apparently ambivalent attitude to social reform and his preoccupation with literature. Sir Walter Scott, for example, is presented as at once a political reactionary and a second-rate writer, for in Maurice's view the two are the same thing. Scott, he says, describes only the surface of life and cannot escape 'the bounds of the present and the actual' to show life as it is, as 'manifestations of still higher principles, and in connection with moral and religious truth'. Unlike Wordsworth and Shelley, Scott does not really tend to promote moral good, for a truly moral author is one 'whose works have the effect of flinging men back upon themselves; of forcing them to look within for the higher principles of their existence; of teaching them that the only happiness, and the only virtue, are to be found by submitting themselves uniformly to the dictates of duty, and by aiming and struggling always towards a better state of being than that which ourselves, or those around us, have hitherto attained'.[12]

Maurice thus rejects political means as a way of effecting the social reform he desires. The would-be social reformer's first duty becomes the task of recognizing the moral principles that are the core of his identity. He must then develop these principles within himself, recognize the similar principles that lie behind the phenomena of the outer world, and encourage others to achieve a self-recognition like his own. Maurice, in that provoking way that was characteristic of him throughout his life, thus appears to sidestep the issue of social change by substituting a theory of education for a theory of political reform.

Yet it would be fairer to say that Maurice had achieved a reconciliation, however temporary, between two of the major forces of his background. His family's political liberalism, with which he had always been in sympathy, demanded commitment to social reform. His sisters' and mother's religious zeal, which he could not ignore, demanded the pursuit of personal salvation and concern for the souls of others. By identifying the soul or essential self with Coleridge's 'reason', Maurice found in philosophical idealism an ally, perhaps a replacement, for evangelical faith. In a minor elaboration upon Coleridge's idea of the 'clerisy' he assigned the task of social regeneration to those who had experienced spiritual awakening. Thus he himself speaks as a prophet, one with a fresh view of the social problems that concerned him and conventional liberals, but a view that set him firmly in opposition to conventional liberalism. It is perhaps in this sense that we should understand his own account of his early development: 'I did not, however, at Cambridge or London, wear the proper Liberal livery, though on practical questions I shouted with them. I was still under the influence of Coleridge's writings – himself I never saw. His book on the "Ideas of the State," [*sic*] which appeared at this time, interested me very much. I accepted to a great degree the principle of it, though not all the conclusions. With the Benthamites, therefore, I was still at war.'[13]

Whatever one may think of Maurice's early beliefs as a guide to political behaviour (or for that matter as a guide to Coleridgean principles), there is no doubt of their value as educational theory, for they are based on a profound sense of the psychological needs of young men like himself. In place of the self-denying accumulation of factual knowledge demanded by the Honours degree system, in place of the self-indulgent idleness encouraged by the Ordinary degree system, in place of the self-assertive rant enforced by the Union's traditions, Maurice offered his fellow-Apostles a justification for personal growth through contemplation, a process based on the individual's own assessment of his needs yet shared with others pursuing the same ideal. The Society did not merely fill a gap in the University's curriculum by providing informal discussion of contemporary culture. Its more essential educational role was to promote the individual's sense of his identity and personal worth through exploration and definition of his most deeply held beliefs. Again, one notes the Society's similarity to what I have called the confessional group, in which soul-searching and public confession of belief are the group's main business. Of course if one searches the souls of a number of the more talented undergraduates of any period, one is likely to discover a preoccupation with the society of the day and with contemporary problems. But for the Apostles the question of their relation to the outer world was a secondary if important concern, following on the attainment of self-knowledge. And Maurice's ideas justified this attitude, for society was to be regenerated by a small group of right-thinking men, by men who, having seen deeply into themselves, could teach others to see, in short by men like themselves.

The *Literary Chronicle* and *Athenaeum* thus strongly emphasize the need for social reform, but the goal desired by Maurice and Sterling was essentially a spiritual change, one to be achieved through education. Sterling perhaps best expressed their common belief at this time: 'A change of institutions is necessary; and this change cannot take place without an alteration in the mind of the country. To this reform of thought and feeling, it is not likely that England will arrive, until she has been taught by much sorrow, been disciplined into wisdom by suffering, and learnt to listen to the voices of the teachers, of such men as Wordsworth and Coleridge'.[14]

From this point of view, the true reformers are those who can 'so instruct the crowd as to give them principles, not opinions', the few who 'though in the age, are not of it, who partake not of its spirit, worship not its idols, but who have proposed to themselves a more sublime idea of intellectual excellence and moral purity than any it will supply them with, and who, with all the power that has been given to them, labour to induce their fellows to exalt their minds to the same standards'.[15]

Evidently the Apostles had their own idols at that time, chief among them Coleridge, whom an editorial note in the *Literary Chronicle* identifies, for the benefit of uninstructed readers, as 'the greatest man now living'. When J. C. Hare and his brother Augustus published their *Guesses at Truth*, they were enthusiastically hailed by Maurice as 'profound reverers of Mr Coleridge', and the book itself was praised as second only to Coleridge's *Aids to Reflection.* Such books, Maurice explained to his readers, are necessarily unpopular. Referring to a celebrated prophetess of the day, he suggested the likely fate of the true oracle in an age addicted to false ones. 'If Mademoiselle Le Normand and Mr Coleridge,' he wrote, 'would each of them advertise to answer questions at the Egyptian Hall, we would wager that the lady would be as generally visited as if she had a pig-face or a Hottentot protuberance; and that, after the first three days, the teacher would be as completely deserted as if he were really inspired. Those who, like the authors of the "Guesses at Truth," make it their great object to set free their own minds and those of their fellow-men, to feel as deeply and think as earnestly as they can, and to teach others to do so. . .such persons as these, whether in Rome, London, or Cambridge, are very certain to meet at first with but scanty audiences, jealous reception, and niggard entertainment.'[16]

The Apostles sometimes satirized their own tendency to self-righteousness, but they more frequently revelled in the sensation that they were among the few spiritually liberated men of the age, those who tenaciously held to the true faith while the world in general went on its misguided way. The period of Apostolic journalism marks the appearance of that Apostolic rhetoric that was to prevail for at least a hundred years – a humorous derivation from philosophical idealism, in which they alone are noumena, the outside world is dismissed as mere phenomena, and election to the Society is an attainment to 'the category of Being'. This rhetoric has always had a serious undertone, and the Apostles of Maurice's time plainly believed that the main characteristic of their age was a vicious, self-destructive sectarianism from which they themselves had fortunately won release.

A character sketch in the *Literary Chronicle* gives a vivid description of the pattern of conversational thinking that they saw all around them. The subject is 'The Sectarian'; the author, probably John Sterling:

His character is compounded of two elements – worldliness and fear. He has no spiritual apprehension; no sense of a life within the material objects around him; no faith to look beyond the outward and the visible; in short, he has no feeling of religion whatsoever, and so far he is merely a worldling. But he is more, for he has a consciousness of this great want, and a fear of its consequences. This fear teaches him that there is an eternal immutable truth which it should be the purpose of our lives to seek after, if haply we may find it; but it teaches him not that this truth is essentially spiritual, has its origin in the bosom of God, and its seat in the heart of man; for this he could only learn from the sweeter voice of love. He seeks, therefore, amidst dry and mouldering forms for. . .a relief from all his terrors. He picks out from the innumerable creeds in which men have attempted to enclose the infinity of truth, some one which suits his temper or squares with his convenience better than the rest; and in the peaceable enjoyment of this, his worldly temper would easily rest content. But the vulture Fear, which there is nothing in the dry husks of theology to satisfy, preys upon him still, and to quiet its restlessness, he becomes a zealot and enthusiast. He pacifies the gnawing suspicion that he is not right with the certainty that others are wrong.

. . . .

Yet with all his industry in digging at the roots of other people's opinions, there is no one more fearful of investigating the foundations of his own. He dare not go down into the chambers of his soul, to inquire how many of the opinions, of which he talks so much, are really living and abiding convictions there; fear is the origin of his character, and its result – cowardice is its prevailing characteristic.[17]

To do the Apostles justice, this is by no means an inaccurate description of conventional belief of many kinds, and their own belief in the unity of human truth underlying varying opinions is, no doubt, an improvement on the narrow-minded attitudes they attack. But one is likely to encounter difficulty in persuading others of the superiority of one's own beliefs, especially when the relation between belief and action is somewhat nebulous. To discover the limitations of Apostolic theology as expounded by Maurice and his followers, we need merely trace the careers of any of its exponents, including Maurice himself, who soon despaired of what he later called his 'sham creed and pretentious toleration'.[18]

Maurice's uncertainty at this time was intensified by financial problems within his family. His father had invested heavily in the Spanish liberal cause, the bonds he held suddenly became worthless, and his older children were concerned to find some way of supporting themselves. Partly in the hope of making money, Maurice made a pact with Sterling and his old friend Whitmore that each should write a novel. The plan had complications they had not foreseen: Whitmore's novel was never published, perhaps never written, Sterling's *Arthur Coningsby* did not appear until 1833, and Maurice's *Eustace Conway* until 1834. Neither work proved a landmark in its author's career: Sterling and Maurice were not cut out to be novelists, although their novels have a certain interest as showing something of their thinking at the time they were written.[19]

In the figure of his hero Eustace Conway, Maurice dramatized the sort of development that he, Sterling and other Apostles were experiencing. Eustace Conway is a young man who spends his first year at university reading hard but soon learns to avoid both the reading and the rowing sets. He associates with an unusual group that sounds very like the Society of the mid-twenties: 'above all, he seemed to delight in a group of which he was the centre; though, judging from his report, the only attraction amongst its members must have been an utter unlikeness in birth, tastes, prospects, dispositions, every thing except a habit of talking about society, poetry, metaphysics, politics, religion, or whatever else they did not understand'. A rebel against the university system, he is delighted to leave and plunges into an active political life in London, although he finds that he has nothing in common with the liberals of that time except a desire for social reform. He becomes greatly disillusioned with them, especially because they seem to lack any imaginative faculty, and he passes from Utilitarianism to 'Spiritualism' – a faith in the effect of education on the human will that corresponds to Apostolic theology as revealed in the *Athenaeum*. But this solution also proves illusory, and he is then faced with a long struggle against his own 'horror of becoming one of the majority'. 'Some men,' the narrator comments, 'think it an act of great moral daring, to proclaim their doubts, whether an Aristocracy is not mischievous, and a Church establishment abominable. Eustace Conway endured many a fierce conflict, before he could find courage to acknowledge that either was necessary. To look evidence stedfastly in the face...to abandon what seemed the firmest standing-ground, and balance yourself for a time on feeble twigs, he found was cruel labour: but it grieved him still more to think, that if he did unfortunately adopt the popular conclusion, he would find himself rank-and-file with the comfortable pluralists, and grinding landlords.'[20]

Gradually Eustace Conway comes to recognize the spiritual pride that underlies his position: 'Practically, he had enlarged, not narrowed the circle of his contempt. . .He said to the Liberal, – "Stand by, I am holier than thou art!" he said to the Tory, – "Stand by, I am wiser than thou art!". . .He had thought within himself. . ."how totally unlike I am to that snail who crawleth every Sunday to his parish church, and every week-day to his counting-house! Poor Whigs and Radicals! I know all your arguments, and how easily I can smother you. Poor churchmen! I know what exceeding fools you are –". . .

'And what remained for him? – He had run the gauntlet of opinions – he had acknowledged Society as God, with the Utilitarians – he had acknowledged Self as God with the Spiritualists – he now confessed that He is God whose praise is in the Churches; and at each stage he seemed to have gained more arrogance. . .At length the light, the painful agonizing light, began to enter the dark places of his soul. He saw, with amazement and shame, that instead of having a right to boast that he had really tried many faiths, he had never fairly tried any. . .A Spiritualist he could not be again, for that faith is always tending downwards or upwards, always merging either in devotion to something above ourselves, or to something below ourselves. But the other two courses were still open. He might become wholly the slave of the opinion of mankind, whom as yet he had only partially served – or he might ascend to that service which is perfect freedom.'[21]

Maurice's own pursuit of that service led him to go to Oxford to complete his degree – apparently an act of self-mortification and penance, for the task would have been an easier one at Cambridge, and he would have been among friends. But an acquaintance of Sterling's at Exeter College took him under his wing, and his friendship was cultivated by Gladstone, acting on Hallam's injunction to make the most of him. At Oxford Maurice was baptized into the Church of England (much to his father's distress) and began a programme of studies that led, in time, to ordination and the beginnings of a clerical career in an obscure rural curacy. He was elected to the essay club that Gladstone had established in imitation of the Society, but this was a short-lived affair, plagued by poor attendance and dispute among its members. Maurice was chosen as President early in 1832, and at least one of his papers was received with great enthusiasm, but he certainly did not influence this group as he did the Apostles.[22]

Essentially, leadership seems to have been the last thing Maurice then wanted. Submission to external authority – specifically, to Christian orthodoxy – was his main goal, and in his pursuit of it he seems to have carried humility to an extreme even for him. His letters to his family suggest that this spiritual struggle had become almost an obsession, so much so as nearly to obliterate the sense of social evil that marks his earlier writings. 'I do not wish you to understand,' he told his sister Priscilla, 'that I have been assaulted with doubts respecting any of the great doctrines, but only that I feel it most necessary to gain a more thorough and vigorous grasp of them as the only protection against the lusts of my own heart and the thousand, ten thousand enfeebling, perverting influences that are continually trying with too much success to twist it aside. I think I am beginning to feel something of the intense pride and atheism of my own heart, of its hatred to truth, of its utter lovelessness.'[23]

To his mother he wrote, 'I have been driven to ask myself what I am myself, and I find that all the mischiefs I discovered in others and in the age were really rioting within myself. Of all spirits, I believe the spirit of judging is the worst, and it has had the rule of me I cannot tell you how dreadfully and how long.'[24]

Maurice was now about to launch on what was to be his life's work – a passionate and unceasing struggle to reveal in the Church of England the force for spiritual union that he had always sought. Carlyle, who disliked Maurice personally, spoke to Sterling of the 'misgiving' inspired in him by Maurice's 'vehement earnestness in twisting such a rope of sand, as I reckon that to be', and this negative judgement was to be echoed many times, by Ruskin, by Matthew Arnold, by Frederic Harrison, by Leslie Stephen, to name only a few of those who were repelled by Maurice's teaching. Sterling's friend Caroline Fox was gentler in expressing her disbelief in the Mauricean vision: Maurice's 'notion of Quakerism,' she wrote, 'is, that it is all included in the belief of the Church of England, and therefore George Fox mistook his calling when he separated himself and followers into a sect. Sterling would fain abolish all sects, and desires that all might concentrate their light into one pure Crystal. But I fear that this Crystal will never be discovered but in Utopia or – Heaven.' Nor were the Apostles who regarded Maurice as their spiritual leader able to follow him in his later views, although he remained a great personal influence over several of them and in time became a prophet for a younger set of men, among them some of the Apostles of the early eighteen-fifties.[25]

The Society however remained true to Maurice's most essential teaching. For the Apostles, the most significant form of human communication did not occur at the level of sharing opinion, since at this level misunderstanding and dissension bred easily. Like Maurice, they sought a deeper, unifying level, one of active sympathy for other people and their personal beliefs. This attitude was passed down to successive generations of Apostles, most of whom knew little of Maurice himself and nothing of his family background, many of whom quite lacked the passionate concern for religious truth that drove Maurice himself. Yet each was a member of the spiritual family that Maurice created as a substitute for his own. Impelled by the force of Maurice's search for unity, the Apostles learned to become 'the brethren' and never forgot the lesson.

Meanwhile, Maurice himself remained a revered, somewhat distant, almost legendary figure on the edge of the Apostolic circle that evolved from the early days of the Society. His writings were discussed and circulated among them. When he had gained a London pulpit, they came to hear him preach and brought others. He appeared at their annual dinner – a distinguished and strangely compelling figure, his face deeply marked with the spiritual suffering he had passed through, his speech intense and passionately earnest. After Maurice's death his old associate Gladstone found the right phrase to describe him, in a letter to Maurice's son. He was, wrote Gladstone, 'a spiritual splendour', and the tribute is the more striking for coming from someone who could never really sympathize with Maurice's distinctive views. Maurice is far more significant than the nineteenth-century liberal Anglican cause he spoused. He was one of those who decisively shaped the moral consciousness of his time, and his role in the development of the Society was merely an early phase in the career of one of the most extraordinary spiritual leaders and teachers of the Victorian age.[26]

CHAPTER 6

THE MYSTICS

As F. D. Maurice passed through the climactic stage of his personal development in the late eighteen-twenties, his progress was watched with anxiety and admiration by John Sterling and his fellow-mystics. By mid-1829 Maurice had left the *Athenaeum* to visit his family for a few months, and had told Sterling that he planned to resume his legal studies on his return to London. 'He will make a brilliant and profound lawyer,' Sterling told Trench; 'but philosophy will lose a wise man; and he himself will, I fear, have little chance of happiness. If there be any one fit to make the craft something more than a trade, it is Maurice; but he will always, in obedience to what is almost a necessity of his character, persuade himself that he is is a mere mechanic, and be rendered miserable by the belief.' Within a few months, however, Sterling was able to report to Blakesley that 'Maurice is going to Oxford and then probably into the Church'. In Sterling's view this decision meant that there might still be hope for Anglican theology, for he reverently added, 'While he lives the breed of the Hookers and Taylors is not quite extinct.'[1]

Sterling's own development was by no means so encouraging. 'I feel myself growing back into Chaos, and the deadness of that ancient Night,' he had confessed to Blakesley; 'a mode of extinction which is just as foolish and wrong though not nearly so rapid, energetic, or satisfactory as a pistol-ball or a precipice. I envy you exceedingly when I hear of your going in for scholarships, and reading and writing, and talking as if you found some comfort in so doing. Sleeping seems to me the perfection of existence; and I only lament that I cannot find any cavern wherein I might sleep on for ever. . .I see nothing for it but opium. I have never tried yet that fine condiment of the fancy: and I believe I am now exactly in the right state of mind for using it with effect, either in the way of a daily stimulant or a final sedative. . .The great necessity is to feel. I am an iceberg that wants to be awoke by a red-hot-poker, – and I would rather it were that of hell than none at all. . .As yet you cannot understand this. In a year or two you will be wiser, – and if possible we will take counsel together.'[2]

As the senior members of the Society left Cambridge and tried to launch their careers, they encountered difficulties not readily apparent to those still engrossed in student life. For several of them the intellectual exploration encouraged within the Society merely made their transition to practical reality the more painful. Understanding the nature of their beliefs was no longer enough, for the time had come to translate belief into significant action. While Sterling and his closest friends differed greatly in the solutions they found and the difficulties they had to overcome, they shared a single problem – after all that talking, what to do?

For Sterling himself there was a succession of answers, none satisfactory. His name has appeared in this chronicle as that of F. D. Maurice's most devoted follower, but this was only one of the many roles he was to play in the course of his short life. Sterling was one of those men who greatly influence others but achieve little themselves. 'Personal influence is the strongest and most subtle of powers,' Fanny Kemble wrote in her memoirs, 'and Sterling impressed all who knew him as a man of undoubted genius; those who never knew him will perhaps always wonder why.' Reflecting on Tennyson, Hallam and the rest of 'those very remarkable young men' who formed her brother's circle, she judged Sterling 'by far the most brilliant and striking in his conversation, and the one of whose future eminence we should all of us have augured most confidently'. But 'Sterling's genius was his *Wesen*, himself,' she concluded, 'and he could detach no portion of it that retained anything like the power and beauty one would have expected.'[3]

Chronic ill-health had much to do with Sterling's erratic and somewhat unsatisfactory career, but chronic intellectual and emotional insecurity was even more important. He came of a rootless Irish family and throughout his life seemed something of a wanderer, forever in search of his true home, the place that would be the expression of his real identity. His schooling was erratic and unsettled, and it seemed to inspire in him an almost neurotic sensitivity to the opinions of others and an anxious desire for their approval. An orthodox Christian upbringing had instilled in him a strong sense of duty but no deep allegiance to traditional forms of religious belief. The opposed forces of a demanding conscience and a daring, restless intellect drove him to adopt and reject one system of thought after another as the key to his own salvation and that of society. Whatever Sterling believed, or wished to believe, he expressed with passionate conviction and great rhetorical force. But his assertiveness and ability to influence others cloaked a basic, unchanging insecurity that left him always searching for a new faith. Sterling could believe in anything but himself, as his closest friends came to realize. 'I think him uncertain in the grounds upon which his opinions rest,' John Kemble acutely observed, 'and liable from such uncertainty to constant changes.' The prediction was accurate: only in his final months, when his death was certain, did Sterling ever seem entirely sure of himself.[4]

When Sterling arrived at Cambridge at the age of eighteen, he had been greatly influenced by the Whiggish liberalism of his father, then a rising political journalist. Perhaps led by the example of Charles Buller and other outstanding Union debaters, he struck a boldly Radical stance for a time. But in 1827, when he was about to follow Maurice's example and become a law student in London, he was acquiring an equally exaggerated enthusiasm for Coleridgean thought, as interpreted by Maurice. Yet he and Maurice regarded as merely laughable the idea that their opinions were identical. The agreement was on the level of principles, it seems, and Sterling's mind was then, as always, only too susceptible to new influences and impressions. In Jane Carlyle's cruel summing-up of his character, Sterling 'wanted back-bone'. But his brilliant mind and remarkable gift for imaginative sympathy were to win him the respect and love of such diverse figures as Maurice, J. S. Mill, J. C. Hare, Thomas Carlyle, Francis Newman and Caroline Fox, to mention only a few of Sterling's extraordinary assortment of close friends. Sterling's genius may have consisted only of being himself, but that was a considerable accomplishment.[5]

As a leading figure among the Apostles Sterling was both inspiring and unsettling, for they could never be quite sure what he would think and say next. At the Union he had seemed a fiery Radical ('a Mr Sterling told us we were going to have a revolution and "he did not care if his hand should be the first to lead the way"'). But soon after going down he shocked his former ally John Kemble, then the most ardent of Benthamite reformers, with what seemed a complete about-face. '[Y]ou know what an enthusiastic person he is,' Kemble complained to W. B. Donne, 'and how apt to run off into any system that takes his fancy: this has now thrown him upon religion until I think it has hurt him. He has now adopted that drivelling sentiment of Human Perfectibility, and talks of it like one inspired. He said that a war of

Extremes was now waging all over the world in almost every subject... that it was a contest between the Utilitarians and the Religionists: that Despotism and Aristocracy were engaged in a final effort against Republicanism and so forth: But what most annoyed me was his saying that he did not think our efforts to instruct and Liberate the people, would be productive of Good. – Saul is among the prophets with a vengeance!' Sterling's new ideas included a theory that a religious person was as superior to a merely intellectual one as the intellectual was to a mere animal, and this had not gone down well with Kemble.[6]

Sterling's sudden change of views coincided with his first visit to S. T. Coleridge at Highgate. 'I was in his company about three hours,' he noted; 'and of that time he spoke during two and three quarters. It would have been delightful to listen as attentively, and certainly easy for him to speak just as well for the next forty-eight hours. On the whole his conversation, or rather monologue, is by far the most interesting I ever heard or heard of.' With characteristic malice, Thomas Carlyle later selected only the first of these sentences for his *Life of John Sterling* and added that to 'sit as a passive bucket and be pumped into, whether you consent or not, can in the long-run be exhilarating to no creature'. But the short run lasted longer for Sterling than Carlyle liked to admit. Eventually Sterling became deeply discontented with what he believed to be Coleridge's intellectual cowardice, but during Coleridge's lifetime he was a devoted disciple and, in typical fashion, attributed to Coleridge and Maurice all that he regarded as worthwhile in his own intellectual development. Just as typically, he bent his considerable talents to the task of spreading the new gospel at the London Debating Society and in the *Literary Chronicle* and the *Athenaeum*.[7]

But in late 1829, when the younger Apostles at Cambridge wrote to Sterling about their efforts on behalf of Wordsworth at the Cambridge Union and asked him to take part in their plans to bear the news of Shelley's poetry to the heathen at Oxford, he astonished them with yet another change of mind. 'I am glad I had nothing to do with your debate on Wordsworth,' he informed Blakesley. 'Almost all oratory, and *all* that of young men is mere lying. I should be still more reluctant to say any thing about Shelley for though I deem as highly as ever of his genius his whole thinking seems to me to have been founded on a mistake, and I believe he has in his time done many of us a good deal of harm[.] I scarcely hold fast by anything but Shakspeare, Milton, and Coleridge and I have nothing serious to say to any one but to read the "Aids to Reflection in the formation of a *Manly* Character" – a book the more necessary now to us all because except in England I do not see that there is a chance of any *men* being produced any where.'[8]

This sudden shift of opinion caused much talk at Cambridge, and Blakesley felt it necessary to reassure one of the most promising of the new Apostles, Alfred Tennyson, that Sterling had not really become an apostate from the true faith. 'I am thoroughly convinced,' Blakesley wrote to Tennyson, after visiting Sterling in London, 'that his opinions are not in the proper sense of the word at all changed, they are precisely the same principles which he has entertained since I have known him.' In Blakesley's opinion Sterling should be seen as a pioneering genius who could not be expected to be systematic in his discovery of truth. Sterling's real problem was the narrow-mindedness of his critics, 'the mousing owls of Cambridge', as Blakesley called them, using the ultimate term of Apostolic contempt. 'He saw the abuses of the present system of things which is upheld by the strong hand of power and custom, and he attacked them accordingly,' Blakesley explained to Tennyson. 'For this conduct he was dubbed a Radical. – He soon saw that the Reforms proposed by that party were totally inadequate to the end which they proposed: that if carried to their fullest effect they would only remove the symptoms and not the cause of evil; that this cause was the selfish spirit which pervades the whole frame of society at present, and that to counterbalance the effects the cause of them must be removed. This end he at first probably thought with Shelley might be effected by lopping off those institutions in which that selfish spirit exhibits itself without any more efforts. He afterwards saw with Wordsworth that this was not the true method: but that we must implant another principle with which selfishness cannot co-exist, and trust that this plant as it grows up will absorb the nourishment of the weed, in which case those wickednesses and miseries, which are only the forms in which the latter develops itself, will of their own accord die away, as soon as their principle of vegetation is withered and dried up. – And it is not wonderful that a mind like Sterling's entering with earnestness and devotion into all that it does, should in this last mentioned stage of development look back with something like sorrow and contempt on the less perfect state from which it has just emerged.'[9]

This ingenious explanation of Sterling's intellectual development may be substantially true, but it avoids the real problem of his emotional instability. Sterling's feelings of 'something like sorrow and contempt' were more persistent than Blakesley might have cared to admit, and at times they amounted to an overwhelming despair.

Sterling's contributions to the *Athenaeum* include a series of meditations on English society – 'Fragments from the Travels of Theodore Elbert, a young Swede' – and these provide a striking record of the impact of his two prophets, Maurice and Coleridge, on his insecure, conscience-ridden mind. His alter ego, Theodore Elbert, is preoccupied with the spiritual and social degradation he observes. Looking out over London from the outer gallery of St Paul's Cathedral, Elbert is struck by 'the size of Mammon's temple, and the number of his worshippers'. 'We scarcely connect the idea of religion,' he says, 'with those churches which are so entirely imbedded among worldly structures, and many of which we know to be completely mere husks and shadows of devotion, scarcely ever entered even by a score out of all those thousands now hurrying past them – empty pretences and solemn mockeries!'

The crowds of London seem to fill him with despair: 'I have, as it were, beneath my hand, a million of living souls; yet, in fact, to moral purposes, dead and decaying. Nurtured in alternations of toil and vice, they are, through life, bound down by the tyrannous necessities of their daily existence, or only loosed at intervals for the relaxations of debasing excess. . .These myriads know scarce anything but the pressure of the hour.'

Why should this be so, he wonders, when he considers that the city also contains some 'hundreds, at least, of expansive hearts and searching intellects', and when he turns towards the 'dim eminence' of Highgate Hill to muse on Coleridge's 'great and circular mind'. Yet those who have achieved spiritual awareness are disregarded, despite 'the nominal supremacy of Christianity' proclaimed by the building on which he stands. Selfishness reigns supreme over English society and dictates its miseries and evils. 'Look at that dark roof,' he exclaims, – it covers a prison: and there the laws of the country proclaim that the most atrocious guilt is collected, – the worst moral diseases. We do nothing to make men self-denying and conscientious. . .We do little towards instructing, nothing towards educating them; and we set them the perpetual example of secure selfishness. A wretched child, born perhaps in a work-house, and nurtured in a brothel, is taught to gain his daily bread by crime. . .at last comes the sudden vengeance of the law; and, to remedy the evil, he is thrown into a prison; probably the only abode on earth worse than his habitual home. He learns still more to glory in criminal enterprise. . .until, before he is yet a man, some consummate outrage brings him to the scaffold. Then through all these streets pours the dense throng of eager spectators. . .to see the horrible removal from the world of a being, who, perhaps, never heard the name of God or duty, or received the sympathy of one human creature. Such is society. Such is London. Such is the perfect working of the Church, which reared the fabric I stand upon.'[10]

Although Sterling tries to end his meditation on a positive note by talking about the beneficial effect of right-thinking men, his sense of futility is the dominant emotion. His sympathy for those who suffer from the social ills of the time was plainly a helpless sympathy – a desire for involvement and action that shows how far he felt he was from real involvement and real action. While he was committed to social reform, he seems to have had no hope for the future but rather a great desire to escape from the world and from the demands of his conscience. In another of these articles we find Theodore Elbert, once more in the streets of London, contemptuously thinking that 'there is more of effective movement in the mind of one philosopher or poet, in one half-hour, than in all Cornhill in a century'. 'It is hard,' Elbert admits, '. . .to retain and cherish the feeling that each of these atoms is in truth a living mind. . .to keep alive the consciousness that we are bound by a thousand sympathies, and by identity of nature and destiny, to even the most degraded things of all the throngs around us.'[11]

The despondency that Sterling felt, even while he was busily engaged with the *Athenaeum* and the London Debating Society, was shared by Richard Trench, after Maurice his closest friend among the Apostles. Like Sterling, Trench suffered from religious uncertainty in his early years, and he believed that it was Sterling, more than anyone else, who helped him through this personal crisis. Yet in almost every other respect the two were diametric opposites, and it was no accident of fate that dictated Sterling's eventual rejection of Christian orthodoxy and Trench's eventual role as a pillar of the Church.[12]

Trench came of an aristocratic background and had been educated at Harrow. The principal influence on him during his early years was that of his mother, an extraordinary woman of cosmopolitan interests and literary talents who died in 1827, while he was still an undergraduate. It must have seemed then that a literary career lay before him. He was deeply involved in the study of Spanish literature, he ran a small literary journal called *The Translator*, he wrote poetry, and he had written a play good enough for Macready to want to stage it. Trench's friend Donne believed him to have greater poetic potential than Alfred Tennyson and hoped that he would devote himself to literature alone. But it was Trench who told the younger poet,

'Tennyson, we cannot live in Art', and he believed what he said. His need for orthodox religious faith was the central principle in his serious, rather melancholy temperament. A literary career was no more possible for him than the many other secular occupations his extraordinary personal talents might have laid open to him. Not that these talents were neglected in the course of his long and active life, for he was to earn high distinction as a Churchman, Biblical scholar, religious writer, poet and philologist. But religion was the primary fact of life for Trench, and if he had known of his friend Blakesley's later regret at the way 'the clergyman. . .swallowed up the poet', he would have thought the sentiment quite misguided. The future Archbishop of Dublin should not, however, be confused with the Richard Trench known to Hallam and the young Tennyson: as a young man and a central figure in the Apostles his most notable characteristics were his intellectual and artistic gifts, his deeply moral attitude to life, and the mental depression and confusion that preceded the final resolution of his religious difficulties.[13]

Although Trench tried several means of escape from the doubt that plagued him, he seems to have known from the first that no secular answer would suffice. Having taken his degree in early 1829 and found himself with time on his hands, he toyed with romantic ideas of travel as a temporary antidote for the acute depression he felt. He was tempted, he told Donne, 'to seek in melancholy earnest some blue sky and Southern mistress: not that I blaspheme the mind, so far as to believe that these last would confirm happiness: but it seems that a form of refined Epicureanism, though not a secure haven, is a refuge at least, for those who fail in their attempt to fulfil the higher end of existence'. Trench was doubtless unaware that this comment might be taken to reflect on Donne as well as himself, since Donne had recently deserted Cambridge for the secluded life of a country gentleman. There may be a touch of gentle satire in Donne's reply, which contains an invitation to visit him at his home in Norfolk, where Trench will find 'a dull and inoffensive race: very little differing from the beasts that perish except that perhaps we eat and drink more and sometimes go to Church'.[14]

By April Trench had set off on a lengthy tour of the Continent, but travel did not appear to lighten his despairing moods or settle his mind. Much of the poetry he wrote at this time reflects his uncertainty, and it seems to have been equally evident from his letters, for Blakesley told Donne that at one moment Trench planned to return to Cambridge to prepare himself for ordination and the next moment was set on 'continuing his travels in Africa, with a view probably of regenerating the Moors and opening them to the influence of Shelley and Wordsworth: or perhaps on setting himself up as a new prophet[,] for which he has a great hankering'.[15]

Blakesley's tone may seem sceptical, but he was in fact a great admirer of Trench. Blakesley's austere, distant manner hid a strong capacity for friendship and a deep loyalty to those few who could see past the façade. Those who knew him superficially and disliked him for his seemingly cold, superior ways might have been surprised to know him capable of such enthusiasm as he showed in praising Trench to one of the younger Apostles, Richard Milnes. 'Great men have been among us in our day,' Blakesley wrote: 'you and I have seen and known many men very far indeed above the vulgar, but none among them come near to Trench. – He blends the deepest earnestness of purpose with the most solicitous kindness and regard for the feelings of others that is possible: the best of men, he distrusts his own goodness and the most completely disinterested he half suspects himself of selfishness. – I know no one who so completely realizes Shelley's words "To fear himself and love all human kind." But enough of this, for I know you laugh at my Trench worship.'[16]

While Blakesley admired Trench and Sterling he was not preyed upon by visions of his moral destiny as they were, and his early development was correspondingly calmer and more mundane. Blakesley was the only son of a London merchant and a product of St Paul's School. There, and at Cambridge, he was an outstanding scholar, distinguished above all for his powers of analytical thought and precise expression. The law would have been his natural profession, but ill-health forced him to accept an academic and clerical career. He taught at Cambridge until the mid-forties, then served ably for many years as a country clergyman and rose to become Canon of Canterbury and Dean of Lincoln. But he was far from ecclesiastical in character. Blakesley was a lucid, exact, logical and unsparing critic, with a great gift for 'discovering a flaw in an argument, or a deficiency in a line of evidence'. Three of the papers he read the Society are extant, and they show careful, cold reasoning of a sort that must have made him a considerable influence on those around him. He is as capable in undertaking a subject entirely new to him, such as the effect of the national debt, as he is in considering whether 'the Mosaic Institutions' were 'adapted to promote the happiness of the Jewish Nation'. The latter paper is a complex and substantial historical essay prefaced by an entirely characteristic remark: 'it is necessary both to the observance of the laws of this Society and to the freedom which is indispensable to a philosophical discussion that I should be allowed to consider the books of the Old Testament merely in the light of ancient documents which have come down to us, and without reference to their real or supposed inspiration'. Blakesley was capable of viewing even his own enthusiasms with amused detachment: when his idol William Wordsworth proved to have political feet of clay, Blakesley told Donne that he hoped 'the Devil always assigns a triple damnation to those who by their back-slidings destroy one's theories. Really it is too bad after having almost bartered one's Salvation for a high doctrine, to have it upset by some cursed fact or other, which ought to have learned to be more accommodating by now.'[17]

Blakesley and Trench were the linking figures within the mystic group, for both were equally friendly with Maurice and Sterling on the one hand and with Donne and Kemble on the other, although these two pairs of friends were not so close to one another. Indeed, Donne was not to meet Maurice for some years, nor did he have direct contact with several of the most important members of the group that formed around Hallam and Tennyson. Nonetheless he remained, through his correspondence and his strong friendships with certain Apostles, a vital member of the Apostolic circle.

Donne's career, like Blakesley's, serves as a contrast to the painful progress of their fellow-mystics. Donne belonged to an old-established Norfolk family and was the only son of a surgeon who had died before Donne came up to Cambridge in 1825. At the end of 1828, after keeping ten terms, Donne left Cambridge without taking his final examinations or his degree, for he found himself unable to profess allegiance to orthodox Anglicanism. (The one essay he read the Society during his active membership would not have pleased admirers of Paley, for it dealt with the 'Evidences of Mahometanism'.) Donne's heretical views proved temporary, but he seems never to have been disappointed in his decision to settle down in the seclusion of country life. He planned to marry a woman he had loved for years, and he was soon successful. Being altogether less ambitious and more stable than many of his Apostolic friends, Donne was content with a programme of private study and a modest career as a critic and occasional journalist. In time he was to rise to positions of some eminence, of which perhaps the most congenial to his temperament was that of Librarian to the

London Library. But as a young man he was much admired and envied by his friends for having willingly accepted a quiet, retiring life. They admired his character, too, for Donne had a warm, charming, gentle personality that is as hard to describe as it is evident from his letters and the fond terms used of him by other members of the circle. A stabilizing factor in the group was Donne's affectionate concern for his fellow-Apostles, above all his unswerving loyalty to the giddy and flamboyant Kemble, who might have tried the patience of the most devoted friend.[18]

J. M. Kemble was a handsome, talented extrovert with a compelling personality, some unfortunate mannerisms and traits, and a flair for all sorts of things. His father, Charles Kemble, was the greatest actor of the time, and John Kemble had a strongly theatrical streak in his character. His family made much of him and expected much, and he grew up to expect much of himself. But he showed little judgement and less caution in finding expression for his extraordinary gifts, and the result was a career of fits and starts that often appeared to be self-defeating and that ended abruptly with death in early middle age. His personal relationships are no more easily summarized, for he could inspire the deepest sort of affection and (sometimes in the same person) the most thoroughgoing annoyance.

At Cambridge, 'Jacky' Kemble was enormously popular and equally active in almost every aspect of student life. He dazzled his fellow-students with his ability to sing, dance, shoot, row, fence, debate and drink. But Kemble did most things to excess and might fairly be called intemperate, both in character and personal habits. When his sister Fanny published her *Records of a Girlhood* in the eighteen-seventies, Charles Merivale noted with amusement her 'sororial view of the racy Black Jack in whom we delighted. . .[F]ancy a life of Falstaff by his sister!'[19]

Merivale's own view of Kemble is valuable if one-sided and condescending. As the smugly successful Dean of Ely, Merivale recalled Kemble as 'very clever, very confident, very wayward; one who took the lead among his companions but did not long keep it'. Merivale went on to explain how his late friend fell behind in the race for worldly success. Kemble, he says, came to Cambridge 'a very fair scholar, with good prospects before him; but he was bitten with politics, devoted himself to the Union and the cultivation of oratory, gave up all his time to newspapers and political essayists, acquired a great mass of information on modern subjects to which he did ample justice with his rare facility both of speaking and writing, and became, as he deserved to be, a great oracle among the more literary geniuses of his day. But of course his classics and mathematics suffered in proportion, and his academic career became a mortifying and I fear a disastrous failure.'[20]

In fact Kemble's reputation today as a scholar far exceeds Merivale's. But a balanced view of such an unbalanced person can hardly be expected from his contemporaries. One can only juxtapose various opinions and allow for the observer's prejudices. Here, for example, is a part of the sororial view that Merivale found so amusing – a teenage sister's description of her beloved but trying brother John while he was still a promising undergraduate who had recently distinguished himself by winning a prize for declamation: 'Dear John is come home with his trophy. He is really a highly gifted creature; but I sometimes fear that the passionate eagerness with which he *pursues his pursuit*, the sort of frenzy he has about politics, and his constant excitement about political questions, may actually injure his health, and the vehemence with which he speaks and writes in support of his peculiar views will perhaps endanger his future prospects.

'He is neither tory nor whig, but a radical, a utilitarian, an adorer of Bentham, a worshipper of Mill, an advocate for vote by ballot, an opponent of hereditary aristocracy, the church establishment, the army and navy, which he deems sources of unnecessary national expense... Morning, noon, and night he is writing whole volumes of arguments against them, full of a good deal of careful study and reading, and in a close, concise, forcible style, which is excellent in itself, and the essays are creditable to his laborious industry; but they will not teach him mathematics, or give him a scholarship or his degree.'[21]

In the event, Fanny Kemble's fears were justified, for her brother not only opted for the Ordinary degree but failed to win it at his first attempt. Dislike of Paley's *Evidences of Christianity* was general among the Apostles, but Kemble carried dislike to the extreme of actually attacking Paley on his final examination. Instead of parroting Paley's arguments, as was expected of him, Kemble described him as a 'miserable sophist' and tried to show the inadequacy of his theology on Benthamite grounds. The surprised examiners, not wanting to allow Kemble the martyrdom he plainly sought, deferred his degree for a year, in the hope that he would acquire in that time the proper reverence for Paley's opinions or at least a more rationally Benthamite view of his own self-interest.[22]

Kemble's later historical scholarship has been characterized as being 'given to exaggeration', and the judgement seems an apt one for his life as a whole. He seemed scarcely to care for his own welfare but rather to follow the passion of the moment wherever it led and then to find an equally engrossing and compelling cause to which to devote himself. Beneath the outrageous dramatic flourishes he allowed himself, however, lay a strong sense of moral responsibility that won him deep respect and love, even from those who deplored many of his actions. As one might expect, Kemble drew mixed reactions from the Apostolic group, being at one and the same time an energizing force, a centre of attention, a source of delight and something of a standing joke.[23]

While Kemble bounded from one extreme to another in the course of his early development, his commitment to social reform was unvarying. 'There never was a more hateful sentence written than that "Suave mari magno" of Lucretius,' he said in an early letter to Donne, in which he explained why he had become increasingly persuaded 'that Byron's character and Poetry have had a most fatal effect upon society'. (The iniquity of Lucretius' sentiment – 'It is pleasant when winds trouble the great sea to watch from the land the great trial of another' – appears to have been an Apostolic commonplace well before Tennyson's exploration of this theme in such poems as 'The Lotus-Eaters'.) Under the direct influence of F. D. Maurice, Kemble abandoned his earlier Benthamite views and adopted the mystics' cause as his own. The change, which occurred in late 1828, was greeted by his friends with delight. 'Give my warmest regards to Kemble,' Sterling wrote to Trench; 'he is a brand plucked from the burning.'[24]

In early 1829, after his first attempt to win his degree, Kemble set off for Germany for a year, for he had a passion for all things Teutonic. According to Blakesley, he spent much of his time reading Kant, while a friend who accompanied him studied magic, and both 'smoke and chew opium and Kemble writes Poetry'. Kemble's enthusiasms were also satirized by Donne, who wrote of him as 'mad for the love of meerschaums, and metaphysics, smoking and Schelling'. Yet his friends trusted Kemble's basic good sense. 'He has an antidote within himself,' Trench wrote, 'and were he to feed on poisons. . .he would turn them to nourishment.' Germany and its temptations could hardly be worse, in Trench's view, than the Benthamism from which Kemble had only recently escaped. 'He is,' claimed Trench, 'the only one who upheld for a long space of time the most degrading system of Philosophy that ever was framed without having his mind or heart impoverished or worsened by it.'[25]

Their Apostolic duty, to know themselves and seek the spiritual regeneration of mankind, was taken very seriously by these young men, whatever the extravagance of their rhetoric or the half-humorous, half-serious tone of their letters to one another. But in the case of John Kemble, the rhetoric is so extreme that one wonders if he is not making fun of himself. His letters from Germany set forth the Apostolic credo of the time with extraordinary bombast. 'One duty I still feel I have to perform,' he proclaimed to Donne: 'it is my last but my greatest: when I think of it, I am full of hope, and to it all my thoughts and feelings turn: It is to lend my hand to the great work of regenerating England, not by Political Institutions! not by extrinsic and conventional forms! By a higher and a holier work, by breathing into her the vigorous feeling of a Poet, and a Religious man, by pouring out the dull and stagnant blood which circulates in her veins, to replenish them with a youthful stream, fresh from the heart: yea so be it, even must the cost be my own life blood. This task not I alone must lay before me. To you, to Trench and Sterling, to Maurice, to all that band of surpassing men is the labour confided, and the commandment given. It is the law of your being: you cannot, must not escape from it. In God's name then on: concentrate your hopes and wishes on that point: you have the power, and I tell you you are bound to exert it: to make yourself great, that you may give greatness to others. . .My hope is in ourselves, and in that spirit of a higher feeling which the young men of this age universally possess: can the great Ideas which are abroad upon the earth perish? I think not: I hope not. Wordsworth has begun the work, he has delivered the sown field into our hand, and is not the harvest ours? Let us believe so. Years may undeceive us: and age bring its disappointment: this should not be! For if we do not live to take the sickle in our hand, we shall at least see the ripening of the ear, and our sons, or our sons' sons will be the gainers by our struggle.'

At this point the peroration momentarily subsides into a confidence: 'My plan of operation I will expound to you when I have perfected it: I will tell you however thus much, that we must strike through Education, and first at the Universities. Is the task not a perilous one, and oh how much more glorious will the struggle be. We shall do nothing till we get rid of Antichrist, and he walks abroad boldly in a Doctor of Divinity's hood, and his thought and cry are "Nego!"' 'This rant amuses me,' Kemble goes on, but within a few sentences he is at it again, describing his message as 'no rhetorical flourish to fill up my paper' and pledging eternal loyalty in the coming battle.[26]

Kemble's self-confidence was infectious, for all his posturing and his florid phrases. Several Apostles, including Trench, planned to converge on Heidelberg (where Kemble and his friend were living) in early 1830. But in the interval financial difficulties within Kemble's family led to his sister's stage debut – a resounding critical and popular success, but one that helped bring John Kemble back to England, resolved to complete his degree and enter the Church. It appears that a living had been found for him, and with this expectation he returned (he told Trench) 'to the muddy banks and intellects of reverend Camus, and B.A.'d with some other lambs in the Cambridge slaughter-house'. The occasion inspired a notable sonnet by Tennyson, who was so impressed by Kemble's determination that he predicted a glorious future for him as a 'latter Luther, and a soldier-priest'. But Arthur Hallam noted that Kemble was 'a man of less calm judgment than honest feeling'; as Hallam later remarked, 'the soldier predominates so much over the priest in Kemble's character' that one could hardly expect him to keep to his professed intention for long.[27]

'The Society here exists,' Blakesley reported to Donne: 'but our meetings are not so good as they were. There is a sort of storminess in the debates and sometimes rather a want of courteousness not arising [from] familiarity is discernible, which betokens somewhat of a want of unity of design or at least no very great frankness of feeling – I wish that you and Trench would come back for a time: much good might be done. Kemble has brought more enthusiasm than good taste with him from Germany; and is somewhat of a stumbling-block to the Neophytes.' Kemble's acting ability was however put to good use in a remarkable production of *Much Ado About Nothing*. 'Conceive Milnes doing the elegant and high minded Beatrice like a languishing trull,' Kemble wrote to Donne; 'also if you can, conceive Hallam and myself setting our faces and taming our eyes into stupidity that we might present some distant resemblances of Verges and Dogberry! I can assure you that if laughing be the criterion, no company ever did better, for from first to last, especially during the tragic scenes, the audience were in a roar.' And Donne heard from R. J. Tennant that 'all three acted extremely well, but Kemble excellently, except that he enjoyed it rather too much himself'.[28]

Though Kemble's dedication to a clerical life might seem questionable, one thing was certain: the time was ripe for action, and surely for something more concrete than journalism. Maurice, Blakesley and Donne had chosen their course of life, but Kemble, Trench and

Sterling needed something to do, some immediate goal to achieve. As it happened, their wishes were immediately met in a way that was to cause all of them deep regret, for it was at this time that the famous Spanish affair began.

Frederick Denison Maurice
(1805–1872)

John Sterling
(1806–1844)

Richard Chenevix Trench (1807–1886)

James Spedding (1808–1881)

Alfred,
Lord Tennyson
(1809–1892)

Richard
Monckton Milnes
(1809–1885)

Arthur Hallam
(1811–1833)

Henry Lushington
(1812–1855)

CHAPTER 7

THE SPANISH ADVENTURE

Everyone acquainted with the facts of Tennyson's life has heard of the ill-fated Spanish adventure of 1830–1 – of how Sterling persuaded his cousin, Robert Boyd, to help finance an insurrection of exiled liberals against the throne of Ferdinand VII, of how Hallam and Tennyson lent their aid to the scheme by carrying messages and money to the Pyrenees, of how Trench and Kemble joined a band of conspirators at Gibraltar, of how this would-be revolutionary movement ended in disaster and the death of most of those involved, including Boyd and the movement's leader, General Torrijos. This episode has been told and retold, usually as an example of the generous, romantic idealism of the Apostles, as a piece of youthful, forgivable folly. But the extent of the folly has perhaps not been fully recognized, and it has been mistakenly attributed to the Society as a whole. Very few Apostles took part in the scheme; many others knew about it but seem to have regarded it with distrust or, as in the case of Maurice, outright disapproval. Even those involved had their doubts, or had doubts thrust upon them as the affair went from bad to worse. Indeed, it appears that they required remarkable powers of self-delusion not to see from the first that General Torrijos' plans were bound to come to nothing, and one may wonder how they came to mislead themselves in this way.

Maurice's opposition to the scheme is not hard to understand. He sometimes appeared naive and unworldly, but he had few illusions about the grand professions of religious or political enthusiasts. He had carried away from his family's internecine battles a shrewd sense of the motives that too often underlie the rhetoric of ardent belief and a painful habit of judging his own motives harshly. John Kemble, on the other hand, seems to have been quite incapable of such introspection. Throughout his life Kemble was addicted to extravagant speech and behaviour: it seems quite reasonable to find him striking military poses at the side of General Torrijos, a man whose faith in himself and his cause approached the suicidal.

Richard Trench's problem was that he entirely lacked faith in any cause and yet desperately needed one. Trench was born to be a believer, but at this point in his life could achieve nothing but disbelief and was apparently in an unvarying state of acute depression. His knowledge of Spanish and his travels in Spain in the winter of 1829–30 had given him unique qualifications among the Apostles to judge Torrijos' scheme, and he knew very well that the Spanish liberals were most unlikely to regain power. But Trench needed a crusade, even a pointless one, as he admitted to W. B. Donne: 'You will say that all this is very foolish, but anything seems to me preferable to rotting in England, one's energies turning inward and corrupting: it is action, action, action that we want, and I would willingly go did I only find in the enterprize a pledge of my own earnestness.'[1]

John Sterling seemed superficially to be a born enthusiast like Kemble. But Kemble believed in himself, whereas Sterling merely tried to and failed. His problem was well understood by Trench. 'Sterling I have not seen much of,' Trench told Donne, 'as he is the prime mover of the conspiracy, and is engaged with the Junta all day – as usual, he is "laboring for his kind in grief." He reminds me often of Prince Athanase, especially in that core of despair which only his nearest friends can discern. He has no hope.'[2]

Shelley's Prince Athanase, who suffers from a nameless, inexplicable sorrow and sits 'Apart from men, as in a lonely tower, | Pitying the tumult of their dark estate,' is a romantically exaggerated figure, but his spiritual malaise resembles Sterling's. Though Sterling could persuade himself of his absolute belief in one cause or another, he could not remain persuaded, and yet each disillusionment he suffered was immediately followed by fresh illusions. But on this occasion he had very good reasons for doubting his dreams, for as Trench said he was far more than a mere abettor of the Spanish exiles' plan. Trench feared that if the plan failed Sterling would 'accuse himself as the cause of all' and commit suicide. Indeed, Sterling never forgave himself for his part in this calamitous scheme.[3]

In the first place Sterling misread the situation in which the Spanish exiles found themselves, though perhaps he was not so very much to blame for the mistake. The group of exiles in London had been there since about 1823: for about a decade before that, Spain had been in a nearly continuous state of civil disorder and party warfare, the liberals uniting around the progressive principles of the Constitution of 1812, the royalists around the tyrannical figure of Ferdinand VII. In 1823

French intervention tipped the balance in Ferdinand's favour, and the prominent members of the liberal group were faced with the choice of becoming exiles or victims of the king's revenge. In 1828 the French troops were withdrawn, but by then Ferdinand had increased his power by moving somewhat closer to the political centre, thus strengthening his hold on the majority of the Spanish people. The leader of the exiles in London was a moderate liberal, General Mina, who maintained an effective intelligence service in Spain and very correctly judged that the liberals did not have enough popular support to make an insurrection practicable. But the exiles in London – some 1,000 families by 1830 – were not prepared to listen to a counsel of despair, and Torrijos, a more radical and optimistic man, gradually won their favour. There was, however, much jealousy and little real unity within the group: only their poverty and the unpleasantness of their position drove them together.

Sterling had been acquainted with these exiled Spanish liberals for several years, for his contributions to the *Metropolitan Quarterly* of 1825–6 include translations of two Spanish songs taken 'from the dictation of exiles, who have felt the enthusiasm they breathe, and who have been engaged in the scenes they celebrate'. The Apostles had helped to raise money at Cambridge for the support of the exiles, and in January 1829 Kemble had confided to Donne 'that we are on the eve of a vast explosion in Spain; that arms and ammunition are provided, and that as soon as £5000 can be procured, a rise may be looked for there; and a word in your ear, that the first Constitutional banner that is waved over the Trocadero will number more than one young Englishman among its defenders...Think of Trench seriously requesting me to give him lessons in the broad sword, and regretting that my pistols are not at Cambridge, and that he should so be prevented from practising: conceive that quietest of human beings having become so splendidly ferocious.'[4]

When a year later Sterling's cousin Robert Boyd appeared, with time and a recent inheritance on his hands, Sterling did not hesitate to suggest that he finance the schemes of Torrijos and his junta. The junta itself, of course, was happy to accept Boyd's offer: Sterling and Boyd met with them on 10 January 1830, and plans were speedily under way. With part of Boyd's money they bought an English frigate, the *Mary*, and under the pretext of preparing for a voyage to Brazil, set about equipping her where she lay in the Thames above Greenwich.[5]

In the meantime Sterling spread news of the scheme among his friends, including John Stuart Mill, to whom he revealed his plans for raising still more money. 'In all respects the chances are most satisfactory. . .,' he claimed. 'What is now of most importance is to make an arrangement with some commercial House in London for obtaining if possible present credits – but at all events for managing the future business of the Adventurers and all the financial concerns of the New Government – which even if they should ultimately be defeated is likely to turn out in the mean time a most profitable concern. Counsel me on this matter – and tell me whether Joseph Hume would not be trustworthy and likely to give good advice in such a business. The chances are five to one that the House which should engage in it would make immense profits, and would continue to be the agents for the Government of Spain – and there would be no possibility of much loss.' Strangely enough, the expedition eventually found such backing, from the banking house of Calvo, in Paris.[6]

News of the adventure particularly interested Kemble, then languishing at Cambridge under the pretence of reading for the divinity lectures he meant to attend the following autumn. He came up to London to join Sterling in planning the conspiracy and then, telling his family he meant to spend the Long Vacation reading theology at Donne's home in Norfolk, the 'soldier-priest' sailed for Gibraltar on 7 July. Hallam and Tennyson had left England just before him, with messages and funds for some of Torrijos' associates in the Pyrenees; Trench left just after him with a group of Spanish officers who seem to have taken a circuitous route, for they took over a month to reach Gibraltar.[7]

While Sterling remained firmly committed to the scheme and was active in recruiting and despatching these fellow-Apostles, the despair which he expressed about political reform suggests that he was already finding it difficult to cling to his faith in the Spanish liberal cause. 'I have seen Hallam whom I like much,' he wrote to Blakesley in early June. 'We have been discussing the prospects of mankind whom I believe to be travelling on a rail-road and by steam hard and fast to damnation. What hope is there of doing much good by institutions when most of our common friends[,] placed in a far more favourable outward position than any in which we can ever hope to see the mass of men[,] are vibrating between living the life of rascals and debauchees and dying the death of cowards. From what I see of Kemble and hear of many of his friends and above all know of myself I own I have but little faith in men however kind-hearted and instructed. We are above all so damnably addicted to self-indulgence, intellectual and physical.'

Nonetheless he added that the 'Spanish affairs are going on well'.[8]

From this letter and others quoted above it will be apparent that the English participants in the conspiracy made no serious attempt to preserve secrecy. Letters went back and forth in which Ferdinand was mentioned by name but Spain disguised under its initial. Mere acquaintances of Sterling were told that he had on hand some momentous business which would in time be revealed, to the astonishment of the British public. But these indiscretions may have been harmless, for from subsequent events it appears more than likely that Torrijos' followers included at least one Royalist spy, and this infiltration might have occurred however careful Sterling and his friends had been.

By late June the *Mary* was ready. Arms, military equipment and the chief officers of the expedition – Torrijos, Manuel Flores Calderon and Juan Palarea – were to be picked up at a port in the Thames estuary, in order to escape detection. But by one of those errors that plagued the affairs of the junta, the arms and equipment were sent directly to the ship at about the same time that the corps of volunteer soldiers were embarking, and Palarea had to be sent on board to straighten out the confusion. It may be that the arrival of an arms shipment and the presence of Palarea gave away the junta's secret, or perhaps they were betrayed from within. In any case, the Spanish consul complained to the government, and, just as the *Mary* was about to weigh anchor, she was seized by the police. Palarea and two others were arrested for falsifying the ship's sailing orders, but Sterling coolly escaped and took news of the disaster to Torrijos and Calderon. As Carlyle tells the story, 'Sterling, whose presence of mind seldom forsook him, casts his eye over the River and its craft; sees a wherry, privately signals it, drops rapidly on board of it: "Stop!" fiercely interjects the marine policeman from the ship's deck. – "Why stop? What use have you for me, or I for you?" and the oars begin playing. – "Stop, or I'll shoot you!" cries the marine policeman, drawing a pistol. – "No, you won't." – "I will!" – "If you do you'll be hanged at the next Maidstone assizes, then; that's all," – and Sterling's wherry shot rapidly ashore.'[9]

The fortunes of the expedition were both dashed and raised at the same time, for on the very day the *Mary* was confiscated – 29 July 1830 – Louis Philippe came to power in France, and for a time the new French government was prepared not only to condone liberal insurrections in Spain but actually to help pay for them. On the night of 3 August Torrijos and Sterling left London for France, crossing the channel in an open boat. In Paris Torrijos obtained a loan –

49,000 francs and 170 ounces of gold – from a committee headed by Lafayette, and a further loan of 95,000 francs in promissory notes from the banker, Calvo. He then sent Sterling back to London, met Robert Boyd and in heavy disguise accompanied Boyd to Marseilles, where they embarked for Gibraltar on 19 August.[10]

In the meantime other Spanish exiles were flocking to Paris, and a new junta was being formed, ostensibly under the leadership of General Mina, who had been persuaded by events to attempt an invasion of Spain from the north. But this new movement, like Torrijos', was doomed from the first. Open jealousy divided its ranks, and the popular support it counted on winning in Spain simply did not exist. It was at this time, while bands of insurgents were gathering in the Pyrenees in preparation for an attack over the border, that Hallam and Tennyson made their visit to the area, apparently with money from Lafayette's committee as well as that originally supplied by Torrijos' junta. The only rebel officer they seem to have met was a very junior one, Ojeda, but the man was so plainly untrustworthy that their doubts were aroused, if they had not been before, and this doubt was increased by signs of jealousy among the rebel leaders.[11]

Meanwhile the Apostles waited anxiously for news. 'To me this is a situation of particular distress,' Donne wrote to Blakesley, 'since Kemble gave his family to suppose he was to visit me, and made me in a measure responsible for his absence.' Understandably, the Kembles were bitter about the trick that had been played on them, and Donne's attempts to soothe them do not appear to have been effective. Nor were the first letters from Kemble and Trench very encouraging. Kemble had been on his own in Gibraltar for some time before Trench arrived in late August and had not been pleased by his first experience of plotting an insurrection.[12]

'I have now been more than a month upon my perilous duty,' wrote Kemble; 'and a month in Hell would have been more agreeable... The object of my coming here was not an agreeable one; it was to keep a parcel of quarrelling Spaniards in order; and to prepare all sorts of matters for the future and speedy arrival of our friends. As it might have been expected I have had as unpleasant a time of it as possible; but I thank God I have accomplished the objects of my mission to my own satisfaction, and got things into something like readiness...The loneliness which I have had to encounter has been more dreadful to me than the selfishness and treachery of those with whom I have been obliged to work; it was sad heart-breaking work after struggling all day against every difficulty which soi-disant friends and real enemies were throwing in my path, not to have one person to whom I dared communicate what I thought and felt. . .Yesterday morning Trench came here, and my heart is as light again as it was. It is now as certain as it can be that we shall have fighting: and God only knows what fate is reserved for us: I can speak for myself, and I am much mistaken if I cannot say as much for him, that on such an errand as ours, Death is no fearful visitant. That we must be parted from our families and friends is a painful thought, but it was well considered before ever we set foot on board; and painful as it is, the man who cannot master that and every other such feeling has no business here. In case I fall prematurely, you must place in your library a small copy of the Iliad and Odyssey which I have directed my sister to present to you as the last remembrance of a friend who looks back upon the years of our converse as some of the happiest that have been vouchsafed to a man most fortunate in the number and affection of his friends.'[13]

Both Kemble and Trench complained of the lack of energy and honesty among the Spanish sympathizers on whose support Torrijos had depended. But there was little they could do until Torrijos himself arrived, and in the meantime they made some attempt to disguise the fact that they were there as his agents. Fanny Kemble, who had a disapproving eye for her brother's antics, wrote that they 'hired a house which they denominated Constitution Hall, where they passed their time smoking and drinking ale, John holding forth on German metaphysics, which grew dense in proportion as the tobacco fumes grew thick and his glass grew empty'. Literature seems to have been as much a diversion as metaphysics, for their letters from Gibraltar are a curious mixture of political news and literary criticism. According to an account sent to Blakesley, they played the public role 'of a couple of careless, gay, and profligate Englishmen, as much as possible: – associating chiefly with the Officers, and entering into their amusements: (which Kemble, at least, evidently does with much relish). They speak with pleasure of the agreeableness of their society.' But Blakesley also heard that 'some of the Officers have entered with spirit into their cause' – perhaps a sign of indiscretion on the part of the two conspirators, for the officers of the British garrison at Gibraltar were the same whose duty it would become to arrest and deport Torrijos on his arrival.[14]

Indeed, Torrijos had great difficulty avoiding the British authorities. He arrived at Gibraltar on 5 September, but four days passed before he could be smuggled ashore. The Royalists on the mainland were well aware of his presence, and the Spanish consul repeatedly tried to have him arrested, so that he was forced to live in hiding throughout his stay and constantly moved from one hideout to another. On several occasions only his command of English and his unSpanish appearance saved him from deportation.[15]

But these were the least of his difficulties, for his liberal allies in Gibraltar proved, according to Trench, to be 'a rout of the most lying imbeciles that ever formed that most imbecile of associations, a Spanish Junta'. They had apparently assured Torrijos that the only thing wanting in their preparations was his presence, but on his arrival he found that the work of organizing the insurrection had to be done from the beginning. Since he himself had only a handful of men, his plans depended on touching off simultaneous uprisings throughout southern Spain, for he was persuaded that the liberals had only to show themselves publicly and wholesale defection from the Royalist army would follow, as the Spanish people flocked to the cause of restoring their Constitution. But such a coordinated flourishing of the liberal tricolour could only occur with the agreement of all the various liberal bands in the area. He made a firm agreement with a local leader, Salvador Manzanares, and expended much money and effort in establishing relations with the twenty-two liberal juntas on the mainland. These groups gladly accepted the arms he sent them and replied with fervent protestations of support, most of them unreliable. By this time Boyd's money was almost entirely gone, and the promissory notes Torrijos had received in Paris proved worthless.[16]

Nevertheless Trench's early accounts from Gibraltar were written in a hopeful mood. News of attacks over the Pyrenees had reached the ears of the conspirators in Gibraltar (they could not know as yet that the attempted invasion was to end in utter failure). It appeared that uprisings were occurring in other places and that their own would be under way within a few days. 'I do not think the attempt can fail,' Trench wrote: 'nor do I think we shall experience any resistance, unless indeed some mismanagement on the first day, whereby there would not be a sufficient body of men collected to cover our landing, should render blows then necessary. After that I apprehend we shall have nothing but a bloodless march on Madrid. – Should this be the case and that city send in its submission, I shall quit the army at Seville, renouncing the pleasure of riding up the Prado, and return immediately to England.' Torrijos had offered Trench and Kemble captaincies in a cavalry regiment to be commanded by Boyd, but Trench did not plan to accept the honour, even if it should ever prove a reality.[17]

At the same time that the first news arrived in England Hallam and Tennyson returned from their expedition to the Pyrenees, with no high expectations for the success of the insurrection. 'I doubt not but you, in common with us all, are very anxious concerning Kemble and Trench,' Hallam wrote to Donne. 'The chances are fearfully against them. Yet if one tenth part of the favorable intelligence which Sterling used to receive from all parts of Spain had been correct, who would not have been certain of a prosperous issue? I fear much from Kemble's rashness of temper. A man who never could command himself in the Union society must be exposed to perpetual danger in an Insurgent Camp. Trench, who has far less of that practical, and outwardly developed power, which is never content save when realizing itself in action, is less likely to come to harm. But both are in extreme danger; and suspense till the next accounts will be cruel.'[18]

Overwork and anxiety had reduced Sterling to a state of very poor health, and his mental condition while he waited for news was a curious mixture of positive and negative feelings. 'I have only learned by to-day's post that they [Kemble and Trench] are both of them safe at Gibraltar – and that affairs there look well,' he wrote to Blakesley. 'I have no detailed information about them or any one else concerned in the same business – but I have hope. As to the establishment of a Constitution in Spain that is rendered perfectly certain by the affairs of France – and all for which I now care with reference to the Peninsula is the question into whose hands the power will fall – and at what loss of life and tranquillity it is to be obtained. If three or four of my own immediate friends were safe I should trouble myself not at all whether the Spaniards reach the gates of Hell – to which all Continental nations (and England too) seem to me to be tending, by a shorter or a longer path. The Revolution in France has settled that the world shall hold no aristocracy whatever – until the reign of the Saints – and I do not see that we have any thing for it but to sink with decency in the rising spring-tide of democracy, clubs and newspapers. However it is something to see the waves go over at the same moment the thrones of the Papacy and the Caliphate, and the Arabian and Roman tyranny drowning together – even though it be uncertain whether we too are to perish in the deluge or be saved alive in the Ark. – Bah – I am sick of politics – As to private affairs – hear – what perhaps may not be news to you – I am going to marry Miss Barton.'[19]

The agents of the juntas on the mainland had suggested to Torrijos that he should lead off the insurrection with an attack on Algeciras, a fortified town on the Spanish coast across from Gibraltar. News of the plan reached Trench on 24 October, as he was in the midst of a letter to Donne. 'In less than twelve hours we strike,' he wrote. 'I shall carry this letter with me, and if I am still in the land of the living, you will find the result in the P[ost] Script. I assure you the end is sufficiently dubious. The state of our prospects is nearly this. We are promised the co-operation of most of the subaltern Officers and soldiers who form the small corps of observation on the opposite coast. They are to arrest their superior officers, and join us immediately on our landing, which will be at midnight. We land, a party of rather more than a hundred men, well armed of course, and as a gallows is behind us, desperate enough. The majority are General Officers, and I believe, the flower of Spain. For Ferdinand this push will cheer him ever or dis-seat him quite. If these men, educated by the war of independence and the Constitution are cut off, there will remain no hope for Spain – not that I believe there is much even now – however let her have a fair chance, and her misery and degradation, if she must be miserable and degraded, lie at her own door. You would scarcely believe what a dead, stirless pool my mind is at the present moment – I feel neither enthusiasm, nor hope, nor fear, nor exultation. . .All I wish now is that a man might know the end of this day's business.'

That evening, Torrijos and over one hundred armed supporters embarked, only to find that none of the expected preparations had been made (they later heard that a nervous soldier had given the plot away to his superior officer). The group retreated without ever having been noticed by the garrison they had meant to overcome, and Trench added the promised postscript to his letter to Donne: 'I want words to express to you the bitterness of feeling with which I take up my pen to announce to you the present failure and probably, entire wreck of our hopes in this part of the country, and all without a gun being fired.'[20]

But Kemble enclosed a letter of his own, which took a rather more hopeful view: 'We have begun ill,' he told Donne, 'but what of that[?] We are all sound in heart and limb, and for my own part I see no evil but what may easily be repaired. The cause of our failure was the want of coöperation on the part of the troops at Algesiras [*sic*], and that arose from no treachery on their part. How the secret was discovered I know not. But at 1 p.m. Sunday, the Governor of Algesiras received news that we were to land between 8 and 9. He immediately called out all the troops, put them under arms, and ordered the ships of war on which we counted to place themselves under a tremendous Battery of 42 pounders before the Town. The troops were taken by surprise and could not act: consequently when we expected that the avenues to the town were in our possession and made our signals, none were returned. We waited with our arms in our hands on board the boats 'til eleven, and finding nothing could be done gave up the attempt. Of course we might have landed our small force, and made off for the mountains, if we had chosen, but that is our last resource. The General and ourselves are safe in the Garrison, and in a few days we will go to work again.'[21]

These letters reached Donne at a climactic moment in his life. A day or so before they came he had written to Blakesley to share with him his fears about Kemble and Trench and his elation about an imminent event – his marriage, which was to take place within a week. He confessed to having suffered from a deep depression, now at last dispelled, and he judged from Trench's letters that Trench was suffering much as he had done. 'He has a hunger and thirsting,' Donne wrote, 'for some steady and constant occupation which shall be the aim of his Being – Why does he not in Heaven's name give up every thought of professional employment and bind himself by strong indentures to Poetry alone?'[22]

The letters describing the fiasco of 24 October quite overwhelmed Donne with their 'noble fervent feeling, heroical devotion and perfect loveliness of spirit', and drew from him a rare distraught outburst: 'O dear Blakesley what a fearful hazard for the wise, the brave the truehearted ones. The world is very hollow and, emptied of Goodness and Genius, a tomb, until we awaken on the great day of Eternity, or, as some say, sleep on while Eternity passes over us. I am indeed at this present time most happy, happy beyond my deserts above my hopes. Yet these things cast a shadow even upon blessedness.'[23]

At Gibraltar it had become impossible for the conspirators to know whom to trust. The local juntas continued to give difficulty, and several complained of obstructive behaviour from supporters of General Mina. The junta at Cadiz seemed particularly weak, while that at Malaga was thought quite solid and well advanced in their planning. Suddenly it was learned that they too were pro-Mina and hence uncertain in their support. Torrijos, however, was quite incapable of uncertainty, even when uncertainty was the only reasonable response to the situation.[24]

A short time after the failure at Algeciras Torrijos, disguised as a fisherman, went aboard a ship in the Bay of Gibraltar, in preparation for another excursion against the mainland. But this too was a failure, and he remained afloat for another two months, in company with Kemble and his chief officers. Finding that their ship, a schooner, was being dogged by two Royalist brigantines, they determined to capture one of these, succeeded in subverting some of its crew, and for three consecutive nights lurked in small boats, fully armed and ready for the signal to board. Again it never came, and eventually their sympathizers among the crew were arrested. The Royalists then attempted to lure Torrijos into their reach and mounted surprise attacks on his ship that were only foiled by keeping constant guard and appearing on deck with drawn swords whenever an enemy craft approached. Salvadore Manzanares, with about one hundred men, managed to land near Algeciras, but on the very evening that Torrijos planned to join in concerted attack, and just as he was raising his anchor to leave, the Captain of the Port appeared and placed them and their ship under arrest. The conspirators managed to delay the British officer and his men, in the hopes of cutting their anchor cable and setting off for the attack once the signal came. The British, it appeared, were to be taken prisoner, respectfully treated and eventually released. But once again the signal did not come, and Torrijos barely escaped deportation.[25]

A series of similar misadventures overtook each of his plans. Late in January he and thirty-four men attacked the garrison of two hundred men, including cavalry, at La Linea, the post on the narrow frontier with Spain. The scheme was successful, but the uprisings that were to coincide with it did not materialize, and Torrijos had to retreat. In March his followers at Cadiz assassinated the Governor of the city, and several thousand troops mutinied, only to be ignominiously overcome by the Royalists, who instituted a reign of terror to keep the civilian population in its place. Manzanares, still on the mainland, formed a guerilla group, attempted to lead it across the mountains to join the rebels at Cadiz, but was caught in a Royalist trap, and killed himself. Only seven of his followers escaped to reach Gibraltar with news of the disaster; those who were captured were taken to various large towns in the area and there publicly executed by crossbow.[26]

In early February the Apostles learned that Kemble and Trench planned to return to England. Kemble resentfully described the Spanish as 'willingly and exultantly enslaved', and (Hallam wrote to Donne) 'abuses all actual and possible generations of mankind, and seems to think them hardly worth a "latter Luther's" while'. Kemble was now considering a legal career, and Hallam thought the change of intention a wise one, in view of Kemble's unpriestly character.[27]

In early March Trench reached England alone, for at the last moment Kemble had felt he could not forsake Torrijos. By the end of March bad news from Gibraltar had reached Sterling, who passed it on to Trench. 'I have heard from Boyd,' wrote Sterling, 'and all is over in the south of Spain. He says that if any one had put himself at the head of the people at Cadiz the question was settled as to Andalusia, as the town was for twenty-four hours without a government, which simply means, I suppose, that there was an interval before the appointment of the new governor. From blundering as to the signals, the troops at La Isla supposed the constitution proclaimed at Cadiz, and declared themselves. They were repulsed in an attack on the Cortadura, and then, to the number of eight hundred, sallied out and went to Vejar, where, instead of marching on Algesiras [*sic*] they remained till Quesada surrounded them and forced them to lay down their arms. The two hundred who were in the Sierra with Manzanares, and who had gone out from Gibraltar, are also all destroyed. Manzanares killed the two spies who betrayed him, and then fell on his own sword. Torrijos is in Gibraltar, and Boyd with him, who thinks he will probably determine on going to France. Boyd himself had enlisted the party of Manzanares, and their wives and children now come to him constantly for bread. He has been dismissed from the Indian army, and I have the comfort of knowing that the whole is my doing. He does not mention Kemble. I am very thankful that you, at least, are in England. God bless you!'[28]

Two months after Trench's return Kemble had still not appeared, and his friends' fears deepened. 'Why does he remain behind with a hopeless cause? and with the season for his own prospects in England passing away?' Donne asked Blakesley. 'I do not mean church prospects – though I am grieved they must be given up, but any prospect for the support and stability of his outward life which he may yet have. I have heard nothing of him, or from him, this year, except a brief and immaterial letter from his brother – it is almost as if my worst fears were true, and the grave had inherited him.'[29]

At the end of May they were relieved to hear that Kemble was back, with what was for him an unusually sober and accurate assessment of the situation he had quitted. 'Poor Boyd remains in Gibraltar,' he told Trench, 'and, indeed, I hardly know what he could do were he to leave it. Yet he is, I think, quite as hopeless as myself for the event; at all events, I am sure it is not the infatuated confidence of Torrijos, which, marvellous to relate, only increases with every fresh misfortune that imposes upon him. But he feels that for him the die is cast, and that he must sink or swim.'[30]

In Gibraltar the stage was set for the final catastrophe. Torrijos and his officers were in such financial straits as to be reduced to selling their watches and clothes in order to support their followers. Palarea and other officers had been caught by the British and deported, and Torrijos was placed under increasing pressure to leave Gibraltar. After many miserable months news came from Malaga that the Governor, Gonzalez Moreno, was a secret sympathizer and would support them if they landed there. Torrijos desperately grasped at this straw and with Boyd and fifty-one others embarked on 30 November 1831 in two ancient ships. The first sign that Moreno's invitation was a trap came on 2 December, when two coast-guard ships attacked them and forced them to land a few miles from Malaga. Torrijos and his group stopped on the beach to perform the ceremony of raising the liberal tricolour on Spanish soil, then set off inland, where the appearance of Royalist troops finally forced them to take refuge in a farmhouse. Moreno himself arrived to negotiate with the besieged liberals and apparently tricked them once again, for on 5 December they surrendered without firing a shot and were led into Malaga. Five days later the orders came from Madrid for their immediate execution, and that Saturday evening, 10 December 1831, the prisoners were told of their fate. The rest of the story may be told in the words of a Capuchin friar, who personally helped to attend the condemned men:

They all as good Catholics that night [confessed] and received absolution, except a Milord Ingles [Robert Boyd], who said he was not an R.C., he had nothing to do with the spiritual Fathers or Ministers of our Holy Religion, adding that for his part he had always endeavoured to adore the Almighty with a pure heart, and to avoid all crimes as could give rise to remorse of conscience, and as he was free from scruples he relied too firmly on the mercy of God to feel unmanned at the approach of death. This person had lent 55000 dollars to Torrijos. All these poor creatures passed the night, some occupied in writing to their wives, others to their families. They all gave up to their Confessors such money as they had contrived to conceal on their persons, some ordering it to be remitted to their families, and others directing it to be laid out in masses for their souls, and one in particular gave his Confessor 4 thousand reals to be invested in the purchase of wax lights for the purpose of illuminating the blessed Sacrament. Several of them subscribed different sums to be paid to the soldiers employed to shoot them.

The Convent bell at last announced the approach of the aurora of the Holy Sabbath Day, and of the hour for the bloody sacrifice. . .At exactly half an hour past ten o'clock 25 of the prisoners had their irons taken off, and being pinioned were taken under a strong military escort down to the sea beach. . .When they had reached the beach they were blindfolded, and being placed in a line on their knees there was a terrible discharge of musketry fired among them, by which they were either killed or wounded except my Lord Ingles, who did not receive the slightest injury, but soon despatched by the subsequent shots, a number of which it was necessary to fire as the greatest part of the victims had only been wounded by the first discharge. Ten. . .carts were waiting to carry off the bodies to the place of interment, five of which were loaded with them, only leaving that of my Lord, which had been claimed by the English Consul. . .It was now necessary to bring some sort of gravel to cover the excessive quantity of blood which remained on the ground in consequence of the repeated wounds received by the greatest part of the unfortunate men. Thus arranged the remaining 24 were brought from the convent, shackled as the former, to the same spot, where they received the same fate. . .They had all ceased to exist before the hour of 1 o'c. . .Thousands of persons flocked to the place of burial, where a large trench had been [?dug] to receive the bodies, and such was the general curiosity to see Torrijos that it [i.e. his body] was not thrown into the ditch for some time. The body of Milord, which remained on the beach, was removed in one of the English Consul's carriages, in which his son, the vice Consul, went in person, carrying with him an English colour in which the body of his noble countryman was shrouded. On arriving at the Consul's house the body was laid out in great state until the evening of the following day, Monday, when it was taken to the E. burial ground and interred according to the rites of their religion, the ceremony being performed by the Consul, who is a priest, some say a Bishop.[31]

The news reached Sterling in the West Indies two months later. 'I hear the sound of that musketry,' he wrote to his brother; 'it is as if the bullets were tearing my own brain.' The death of Torrijos haunted him. 'I thought I had made up my mind for the worst,' he wrote to J. S. Mill, '– but this horrible fate of such a man and one whom I had known as well as you and I know each other – has overpowered me completely. I can think of nothing else – and cannot write of it without excessive pain.' His friends, according to Carlyle, were warned never to mention the subject to him again.[32]

Shortly after his marriage in November 1830 Sterling had fallen dangerously ill and on recovery had hit upon a new scheme of action. To protect his family's financial interests and his own precarious health he would go out to St Vincent and manage his great-uncle's sugar plantation there. Moreover, he had great plans for educating the West Indian slaves against the day of their emancipation. His first setback was a hurricane that devastated his new home; his second the active hostility of his fellow-planters, many of whom (he reported to Mill) 'consider every attempt to benefit the negroes a direct blow at their own interests'. The news of the catastrophe at Malaga seems to have completed the process of his disillusionment. He was, he confessed, 'less and less anxious as to doing any thing outward beyond securing humane treatment and some mental cultivation for the negroes under my Controul. . .[M]y only aim is to realize a new life – and I think (so far as I can) solely with reference to that end.' In this repentant mood he left St Vincent for England in the summer of 1832. The Spanish adventure had ended in disaster, the West Indian scheme had been a failure, and Sterling was no closer to realizing his dreams in action.[33]

CHAPTER 8

THE SOCIETY IN THE EARLY THIRTIES

The failure of the Spanish adventure coincided with a deepening sense of dissatisfaction with the age among the Apostles. Apostolic expressions of alienation from the outer world were not merely a matter of youthful arrogance, for the years preceding the Reform Bill were marked by virulent factionalism, increasing political confusion, and frequent outbursts of violence. 'The country is in a more awful state than you can well conceive,' Arthur Hallam wrote to Trench in December 1830, when Trench was still in Gibraltar. 'While I write, Maddingley [*sic*], or some adjoining village, is in a state of conflagration, and the sky above is coloured flame-red. This is one of a thousand such actions committed daily through England. The laws are almost suspended; the money of foreign factions is at work with a population exasperated into reckless fury.'[1]

'Captain Swing', the legendary leader of the rickburners, had appeared in Cambridgeshire. Many students, among them several Apostles, turned out to quench the fires in the surrounding countryside, and for a day or two the University was in a panic at the rumour of impending invasion of the town by a mob of rebels. Among the *Joint Compositions* of Henry Lushington and George Venables is a poem, apparently written in retrospect, that describes this incident. 'Swing, at Cambridge' is the merest of light verse, but it vividly recreates the atmosphere of the time:

> Within our old religious walls,
> In statued courts and pictured halls,
> There dwelt an anxious band:
> For nights were long, and days were drear,
> And rumours dark of aimless fear
> Ran whispering through the land.
>
> 'Twas said there passed from town to town
> On dangerous errands, half unknown,

Strange men of doubtful lives;
In cottages, and city lanes,
They spoke of toil and niggard gains,
Of children and of wives.

. . . . . .

The landlord's rents at Christmas came,
His fields and woods were crammed with game,
The farmer's barns with wheat;
The parson had his glebe and tithe;
While they who held the plough and scythe
Must beg or steal to eat.

Strong men were changed beneath the curse,
The good were bad, the bad were worse;
In reckless suffering
They named with hope a sordid name,
With terror linked, and midnight flame,
The stern reformer, 'Swing.'

For through the land, and here and there,
Seen like a spectre everywhere
A form of ceaseless change,
He lived without a known abode.
In a green gig he always rode,
With chemic mixtures strange.

At noon the homestead passed he,
At eve the farmer came to see,
And all was well and still –
At midnight Swing was far away,
Then blazed the ricks of smouldering hay
Far over vale and hill.

The poem recounts a sequence of events that began one evening when the students emerged from chapel, discovered the signs of Swing's handiwork at nearby Coton and rushed to the rescue:

By road and path
O'er hedge and ditch, in fear or wrath,
We ran, a panting crowd;
The fire before us larger glowed,
Behind the swearing firemen rode,
With lumbering engines loud.

In order meet of double line
We formed with ready discipline,

And fast the buckets sped;
Some to their knees in water stood,
The most were ankle-deep in mud,
Some climbed on roof or shed.

While from each sullen gazing block,
With idle hands beneath his frock,
Malignant mutterings fell;
'See, where the farmer's harvest goes,
'The fires flare up – as hot as those
'Shall roast the rich in hell.'

The screaming poultry burst the hatch;
The pigs were scorched with burning thatch;
In stall the horses died
With hideous shriek...

Returning from their night's work fighting the fire, the students were confronted by the news that 'starving stalwart men...|Were marching on the town...|With fork and scythe and flail,|And bills, and hooks of all degrees'. With great enthusiasm the students prepared themselves for battle:

At dawn we heard – that night by six
Nor love nor money purchased sticks.
Quick ranged in numbered bands
We watched each post and passage strait,
From Jesus to the towered gate
Where sceptred Edward stands.

. . . .

Scholars threw by their Grecian lore,
The algebraist worked no more,
One primal science thrives;
Deep thinkers left their whys and hows,
And stood prepared to solve with blows
The riddle of their lives.

Unto the poet wise we spoke,
'Is any law of battle broke,
'By pouring from afar
'Water or oil, or melted lead?'
The poet raised his massive head –
'Confound the laws of war.'

The patriot sat with brow of care
With pistols close beside his chair;

And if we handled one,
'By heaven!' he shouted 'mind the lock,
'The pistols both are on the cock,
'The caps are ready on.'

The bloody-minded poet was Tennyson himself, but it should not be thought that the Apostles' reaction to popular discontent was merely one of fierce repression. Lushington and Venables pause in their comic treatment of these events to reveal their real sympathy for the distressed and rebellious agricultural workers and the concerned perplexity with which the Apostles viewed the age:

So, all looked gladly for the morn;
And, yet I know we did not scorn
The hungry multitude;
Or hate them, that their evil chance,
Of want and woe and ignorance,
Had made them fierce and rude.

But doubtful in our dazzling prime,
We watched the struggle of the time,
The war of new and old;
We loved the past with Tory love,
Yet more than Radicals we strove
For coming years of gold.

With loyal heart and eager mind
Saw light before us and behind –
But none could hope for good
From blazing ricks, and lawless force –
So followed we without remorse
The stirring of our blood.

And the poem concludes with the disappointment such students as the Apostles felt when no rebels appeared for them to fight, and the chance for decisive, meaningful action once more eluded them:

So with a jar we all sank back
Into life's daily beaten track,
To think, and not to do;
The spider custom crawling out
Wove round again the web of doubt,
Which deeds had broken through.

We went about, and said or thought
How gallantly we would have fought,

And peace seemed dull the while;
Or if we said we should have grieved
At civil broils, and men believed,
We could not choose but smile.[2]

When in early 1831 J. W. Blakesley graduated with high distinction in classics, John Sterling suggested that he melt the medal he had won 'into bullets or other revolutionary engines for destroying Bishops and Tutors of Colleges – as under the new system we intend to abolish learning and all that – and if such an article as a medal were found about you it would inevitably bring you to the lamp-post. We would suspend you if it were only to prove that Greek is not as luminous as Gas – a truth of great importance to the progress of civilization.'[3]

But the progress of contemporary civilization was no joking matter for Richard Trench when he arrived back from Gibraltar in a state of despondency unusual even for him. 'I cannot think you have done wrong in returning,' Hallam reassured him in reply to one of the sad, self-reproachful letters Trench wrote his friends at this time, 'nor do any of your old and good friends, so far as I know, think so, for whose judgment I should, of course, expect you to care more than for mine. But I do not wonder you should feel these misgivings and backward yearnings of mind. I only trust you will find England is not yet so sunken but that many duties, many privileges, and many hopes remain for her sons.'[4]

In May Trench was relieved to hear that Kemble had returned, but his letter of welcome was far from encouraging. 'You must wonder,' he wrote, 'after the wreck of our late hopes, what new object or aims one can have for one's studies. I give myself pretty assiduously to modern history, and attempt to hear the flowing of the great stream of tendency, though I cannot say with much success. From it, more than aught else, I feel there is a hollowness at the heart of all things, which conviction one is unhappily too apt to entertain without the aid of these studies.'[5]

The next few months were a time of great uncertainty for Trench. He found himself unable to compose poetry, to pursue any settled course of reading, or to fix on any worthy vocation. 'What do you intend to play on this humorous stage of the world?' he asked Kemble. 'I cannot find a part to suit me, but one must fill up some or other. We have traded long enough in self-conceits, and a few months ago became both of us sheer bankrupts – what remains for us? Luckily, the world is going to pieces and perhaps when it forms again we may find ourselves in more satisfactory situations. I have given over despairing, and reading Shelley, and am beginning to acquiesce in things just as they are going on; in brief, to the great satisfaction of all my friends and relations, subsiding into a very respectable worldling.'[6]

The following October, however, found Trench at Cambridge, still preoccupied with contemporary problems and closer than ever before to the affirmation of religious belief that had so long eluded him. He wrote to Maurice to ask him for 'a key to a system of theological studies', but he seems to have found his own key in the theology of that remarkable prophet of the eighteen-thirties, Edward Irving. He discovered 'new worlds of thought' in Irving's writings and became fascinated by the man and his beliefs. His daughter did her best to minimize this intellectual debt in her official biography of Archbishop Trench, but the fact is that Trench was greatly influenced by Irving and remained a devoted disciple of his for many years.[7]

Edward Irving was a liberal Scottish clergyman who had established himself in London as an immensely popular preacher, but his interest for Trench lay in his fervent Millenarianism. Christ's return, Irving taught, was imminent, and the Christian Church had a vital role to play in the upheaval that would accompany his return, a spiritual revolution that would utterly destroy the known order of things. Irving was a sincere and profound religious teacher, whose writings commanded respect from many thoughtful men, but his personal following also included a fanatic element, by which he himself was too inclined to be swayed. A series of reputed miracles and the phenomenon known as 'speaking with tongues' swept Irving and many others away in a wave of religious hysteria – a nine days' wonder that caught the Apostles' attention as much as anyone's. People thronged to his church, among them Hallam and Milnes, who went together in May 1831, when 'the tongues' were just beginning. In November Hallam and Trench planned to spend a day in London, both being 'very anxious to hear the tongues'. James Spedding was among the Apostles who went to hear Irving and, with characteristic coolness, remarked that he 'is a splendid declaimer: but his eloquence is too little allied to logic for my taste'. Many of the Apostles were deeply impressed, and they eagerly discussed the subject among themselves.[8]

If Irving's teachings met Trench's hopes for a new age, another cult of the time, the St Simonians, met his worst fears for the present. Led by their self-styled 'Supreme Father' Enfantin, the followers of St Simon had established themselves as a church in 1830 and had won widespread attention for their revolutionary ideas and the fanaticism of their dedication to the cause. Internal discord had seemed to destroy the movement in 1831, but in the following year two weirdly uniformed missionaries of the new religion appeared in London, amid wild rumours, and hired lecture rooms in Burton Crescent. To the Apostles the St Simonist faith must have seemed a demonic parody of their own. Like the Apostles, the St Simonians hoped for a new social order, to be won not through political manipulation but spiritual regeneration – through the victory of the principle of cooperation over that of competition. But the future they prophesied seemed to the Apostles not so much a recapturing of lost values as the creation of a brave new world of their own devising.[9]

Although the other Apostles did not necessarily share Trench's opinions, they could not help but be impressed by his deep concern for spiritual matters and his horror at the tendency of public affairs. The letters he wrote to Donne during his first few months back at Cambridge suggest the preoccupations and personal qualities that helped make Trench a central figure among the Apostles at that time. 'Do you share in the general despondency of wise and good men at the present aspect of the world?' he asked Donne. '. . .I live in the faith of a new dispensation, which I am very confident is at hand – but what fearful times shall we have to endure ere that – we must pray earnestly not to be swept away by the great torrent, for its semblances will be goodly and specious to look at, and it will come with signs that shall wellnigh deceive the elect. What think you of the St Simonians? to me they seem the most perfect expression of the Spirit now at work – primogeniture, aristocracy, heredity, all that rested on a spiritual relation, which relation will no longer be recognized, must be swept away before the new industrial principle – *à chacun selon ses oeuvres*.'[10]

'I purpose residing here and reading Divinity for the next two terms,' he told Donne, 'though I think that in these times it is a question of especial difficulty to what profession one should betake oneself. Literature will not do for me. . .there is always the central hollowness, the cold black speck at the heart, which is spreading and darkening, and which must be met by other arms than those which Letters supply: we are now moreover on the eve of the mightiest change, which the world has ever known – all forms and institutions, which however little we recognized it, supported mightily our moral being, all these must give way: and if we stand not on our own or in God given strength, we must fall, or which is yet more fearful, become weapons of mischief in the hands of Him, the false Prophet, who with lying signs and wonders is about to be revealed. You see that I am a believer in the approaching Millennium and personal coming of Christ, but I know that before it, the nations will endure such things as never have been endured. Henceforward there will be no more peace, but revolution on revolution, and war on war: all the cement of Society has fallen away, and it is vainly attempted to be supplied by a well enlightened self-interest, which is a principle of enmity, and not of union. Have you read any of Irving's later works? if not pray do it. I feel sure that he is *the* man of the Times, the man who sees most clearly, on whom rests most of the Spirit of Prophecy: for his *vision* has almost arrived at that.'[11]

It was almost certainly at this time, before Tennyson left Cambridge in February 1831, that he was so impressed by Trench's dictum: 'Tennyson, we cannot live in Art.' Tennyson's poetic dramatization of this principle, 'The Palace of Art', seems to have been a direct response to Trench's statement. A prefatory poem, addressed to Trench, expounds the Apostles' belief in the moral nature of true art and their conviction that 'he that shuts Love out, in turn shall be | Shut out from Love'. The principle of spiritual affinity with one's fellow human beings remained an Apostolic ideal, however hard it may have been to realize in practice, and Trench's deeply serious pursuit of spiritual solutions to the dilemma of the age made him an inspiration to several of his fellow-Apostles, among them Arthur Hallam. 'I thank God,' Hallam wrote to him, 'that at so critical a moment of my life He has brought me into daily intercourse with you.'[12]

Trench himself was well aware that the group shared his distressed concern, although he was capable of viewing the subject satirically. 'Hallam, Blakesley and myself and one or two others sit like a congregation of ravens, a hideous conclave, and croak despair,' he told Donne, 'which however does not prevent us from smoking a multitude of cigars and drinking whatever liquor falls in our way.'

But this letter to Donne is accompanied by one from Blakesley that affords a rather different perspective. 'Trench has been here all the last term in a terrible state of anxiety at the prospects of Society,' Blakesley wrote. 'He is quite furious with me for not manifesting a similar degree of fidget, although I pretty nearly agree with him as to our desperate state and the only difference is that he makes himself ill by going daily to the Union and reading all the papers spawned by the press, while I being much too lazy for any such proceeding, escape the irritation which it regularly produces in him. I hear that you are acting more wisely than either of us, and reading classics steadily and earnestly.

Certainly it is much better thus to "work linked armour for one's soul" before it "shall go forth to battle with mankind," than like me to grow stupid with draughts of intellectual laudanum or like him to voluntarily take every day an emetic of St Simonism or Westminster Review.'[13]

Despite such differences in attitude the Apostles were in substantial agreement in being dispirited by the fever pitch of political controversy and the eruptions of social disorder that preceded the passing of the Reform Bill. They viewed the Bill itself most unfavourably and seem to have thought civil war a real possibility. Discussion of such topics, and of Irving and the St Simonians, continued throughout the early eighteen-thirties, in a steady flow of correspondence that kept the Apostles aware of opinions and activities within the group.

In the spring of 1832 they were delighted to hear that Trench, then at his family home in Ireland, was on the point of marriage. 'He still gives utterance to low thunders about S [Simonians],' Hallam said, 'but it is evident such Hecubas are [not] so much to him now as they were. [A] man, about to be married to the woman he loves, is not easily to be persuaded that wars and revolutions will disturb his honeymoon.' Perhaps, Donne wrote hopefully to Blakesley, his marriage would at last bring Trench relief from the unhappiness that had plagued him for so many years.[14]

In fact, marriage made no immediate change in Trench's concerns. He made several trips to London in the course of the year and while there attended Irving's church whenever he could. The anxiety with which he followed the ebb and flow of current events did not lessen, and the vital question of one's spiritual development in such an age remained a constant theme in his correspondence with his fellow-Apostles. By 1833, however, he had been ordained and had acquired his first curacy. Happiness was never to be his lot: his life was haunted by personal misfortunes, and a long struggle against ill health greatly hampered him in beginning his chosen career. But the direction of his life was henceforth fixed, and his commitment to his faith and to the Church was absolute.

Such commitment was quite beyond the reach of John Sterling, for all his efforts. While still in the West Indies he had responded with great interest to Trench's letters, although he viewed certain of his opinions with scepticism. 'I feel with you,' he wrote, 'that the great difficulty, and the one the solution of which would end all others, lies in the Will; and there is no resource but obedience, patience, and prayer. As to your view of our nearness to the end of this dispensation, I have often been inclined to entertain it; but I know that this belief is a ready means of self-delusion. . .Moreover I cannot see my way to any such certainty as Irving derives from the Prophecies; and I have scarcely the trace of doubt that the unknown tongues are the familiar and easily intelligible language of mere human vanity and superstition.'[15]

During his voyage to England Sterling experienced a sudden overwhelming sense of religious conversion and, he told Trench, was able to feel for the first time 'a lively and increasing hope that I may be able to overcome the world'. This change was of course welcome to his fellow-converts, Maurice and Trench, but Sterling found that it required some cautious justification to his more sceptical friends. '[Y]ou will readily believe,' he wrote to J. S. Mill, rather stiffly, 'that the prospect of escaping from Remorse and Anxiety and of maintaining my will in conformity to that of the Supreme Reason is one which renders all outward difficulties easy and which I would not sacrifice for the most brilliant worldly object. I think you know how far I have always been from contentment or even resignation and may therefore judge how highly I value the means by which I have been brought not only to present satisfaction but to lively and ardent hope for the future. Christianity has done for me what no pursuits of Curiosity or Ambition – and not even sacrifices for others [–] ever did. Not that I regard myself as having made even as near approaches to the Christian Ideal as many men but that I now know myself to be in the right way and have good hopes of daily progress. I am sure you will not now be inclined (whatever theories you may adopt) to undervalue the practical importance of a system in which alone I have been able to find Rest[,] Comfort and Cheerfulness. . .I hear that C. Buller amuses the universe at the expense of my religious views. I wish that his gave the same handle to other jesters.'[16]

Sterling's attempted progress towards 'the Christian Ideal' was characteristically impetuous, enthusiastic, erratic and ultimately self-defeating. Although Blakesley was himself about to be ordained, from Sterling's new position Blakesley seemed insufficiently orthodox in his views of the human will, a faculty which Sterling was inclined to judge harshly (having been much disappointed in his own). He recommended that Blakesley read more deeply in Luther and Irving and urged on him 'a clearer or at least a stronger and deeper view of the nature and reality of Sin – as not consisting in acts or any particular determinations of the Will – but in the absolute corruption of the Will. . .the destruction of which is the only worthy object of Prayer – and all that we need care or wish for'. At the same time Sterling became preoccupied with those modernist tendencies in religious thought that were in time to lead him to reject orthodoxy. Coleridge's views on Biblical inspiration fascinated him: he visited him repeatedly and told Blakesley that he would 'spend a week or more at Highgate in order to be near him – and hope to write down for publication some of the volumes that live like the Bible in the "Monastery" in the gentle flame of his brain'.[17]

Before Sterling had been back in England a year he decided that a first-hand knowledge of German metaphysics and theology was a prerequisite for the ministry. In order to learn the language he moved his growing family to Germany, where Blakesley paid a visit to him in the course of 1833 and reported the event to a younger Apostle, W. H. Thompson. 'Sterling was at Bonn with his wife and children,' he wrote, 'reading German and running rather mad on the Idea of Christianity. He has heterodox views on the subject of a redeeming Sacrifice, in which he considers, I believe, the first teachers to have had very limited views. He also talked to me about the various readings of the New Testament and the interpretation of others in terms which prejudices derived from a classical education made me think absurd. However he called me microscopic and other hard names; so that I shrunk into my shell and held my tongue.'[18]

Another visitor to Bonn in mid-1833 was Sterling's former Lecturer in classics, J. C. Hare, who had recently left Cambridge to succeed to the remunerative family living of Herstmonceux in Sussex. He spent a day in conversation with Sterling, heard with pleasure that Sterling planned to take orders after preparing himself with one or two years' study abroad, and promised that Sterling should have the curacy at Herstmonceux, if it was free when Sterling was ready to be ordained. Curacies were by no means easy to obtain at that time, as Trench had found in the previous year. A few months later Sterling abandoned his German studies for this new scheme. He returned to Cambridge to study for his degree examinations, which he had not bothered to take when he left the University in 1827. In 1834 he graduated, was ordained deacon and took up his duties at Herstmonceux with all the vigour and excitement that a new task always inspired in him.[19]

At Cambridge Sterling found himself once more in the company of John Kemble, still talking of a career in the Church but in fact wholly engrossed in academic research. On his return from Gibraltar Kemble had plunged into philological studies and in 1833 published his edition of *Beowulf*, a pioneering work in the field of Old English. Now he proposed to take the University by storm with a series of twenty lectures on the early history of the English language, in the hope that a professorship would be created for him. Quite unpredictably, the 'soldier-priest' had been transformed into an innovative scholar.

While Sterling and his fellow-mystics were engaged in their struggles to establish themselves in the outside world, the Society itself had entered a new phase. Maurice had never accepted the fact of his leadership, and his self-banishment – first to Oxford, then to a country curacy – meant that he was soon little more than a name and a legend for the younger members. His friends, especially Sterling and Blakesley, had done their best to carry on his tradition and to further the mystic cult, and their success had been ensured with the election in 1829 of Arthur Hallam and Alfred Tennyson, for in Tennyson the cultists found living proof of their belief that a new age in literature was dawning, and in Hallam they found a successor to Maurice. For a new generation of young men Hallam seemed the embodiment of the spirit of the Society, and his friendship with Tennyson, the most famous of all Apostolic friendships, was the basis of a new network of relations that developed around them during Hallam's brief lifetime. By 1834, shortly after Hallam's death, Maurice and his friends had become the senior members of a distinct Apostolic set that was to last for decades.

Tennyson was at least as important to this set as either Maurice or Hallam, although his place within it was an odd one. Tennyson was never anything like a leader within the group, and he was strikingly unsatisfactory as a member of the Society, but he was the only true genius they had – in fact, the only true genius to become an Apostle until James Clerk Maxwell was elected in the fifties. Many years later, when W. H. Thompson was Master of Trinity College, he was interviewed about his undergraduate days by a younger Apostle, Henry Montagu Butler, who asked Thompson which of Hallam and Tennyson was at that time believed to be the greater man. Thompson replied that it was Tennyson, 'beyond a doubt', and went on to describe 'the impression produced on the immediate circle of friends by the early Poems'. Thompson may have been thinking primarily of the poems published in Tennyson's volumes of 1830 and 1832, but for the Apostles these simply fulfilled the promise they had seen in an earlier poem, his 'Timbuctoo'. In 1829 Hallam, Tennyson and Richard

Milnes were among the students who submitted poems on this unlikely subject for the Chancellor's Prize in English Poetry, and Tennyson's success in the competition was announced shortly after his name had been proposed for election to the Society. Tennyson's poem caused much comment at Cambridge as a strange and irregular production – for one thing, it was the first prize poem written in other than heroic couplets – but its real claim to attention lay in the certainty and power of the poetic voice that any acute reader could discover in it. Acute readers are not normally impressed by undergraduate verse, a fact that would make even more startling such lines as those describing a vision of the cosmos attained by the poem's narrator:

> I felt my soul grow mighty, and my Spirit
> With supernatural excitation bound
> Within me, and my mental eye grew large
> With such a vast circumference of thought,
> That in my vanity I seemed to stand
> Upon the outward verge and bound alone
> Of full beatitude. Each failing sense
> As with a momentary flash of light
> Grew thrillingly distinct and keen. I saw
> The smallest grain that dappled the dark Earth,
> The indistinctest atom in deep air,
> The Moon's white cities, and the opal width
> Of her small glowing lakes, her silver heights
> Unvisited with dew of vagrant cloud,
> And the unsounded, undescended depth
> Of her black hollows. The clear Galaxy
> Shorn of its hoary lustre, wonderful,
> Distinct and vivid with sharp points of light,
> Blaze within blaze, an unimagined depth
> And harmony of planet-girded Suns
> And moon-encircled planets, wheel in wheel,
> Arched the wan Sapphire. Nay – the hum of men,
> Or other things talking in unknown tongues,
> And notes of busy life in distant worlds
> Beat like a far wave on my anxious ear.

Not all the Apostles approved: Donne claimed that Hallam should have had the prize and for years continued to think Trench a better poet than Tennyson, but the impact of Tennyson's poetic genius on the group as a whole was overwhelming, as their very exceptional treatment of him shows.[20]

Whether the University authorities welcomed Tennyson's prize poem in quite the way the Apostles did is far from clear. One of the examiners was the Professor of Modern History, William Smyth, an elderly, old-fashioned gentleman well-known at Cambridge for one of his annual lectures on the French Revolution. According to Leslie Stephen, this particular lecture 'always drew an audience, because it was known from previous experience that in the course of it he would burst into tears upon mentioning the melancholy fate of Marie Antoinette'. It has been claimed that Smyth marked Tennyson's manuscript with 'v.q.' for 'very queer' and inadvertently predisposed another examiner towards the poem, since he read the notation as 'v.g.' for 'very good'. The story may well be true, for Smyth was himself an occasional poet in the old style, and modern poetry inspired him with nothing but amused tolerance. With characteristic brashness, Richard Milnes attempted an assault on Smyth's prejudices, but to no avail. 'I have just been drinking tea tete a tete with old Smyth and trying to convert him to Coleridge,' he told his parents during his second year at Cambridge, 'but he is too old to be corrected.' After Smyth's death in 1849, at the age of eighty-four, Henry Lushington affectionately recalled him in a letter to Milnes. 'Poor old Smythe [*sic*],' wrote Lushington, '– how well I remember him discussing the Adonais and the Alastor, with a certain tenderness for the misguided enthusiasm of his clever though in his view ludicrously absurd "young friends" – such as you – and with the most total non-perception of even the very minutest justification of any part of their admiration. Peace be with him. We shall not see a Professor of history in drab knee breeches again. The era of gaiters is closed. Clio indues trowsers – and too probably drops versifying together with gaiters. It may be feared that no succeeding Professor will contribute as largely as the late to that description of pieces in the Elegant Extracts headed "sentimental, lyrical, and ludicrous," a classification which always appeared to me exquisitely expressive – so innocently unconscious of absurdity – betraying the turn of mind of a whole generation.'[21]

For the Apostles, self-consciously in revolt against the literary values of the old guard, Tennyson's poetry was the voice of the new era, and faith in Alfred quickly became an article in the Apostolic creed. A comic version of this faith appears in a letter from an Apostle who had met a young lady deserving election to the Society. 'Miss Mellish ought to be sent to Cambridge, and made an Apostle,' he wrote enthusiastically. 'She is in every way worthy, having laid a glorious foundation of Wordsworthianism, and gradually erected on it a palace of Shelleyanism and Coleridgianism, crowning it with the airy minarets of Tennysonianism.' But the Apostles were serious in seeing Tennyson as prospectively a major literary figure and hence, in their view, an important agent in the regeneration of society that they hoped would spring from the growth of individual self-knowledge induced by great literature.[22]

Apostolic admiration of Tennyson was not lessened by his personality and looks. The three Tennyson brothers – Frederick, Charles and Alfred – were notable oddities in the undergraduate world, both for their behaviour and their reputation as poets. And Alfred's appearance was striking: he was a big, shambling figure with handsome features, very dark skin and an unkempt air. Shy, moody, often withdrawn, he was far from being easy to know and something of a mystery even to his friends. Like Maurice, he had experienced a painful, disturbing upbringing that had left him the victim of acutely sensitive feelings and bouts of depression. While he had remarkable powers of imaginative sympathy, verging on the mystical, his insights found their natural medium in poetry. Writing prose was unpleasant to him, and he spoke for the most part in succinct, isolated, rather awkwardly phrased sentences. In refreshing contrast to the smoothly proficient rhetoric and easy wit achieved by so many of the Apostles, Tennyson's conversation was almost childlike in its directness, unpretentiousness, and simple delight in humour.

As an active member of the Society Tennyson did not give satisfaction. He was elected on 31 October 1829 and attended the meeting of that date but failed to attend the next two and was fined five shillings for this offence. The punishment does not seem to have encouraged him to conform to Apostolic expectations. Further absenteeism occurred, and when his turn to deliver a paper came around he had not completed the task and had to resign from the Society. A note by W. H. Thompson in the Society's record book states that 'he wrote and began to read a paper on "Ghosts," but was overcome with nervousness, and tore up what he had written, throwing it in the fire. The same day he resigned his seat in the Society. He thought in poetry, and was not fond of expressing himself in prose.'[23]

Although Tennyson was a member for under four months and seems to have attended no more than five regular meetings, he was nonetheless still regarded as being in some special sense an Apostle, as perhaps no one else has ever been. Douglas Heath, who was elected to the Society just at the end of Tennyson's residence at Cambridge, did not recall Tennyson's attending the regular meetings 'as distinguished from the almost daily gatherings in one man's or another's room'. But Heath retained a vivid image of Tennyson 'sitting with his feet on the hob' at these gatherings, 'meditating verses (I suppose), and now and then mingling in the conversation, and now and then "mouthing out his hollow oes and aes | Deep chested music" with the result of some new poem or fragment, which may or not have afterward been published'.[24]

A letter from another Apostolic friend, R. J. Tennant, shows that Tennyson was not accorded honorary status and the privilege of attending the Society's annual dinner. 'I wish you had been able to read your essay on ghost stories and been elected an honorary,' wrote Tennant after the dinner of 1834; 'for then perchance we might have seen your pipe and shaken your fist at the "great dinner of the elect".' Years later, however, Tennyson did become an honorary member, thanks to F. J. A. Hort, a central member of the Society in the eighteen-fifties, later an eminent biblical scholar and Churchman. In 1855 Hort had assumed the duties of Secretary to the Society and had done some research into its records. The result appears in a letter he wrote to Tennyson when organizing the annual dinner of 1856:

My dear Sir,

You have probably heard many months ago that at the annual dinner of the Apostles in June last you were elected an honorary member: but still I suppose it is part of the duty of the Secretary to give you formal notice of the fact: at all events you must allow me the pleasure of doing that supposed duty. You would doubtless have been elected many years ago, had not a tradition been current that a law made in the mythical ages of the Society forbade the reelection of any one who had not written at least three essays. Fortunately a year ago an impulse seized me to explore the records of those shadowy times, and ascertain the true state of the case. The result was better than we had expected; and at the dinner I was able to tell young and old that your reelection would not be a violation or even a temporary suspension of the laws of the universe. Maurice immediately proposed that Mr Tennyson be elected an honorary member of the Conversazione Society of Cambridge, and acclamation did the rest. So now I hope you will often come and see for yourself whether little Maud or great Diana of the Ephesians is most honoured at our frugal feasts. At all events let us have you among us at our one unfrugal feast at Richmond on June 11 or 18.

It seems unlikely that Tennyson ever bothered to take advantage of his new privileges. He is not known to have attended the Society's meetings at Cambridge, and one of the few published poems omitted from Professor Christopher Ricks' otherwise excellent edition of Tennyson's poetry was written in refusal of an invitation to the annual dinner. Addressed to W. F. Pollock, it reads (in its entirety), 'Dear P. | Can't come. | A. T.'[25]

All the evidence suggests that Tennyson cared a great deal less about the Society than its other members did about him. Though the whole point of the Society for most of its members was the educational experience of a perfectly free interchange of ideas, it did not have this value for Tennyson, for he was not the least inclined to develop his thoughts in the form of intellectual discourse. He was greatly influenced by some of the Apostles' characteristic ideas, especially as expressed by Arthur Hallam, he valued their companionship, and in several ways they were important to his career as a poet. But he was essentially an eccentric element in the Apostolic circle, observed with admiration, amusement and sometimes a certain lack of understanding by his Apostolic friends. Much to the puzzlement of those Apostles who felt that they knew better than he how his talents should be employed, Tennyson was quite persistent in doing things his own way.

Tennyson's resignation from the Society in early 1830 thus made no real difference to his role in the Apostolic set that was then emerging under the careful supervision of J. W. Blakesley. Blakesley was aware from the first of the importance of Hallam and Tennyson in this group, for he spoke of their election as 'a great addition' to the Society and in letters to other Apostles described Hallam as 'worthy of the days in which giants walked on the earth' and Tennyson as 'truly one of the mighty of the earth'. He seems to have looked forward with pleasure to the forthcoming resignations of several less worthy Apostles, and he took pains to replace them with members more likely to contribute to the Society's future significance. During Tennyson's short period of active membership Blakesley went to some lengths to cultivate his friendship and encourage him in 'the proper way of thinking'. In a substantial letter he explained to Tennyson that 'the present race of monstrous opinions and feelings which pervade the age require the arm of a strong Iconoclast. A volume of poetry written in a proper spirit, a spirit like that which a vigorous mind indues by the study of Wordsworth and Shelley would be at the present juncture the greatest benefit the world could receive. And more benefit would accrue from it than from all the exertions of the Jeremy Benthamites and Millians if they were to continue for ever and a day.' This letter continues with Blakesley's elaborate explanation and defence of Sterling's recent intellectual development and ends with the news that R. J. Tennant 'talks of proposing Leighton for an Apostle: I like the man much as a goodhearted and agreeable companion but do not think he has sufficient earnestness to make one of a body which I hope and trust will do much for the world. I had much rather from what I have seen of them have Monteith or Garden especially the latter.'[26]

Blakesley's efforts at moulding opinion were successful, and the Apostles soon elected Robert Monteith and Francis Garden, a pair of inseparable friends who became lifelong members of the Apostolic circle. Shortly before, the Society had lost Tennyson as an active member, but a number of the Apostles less favoured by Blakesley also left at about the same time, and Blakesley did not cease his efforts to improve the Society. He found his next recruit a few months later, during the Long Vacation of 1830, when he was a member of a reading party at Portsmouth that included James Spedding and two younger undergraduates, John Allen and Henry Alford. Allen and Alford had been members of W. M. Thackeray's short-lived essay club during the preceding academic year, and the closest of friendships had developed between the two. But Allen was a quixotic, overly serious man – not at all the Apostolic type – whereas Alford's personality and intellectual gifts made him a likely candidate for the Society. Blakesley plainly had an eye on Alford, and Allen recorded in his diary his jealousy as he watched their growing intimacy. '[C]an such be friends?' he wrote. 'The cold sneering temperament however great the abilities (and in my soul I think the abilities are overrated) can not match with the warm, versatile affectionate (and slightly superficial) temperament of Dear Alford.' For his part, Alford welcomed Blakesley's attentions: to his great delight he was elected to the Society in the following term and joined the little group of those who prided themselves on being Arthur Hallam's intimate friends.[27]

By such deliberate and painstaking means the Society gained only a dozen more members in the next four years, nearly all of them important additions to the Apostolic circle. George Farish, W. H. Thompson, Douglas Heath, Kenneth Macaulay, George Venables, Charles Merivale, Savile Morton, Stephen Spring Rice, Henry Lushington, Arthur Helps, Edmund Lushington, John Heath – the group comprises those who were regarded at the time as among the most talented and promising young men at Cambridge. Time has a way of playing tricks, and at least two of those passed over by the Apostles – Edward FitzGerald and W. M. Thackeray – are now much better known than any of those they elected. But Blakesley and his friends had nonetheless gone a good way towards realizing their dreams of the Society's future significance.

The Apostolic set that evolved from the Society in the early thirties was, as one might expect, highly complex. It consisted of a network of friendships among about two dozen individualistic, unusually gifted young men, each of whom was actively engaged in the process of his own distinctive intellectual and emotional growth. The story of the group could be told, with advantage, from the point of view of any of these members. But during the remainder of his short lifetime Arthur Hallam's leadership was the central principle of the group's existence, and it is from his point of view that their story is most usefully told.

CHAPTER 9

ARTHUR HALLAM

'I long ago set him down for the most wonderful person altogether I ever knew,' wrote Henry Alford, in trying to describe Arthur Hallam to someone who had never met him. Hallam seems to have inspired unqualified admiration in almost everyone who came to know him. From his earliest years he had shown remarkable intellectual gifts, and he had been brought up as a privileged being in a family headed by one of the more distinguished writers of the day. Henry Hallam had the highest hopes for his brilliant eldest son: under his cautious supervision (or perhaps despite it) Arthur developed into an impressively well-read and cosmopolitan youth, with an exceptional knowledge of modern literature and thought. In character he was reflective, earnest, rather solemn, yet he charmed his contemporaries with the openness of his manner and the sympathy with which he treated them. He was far from being merely amiable: indeed, he tended to be a demanding and critical friend, for he was as aware of his superiority as anyone else and was rather too accustomed to being idolized. But his friendship seemed immensely valuable to those around him, and they anxiously, even jealously, strove to please him and be near him.[1]

For all this, Arthur Hallam was a very unhappy person when he first came up to Cambridge in October 1828, at the age of seventeen. His father, with little regard for Arthur's feelings on the subject, had chosen Cambridge rather than Oxford for him, although the decision meant that Arthur was separated from his closest friends and had the alien subject of mathematics forced upon him. From the first, he was lonely, discontented and much in need of affection. His resentment was less powerful than his desire to please his father, and he struggled hard towards the goal that had been set him, but his dislike of Cambridge was intense. '[T]he whole mode of existence here – its society, as well as its midnight lamp – its pleasures as well as its compulsions, are alike in my eyes odious,' he confided to Gladstone during his first term, and to his little sister Ellen he wrote, 'There is nothing in this college-studded marsh, which it could give you pleasure to know; or I would tell it you, my Nelly.'[2]

Although his disapproval extended to the Cambridge Union he allowed himself to be courted by one of its notable figures, Richard Milnes, and demonstrated his consummate skill at oratory among the members of a private debating club to which Milnes also belonged. Milnes was ecstatic about his new friend and eagerly reported to his family how much Hallam meant to him, how his tutor Connop Thirlwall had been entranced by Hallam, and so on. For his part, Hallam told Gladstone that he had not as yet discovered any real friend among his new acquaintances at Cambridge.[3]

By the end of his first year, however, Hallam had found a friend, a cause and a social circle. His first contact with Alfred Tennyson (apparently in early 1829) seems to have helped confirm his preoccupation with modern literature. Hallam's poem on Timbuctoo, which he had completed by that time, shows that he was already an ardent proponent of the literary movement admired by the Apostles. The Apostles' faith in modern poetry and Coleridgean metaphysics was entirely congenial to Hallam, for whom it acted as a bulwark against the negative influence of the Cambridge system. He and Tennyson became known to R. J. Tennant, the Apostle who, with his fellow-mystic Blakesley, had defended Coleridge's *Ancient Mariner* in a notable debate at the Union. Tennant proposed Hallam for membership in the Society: on 16 May 1829 he was elected and attended his first meeting, where he heard Thomas Sunderland speak on the question 'Is the Study of Oratory desirable?' (All seven members present, including Hallam, agreed it was.) A week later Tennant gave notice that he would propose Tennyson as a member; with this meeting the Society adjourned for the Long Vacation, but Tennyson was duly elected at the first meeting of the new academic year. In the meantime, Hallam and Tennyson conceived of a plan for publishing a joint volume of poetry, and Tennyson caused a little flurry of excitement among the literary set at Cambridge with the success of his prize poem.[4]

For the latter part of his first year, however, Hallam was in the throes of acute depression, and his election to the Society coincided with the first signs of the congenital vascular weakness that was to kill him four years later. '[Y]ou have probably heard,' he wrote to a friend, Robert Robertson, who planned to come up to Cambridge, 'that I have been ill lately with a complaint in the head; but you cannot have heard and can have no adequate idea of the miseries I suffered in mind, before that complaint came on; the most abject despondency mixed with vague dread and strong remorse. – Oh, my God! I hope never to know such days as those again. Since my illness I am much better. I see my way out of my glooms when they come upon me, and I despair less of ultimate peace of mind. Cambridge I hate intensely; which however is no reason why you should not like it. You say you have a bent towards mathematics and if so, you are of the happy few, whose intellects the odious system pursued there is not calculated either to crush, or to deprave. Besides there is a sufficiently pleasant society there, to the best of which I can introduce you.'[5]

Throughout the summer of 1829 Hallam poured out his feelings in poetry and in letters to friends, among them Richard Milnes. 'In my fits of gloom,' he told Milnes, 'I so often look death, and insanity in the face, that the impulse to leave some trace of my existence on this bulk of atoms gathers strength with the warning that I must be brief. . .I feel day by day that it is only in the pure atmosphere of Feeling (the word is not that which I need, but I have no better at the moment) I shall find ultimate peace of mind. What are thoughts and opinions? Cher ami, devices to grow cold; ever-acting powers of self-palsy! The reasoning faculties are by nature sceptical: there is no *love* in them: and what *man can be happy beyond his love?*'[6]

'My tour in Scotland is over,' he wrote to Milnes a few weeks later, 'and I am as miserable, if not more so, than ever. I really am afraid of insanity: for God's sake, send me letters, many letters, amusing letters. Mountains, or metaphysics; jokes, or arguments. . .any thing to distract me, anything to give me hope, sympathy, comfort! Do you ask what is the matter? I cannot tell you: I am not master of my own mind; my own thoughts are more than a match for me; my brain has been fevering with speculations most fathomless, abysmal, ever since I set foot in Scotland. As soon as I reach Malvern I must fling on paper what I have been thinking of, in order to know what *I do believe*, *what I can believe*.'[7]

'My last letter to you (that from York) was a strain of madness,' he wrote from his home at Great Malvern. 'I am calmer now. I past some days with Gaskell, which strengthened me: and visited a Lunatic asylum, which gave me a very awful, and elevated sense of sadness: so I am calm for the present. My father found one day my little book of Poetry, and read several pieces that assuredly I never dreamt he should see: on which we had a long, but unsatisfactory conversation, full of kindness on his part, and exhortations to turn my mind vigorously from the high metaphysical speculations and poetic enthusiasm that were sapping its very foundations. It cannot be: whither can I turn? Shall the river complain, that its channel is rocky? I must onward, and Le bon Dieu nous aide! I am seeking Truth – with my whole heart, with my whole being: I pray God that he deny me not light. I am seeking Moral Strength too: and though I have been the creature of impulse, though the basest passions have roused themselves in the dark caverns of my nature, and swept like storm-winds over me. . .I will struggle yet, and have faith in God, that when I ask for bread, I shall not receive a stone. My anathema, as you term it, of Metaphysics was but the whim of the moment: I thought more severely among the Scottish hills, than anywhere ever, and am now employed in committing to paper the result of my strivings in mind. I had many grapples with Atheism, but beat the monster back, taking my stand on strongholds of Reason. But my present convictions are decidedly opposed to all Formal Religion.'[8]

In this emotional crisis his one positive interest and solace seems to have been poetry. 'I tried to convert the nicest woman on earth to Wordsworth, and failed!!' he wrote to Milnes. 'En revanche, I made a convert to Shelley in the Glasgow steamboat, and presented him with a copy of the Adonais, as a badge of proselytism.' Back home at the end of the Long Vacation he reported with delight that the local vicar was not only a devotee of Shelley's poetry but believed Shelley 'to have lived almost the life of a saint'. His plans for publishing his own poetry with Tennyson's were soon to be vetoed by Henry Hallam, but in the meantime the scheme had interested other poetically inclined friends. 'You have my free vote for publishing along with Tennyson, and myself,' Hallam wrote to Milnes: 'but mine alone is not enough, and as he refused his brother on the score of not wishing a third, some difficulty may lie in your way.' To Gladstone he confided his belief that Tennyson might become 'the greatest poet of our generation, perhaps of our century'.[9]

By the time Hallam returned to Cambridge in late October 1829 he was somewhat better in both bodily and mental health, although he continued to cause alarm among his acquaintances. 'This odious place has been less odious to me this term than before,' he admitted to Robertson, and with obvious delight he described his new friends, among them Milnes ('the witty, frank, light-humored Milnes, whose temper was never yet ruffled nor his sauciness abashed, but in whose uniform kindliness of feeling one forgets the extravaganzas of his always random conversation') and Tennant ('the calm earnest searcher after Truth – who sat for months at the feet of Coleridge, and impowered his own mind with some of those tones, from the world of mystery, the only real world, of which to these latter days Coleridge has been almost the only interpreter'). Hallam had recently taken part in the memorable debate on Shelley and Byron at the Oxford Union, and was now planning with some of his fellow-Apostles to join Kemble in Germany. At the end of this term he gave his first paper to the Society, on the question 'Is the existence of an intelligent first Cause deducible from the phenomena of the Universe?' To this question Hallam and nearly all the other members of the Society returned a negative answer: it would seem that Hallam's efforts to define his religious beliefs had led him far enough for him to reject decisively the traditional defence of orthodoxy offered in such works as Paley's *Evidences of Christianity.*[10]

During this academic year Hallam spent a good deal of time learning German and rather neglected his regular studies, especially mathematics. The return of Kemble merely confirmed him in his desire to visit Germany. 'I question whether my Father may not be obstinate against my leaving England this year,' he told Robertson, '– but I shall do battle gallantly for so good a cause, and if I prevail intend being very happy at Bonn, Heidelberg or such like fine place. I am promised an introduction to the principal Burschen Clubs, in which I will drink beer, and clash swords for fatherland with as good a grace as one so green in the business may pluck up for the nonce.' Kemble's rendering of student songs learned in Germany made him, he said, 'feel capable of a terrible quantity of fine things, so that blowing out my brains is by no means so favorite a thought as it became two or three months ago'. Although the trip to Germany did not occur at this time, he and Tennyson made their trip to the Pyrenees during the Long Vacation of 1830.[11]

However helpful the Apostolic circle may have been to Hallam, his growing friendship with Tennyson was even more important. During the academic year of 1829–30 they became the closest of friends, and Hallam made the first of his visits to Tennyson's home at Somersby, where he met his future fiancée Emily Tennyson and was enraptured by the beauty of the Lincolnshire countryside. Here Hallam reached a turning point in his emotional development: his love for Tennyson, for his sister, for their home, became indistinguishable parts of a mood of exaltation as violent as his depression of the previous year. A letter written to Blakesley in April 1830 gives a vivid and somewhat ominous picture of his state of mind and health during one of these early visits to Somersby:

My dear Blakesley,

You have been surprised perhaps at my not writing, and will be still more so to hear that I am not about to return for the Scholarship [examination]. The weather has been playing the devil with my upper chamber, and my life here has been one of so much excitement and enjoyment, that I could hardly expect mere temperance of outward living should secure me from illness. How I am to get through the summer, 'the sweet little cherub that sits up aloft,' only knows. If I die I hope to be buried here: for never in my life, I think, have I loved a place more. I feel a new element of being within me — don't laugh — and if my past follies and reckless life have not clipped my wings, I trust soon to – fly over the moon, unless indeed I tumble into it in the shape of a lunatic. You are perhaps by this time disposed to think the catastrophe is past praying for, and in truth I do feel rather mad at times here – but Wallawaw! (as Tennant has it) sanity after all is a dull, old woman, very plain, and very *blue*. 'But what the deuce have you been doing' must be the question your dialectical soul is putting me all the while. I can hardly tell you: I have floated along a delicious dream of music and poetry and riding and dancing and greenwood-dinners and ladies' conversation till I have been simply exhaled into Paradise, spiritually speaking, while my 'dull brain' by 'perplexing and retarding,' or (to adopt Kemble's method of misquotation in order to come nearer truth) by throbbing and swelling and reeling, takes upon it the odious office of reminding me that I am dust.

This letter continues with a section characteristically concerned with literature and its reception in an unpoetic and unregenerate age. Charles Tennyson had just published a collection of sonnets that was much admired by the Apostles (although he himself seems to have been insufficiently Apostolic to be elected a member). These poems had met with some unsympathetic readers among London society, and Hallam's reaction to this was entirely characteristic of the Apostles' sense of their position as an élite in a hostile world, largely occupied by 'Stumpfs' (an Apostolic term for Philistines):

I heard the other day from Spedding, who was in London – poor fellow! and professed his intention of returning to you on Friday. He had shewn Charles's book to a young lady, who told somebody else he had brought her a strange book all about kissing the ladies! This moves my bile immensely. Gracious God! what an amalgamate of Mephistophilisms that

London society is! If the angel of the Lord appeared to Coleridge, as in the olden time to Abraham, and threatened fire and brimstone to this new Gomorrah, are there ten, think you, whom 'the hooded eagle' could fix upon to avert the storm of death by their righteousness[?] – Possibly at Snowhill or Whitechapel such might be found, but in the Westend, within the sweep of the whirlpool, hardly, hardly! Spedding suggests that as Charles's line about 'finches and thrushes' is abused by everybody, he had better to stop the mouths of the cavillers add a note to the next edition, 'it is a wellknown fact in natural history that finches and thrushes never build in the same nest!' Rather a splendid scoff – but woe to those who revile the line – on their foreheads through a burning eternity 'Stumpf' shall be pecked out by the indignant bills of legioned and immortal finches!!

Hallam's anger had plainly turned outwards against those fools who could not appreciate him and his friends, and this rather dangerous mood predominated in his mind for some considerable time.[12]

The problems of living in an unappreciative age, one that simply refused, for the time being, to be regenerated by literature, became even more acute in mid-1830, when Tennyson's *Poems, Chiefly Lyrical* appeared. Although Hallam had been prevented by his father from publishing his poetry with Tennyson's, he did what he could to promote Tennyson's book and in the following year reviewed it himself in the *Englishman's Magazine*. The review is a brilliant critical essay, yet one that makes no concessions whatsoever to the prejudices of the ordinary reader, who would probably be as sceptical of the ecstasy of admiration to which Hallam gave way in the latter part of the review as he would be puzzled by the extremely complex argument that makes up the first part. If he understood this argument at all, he might very well conclude that on the one hand he was being asked to accept the unknown Mr Tennyson as a great poet, while on the other he was being assured that he wouldn't recognize a great poet if he saw one. The best modern poetry, according to Hallam, 'is likely to have little immediate authority over public opinion. Admirers it will have; sects consequently it will form; and these strong under-currents will in time sensibly affect the principal stream.' Of course Hallam was quite right: from our vantage point in time it is easy to see how such avant-garde cliques as the Apostles served to bring new ideas into general consciousness. But he could scarcely hope to further Tennyson's career by publicly asserting that his poetry was likely to be unpopular with all but a privileged few.[13]

According to Hallam himself 'the communion of Apostles' was generally pleased by his review, but one of the more level-headed of them, James Spedding, did his best to warn him. 'The worst of it is that it is not written for the vulgar,' Spedding complained to Blakesley; 'but it is dangerous to tell him so, for he immediately assails you with cunning sentences and most scoffing periods, proving that if you object to his expressions you are ignorant of the truth of metaphysics.'[14]

'It is true I thought more of myself and the Truth, as I thought I perceived it, than of my probable readers,' Hallam admitted in a letter to James Spedding's younger brother Edward. 'This, you will say, was selfish, because I ought to have done whatever would do most good to Alfred. It is no easy matter however for a man to stop himself when he gets into full swing, and begins to write con amore: in parts I endeavored, as you observe, to put myself in a Magazine humour, and the result was trash that you are very properly ashamed of, and so am I. I am inclined however to think that both you and your brother something overrate the abstruseness of my writing.'[15]

Despite the warnings of his friends and some signs of restiveness among the established critics of the day, Hallam continued to urge Tennyson on the British public. Tennyson himself offered some resistance but was plainly carried away by the Apostles' vision of his duty to the age, for his second volume of poetry, published at the end of 1832, was prefaced by some lines that echoed the injudicious argument put forth by Hallam in his review:

> Mine be the power which ever to its sway
> Will win the wise at once, and by degrees
> May into uncongenial spirits flow;
> Even as the warm gulf-stream of Florida
> Floats far away into the Northern seas
> The lavish growths of southern Mexico.

This poem was one of those singled out for heavily sarcastic praise in J. W. Croker's devastating review of the 1832 volume. In Tennyson's mind Croker's scorn far outweighed the Apostles' approval, and to their dismay he set his face against all further publication. To the Apostles the 'ten years' silence' that followed was interminable and explicable only in terms of Tennyson's generally eccentric behaviour.[16]

In February 1831 Hallam and the Apostolic group at Cambridge lost the active presence of Tennyson, who was called home to his father's death-bed and never resumed his formal studies. Tennyson was overcome by acute depression and hypochondria at this time, but Hallam made every effort to bring him back into ordinary life and was almost entirely responsible for arranging the publication of his second volume.

By this time a complex Apostolic network had evolved. At its centre were the active members at Cambridge, and this group was supplemented by those senior Apostles who continued their studies there, some of whom won fellowships and settled down to academic careers. London was a second meeting-place, especially for the many Apostles who entered law, and other points of assembly were formed by certain family homes, such as the Heaths' at Kitlands, the Monteiths' at Carstairs, the Speddings' at Mirehouse. They visited back and forth, they met at Bonn or at Rome on their Continental travels, and through a steady flow of correspondence they kept one another aware of developments within the group.

The period 1831–3 – the last years of Arthur Hallam's life – were the heyday of the Apostolic set that surrounded him, and their letters to one another seem livelier, more exuberant, than at any other time. Hallam seemed much happier to his friends, and his moods were infectious, for his influence within the group was overwhelming. Letters of this period sometimes speak as if Hallam and the Society were identical, as if Hallam's opinions needed only to be known in order to know what the others were thinking. Richard Milnes, who had left Cambridge by then, had for some reason lost Hallam's friendship, but he was consoled in a letter from Robert Monteith, which referred to the Society as 'a region in which I do not think you know how much you are esteemed – Hallam though very variable and certainly at one time in my opinion very unjust towards you has recovered his amiability of late. He is not so dissatisfied with *himself*, not so morbid as he used to be and therefore more in possession of his naturally exuberant loving kindness towards others.'[17]

In 1832 Hallam graduated and, to his great pleasure, left Cambridge, and soon afterwards he became formally engaged to Emily Tennyson. Henry Hallam had not approved of the connection and maintained his anxious surveillance of his son's development, so that Arthur found himself obliged to study law in London, with a small income and little time for vacations abroad. He was often uncertain, sometimes depressed, and the direction of public affairs continued to worry him, but for the most part he seems to have enjoyed himself, dabbling in law, reading what else he pleased, spending much time with his fellow-Apostles in London and writing long letters to his fiancée and to other Apostles about himself, the group and the news of the day.

'I am about to become a nominal student of law,' he wrote to Donne in early 1832, 'but unless Ministers think fit to pull down the national credit along with their imbecile selves, I have not much thought of practising. The life I have always desired is the very one you seem to be leading. A wife and a library – what more can man, being rational, require, unless it be a cigar? I am not however without my fears that the season for such luxuries is gone or going by: in the tempests of the days that are coming, it may be smoking, and wiving, and reading will be affairs of anxiety and apprehension. Trench considers a man, who reads Cicero or Bacon nowadays, much as he would a man who goes to sleep on a ledge of a mad torrent, and dreams of a garden of cucumbers. I am very glad he visited you at Cromer: it seems to have done both your hearts good; as for him, he was delighted with all about you, except that he fears you are not quite in accordance with the Third and Fourth Councils respecting the nature of the Logos. . .He tells me he has awakened you to some alarm concerning the St Simonians, those prophets of a false Future, to be built on the annihilation of the Past in the confusion of the Present. I too am alarmed at the gigantic atrocity of their idea, at their increased organisation, and the facility with which France appears to imbibe the poison, but I cannot but confide yet in English good sense that it will repel them from these shores with indignant scorn. . .The mission is come however; and according to their instructions they are to call on Sir Francis Burdet, and "the chiefs of the aristocracy" to tell them "that humanity marches"! Bless their five wits – what incurable fools Frenchmen are!'[18]

In mid-1832, much to Hallam's delight, Tennyson paid a visit to him in London. 'I have news for you, great news –' Hallam wrote to Kemble, then in London himself to study at the British Museum, 'Alfred the great will be in town, perhaps today. He lingers now at Cambridge with Tennant. He talks of going abroad instantly, from which I shall endeavor to dissuade him. . .Alfred's coming seems to be mainly attributable to your letter three months ago – at least his answer to questions, why he comes to London, is said to be, "I have never answered John Kemble!" One would have thought taking pen in hand was less trouble than coming 50 miles; but different persons have different estimates of difficulty.'[19]

The visit was a great success. 'Nal seems much the better for this visit to London,' Hallam wrote to Emily: 'he smokes all day with Kemble and me, and very rarely talks, or thinks about his ailments, real or imagined.' The evenings were pleasantly spent. 'Jem and I went to the Kembles last Sunday night,' Edward Spedding told Donne, 'where we met Hallam and Alfred Tennyson. . .and heard French and German oaths and curses set to music, and called Histories of David and Goliath, likewise Fanny Kemble's self singing the two sisters who dwelt in a bower – Edinbroo Edinbroooe which was not a little edifying.' Tennyson's contribution to the evening was a recital of 'The Legend of Fair Women', but he had other social gifts, to judge from another account of the visit. 'You would have heard of Alfred Tennyson's sojourn among us,' Edward Spedding wrote to Blakesley, '– how he read to use the Legend of Fair Women – and gave us bakky – and was so excited by Kemble's mimicry and the clapping of his wings on a rump encased in white trowsers, that he set to work himself and enacted 1stly a Teutonic Deity – 2ndly the Sun Coming out from behind a Cloud 3rdly a man on a close stool – and lastly put a pipestopper in his mouth by way of beak, and appeared as a great bird sitting on an opposite bough, and he pecked in my face and I cried haw, haw! with divers other facetiunculae.'[20]

Tennyson was not to be dissuaded by Hallam from his plans for a Continental journey. In July the two set out for the Rhine country, but Hallam returned to London by a deliberately circuitous route. 'I suppose my own family has left London by this time,' he wrote to Kemble from the Continent: 'at all events I shall not go home, if I can help it, before I go to Lincolnshire; so, in case you meet my father, or the like, you need not give quite so precise an account of my intended proceedings as I have given you. Our journey has not been to me unpleasant; but Alfred swears the Rhine is no more South than England, and he could make a better river himself!. . .We have drunk infinite Rhenish, smoked illimitable Porto Rico, and eaten of German dinners enough to kill twenty men of robust constitution, much more one who suffers paralysis of the brain like Alfred. He has written no jot of poetry.'[21]

On his return from this surreptitious visit to Somersby in late August Hallam was shocked to hear of the sudden death of Edward Spedding. The younger Spedding was an accepted member of the Apostolic circle and would certainly have been elected to the Society, had his illness not prevented him from going up to Cambridge. The news elicited a poem from Tennyson, 'To J. S.', which examines and rejects conventional forms of consolation and culminates in two striking stanzas:

I will not say, 'God's ordinance
Of Death is blown in every wind;'
For that is not a common chance
That takes away a noble mind.

His memory long will live alone
  In all our hearts, as mournful light
That broods above the fallen sun,
  And dwells in heaven half the night.

Vain solace! Memory standing near
  Cast down her eyes, and in her throat
Her voice seemed distant, and a tear
  Dropt on the letters as I wrote.

I wrote I know not what. In truth,
  How *should* I soothe you anyway,
Who miss the brother of your youth?
  Yet something I did wish to say:

For he too was a friend to me:
  Both are my friends, and my true breast
Bleedeth for both; yet it may be
  That only silence suiteth best.

Words weaker than your grief would make
  Grief more. 'Twere better I should cease
Although myself could almost take
  The place of him that sleeps in peace.

Sleep sweetly, tender heart, in peace:
  Sleep, holy spirit, blessed soul,
While the stars burn, the moons increase,
  And the great ages onward roll.

Sleep till the end, true soul and sweet.
  Nothing comes to thee new or strange.
Sleep full of rest from head to feet;
  Lie still, dry dust, secure of change.[22]

Late 1832 was a troublesome time for Hallam, for his father was engaged in the distasteful task of bargaining with Emily Tennyson's dictatorial and mean-spirited grandfather, from whom her dowry would have to come. 'Lately I have been more than ever a prey to anxiety,' Hallam told a friend. 'A negotiation has been going on between my father and the old man whose only good quality is his relation to the person I love best in the world. The wretch makes most shabby, beggarly offers, which my father considers inadequate; and unless I can by hook or crook induce him to bid higher, I am not likely to be married before the Millennium. If I had any means of procuring by any means of my own, literary or others, even a slight addition to the allowance which my father can make me, all would go well; but I do not see such means. Bookmaking is a worse trade than ever; the law, besides being a profession which I hate, could not repay me for many a long year, and then only in case I succeeded in it.'[23]

For all his worries Hallam was sometimes in high spirits during the last year of his life. He did not find reading law as distasteful as the prospect of practising it, and he had ample time for other interests. In a letter to Tennyson he drew a pleasant picture of his daily routine:

'O world O Life O Time.' Have you a clear idea of my Croydon life[?] Listen, about ½ past 8 in the morning, I find myself dressed. I sometimes take a turn in the garden until the great bell summons us to prayers and breakfast. A microscope is then produced if the day be sunny and my Father examines various subjects of the animal and vegetable kingdom, then ½ an hour music by my sister. Inundated with Mozart and Beethoven I go up to my room and read about 'Real Property' till 2, then walk; then talk or German reading or more music with the sister. Dinner at 6. As soon as my Father makes the stir of his chair as a prelude to rising after dessert, I tap my sister on the shoulder, take a candle and up we go to my room, where I smoke and read German till ½ past 8 when we are called down to tea, then I read or write till 11. The last two days Kemble has been staying here. He has been very lively but he is so absorbed in Gothic manuscripts, that however conversation may begin he is sure to make it end in that. If one says 'a fine day John' he answers 'very true, and it is a curious fact that in the nine thousandth line of the first Edda, the great giant Hubba-dub makes precisely the same remark to the brave knight Siegfried.'[24]

Hallam used some of his spare time to write an essay castigating Professor Gabriele Rossetti for the literary atrocity he had committed in his *Disquisizioni Sullo Spirito Antipapale*, which contains the absurdly literal allegorical treatment of Dante that caused D. G. Rossetti to remark that his father had thought Beatrice to be the twopenny post. In late 1832 Hallam was able to tell Kemble that the 'essay on Rossetti is about to come out as a pamphlet, but without my name. I took fright at some things I had said about Christianity and matters appertaining to it, so I mean to avoid the direct responsibility, having no wish to earn the reputation of an Atheist or a Mystic. The secret of my authorship therefore may only be cautiously divulged by you. Do you know if Rossetti is a big man? I flatter myself, if he calls at my house to lick me, I have English stuff enow in my fists to floor a beggerly Italian. The stiletto, though more congenial, he will hardly employ, as it might not be considered Professorial. A duel would be inconvenient, because I am no great shot; but if you will be my second, and load my pistol, perhaps I may contrive to fire it.'[25]

By early 1833 a number of Hallam's Apostolic friends were frequenting London, and they may have had regular meetings of a quasi-formal sort, to judge from a light-hearted account of the group by James Spedding. 'You wish,' Spedding wrote to W. H. Thompson in Cambridge, 'to know about the Fathers – by the Lord so we call ourselves – Well but what do you want to know? Do you want to know whether we are Nominalists, Conceptualists, or Realists? That I really cannot answer till the events of tomorrow night shall have become to be – ("*from* not being, – therefore they must needs exist now" – note by Plato) – But my opinion is that some of us are one, some of us another. Hallam and I agree – and Tennant opposes us – but he will not allow the grounds of his opposition to be stated in any words but his own and they will not bear that test – from which we may conclude that his views are *singularly* true; i.e. there is not another mind to which they will appear so. I need not add that his own words are quite unintelligible. If I were to record all our laws, customs, sentiments, pieces of illumination and analysis, – etc., I suppose that this paper itself would not contain the words that should be written, but it would require at least as much again. Any Father can introduce an Apostle which I look upon as participation enough in our immunities – N.B. I am the most impartial judge, as I belong to both.'[26]

Alfred Tennyson's brothers remained on the fringes of the Apostolic set, their eccentric, Tennysonian behaviour noted with awe and amusement by the Apostles. 'Charles and Frederic Tennyson are beginning to take positive steps towards entering the Church,' Hallam reported to Milnes in 1832: 'they toil not however; neither do they spin (sonnets); very fat prelatical lilies they are like to make.' Frederick managed to avoid this fate, wished on them by their tyrannical grandfather, but in early 1833 Charles, retiring, morbid, self-doubting, gave way to it and, worse, also began to give way to opium addiction. His reappearance in London after his ordination was remarked upon in their correspondence by both Hallam and Spedding. 'Charles made his appearance last night, having been two days in town, *too nervous* to see any of his friends,' Hallam wrote to Emily. Hallam took pity on him and brought him into the social whirl by escorting him to dinner at Douglas Heath's rooms. 'I dined at Heath's on Thursday,' Spedding later wrote to Thompson, '– and whom should I see sitting opposite as I entered the room, but Charles Tennyson? Of course I betrayed as much excitement as could be expected, and inquired with large eyes the when and the whence – but I could hear nothing further than that he came proximately from the Old Hummums [a hotel in Covent Garden] and ultimately from Lincolnshire – He had been three days in London without revealing himself; what doing, – is one of the many things which God is said to know – Doubtless nothing immoral; for he told me only this morning how pure and good he had grown since he took orders – for he had seen in several shops books with indecent titles and indecent pictures, and he had passed by them *quick*. He was so good as to say that some of the pleasantest moments of his curacy had been those in which he thought of me. In short, he is much as he was – looks well – and denies laudanum, except in asthmatical intervals.'[27]

The next month Alfred himself reappeared, this time with his sister Mary, and Hallam had a pleasant time showing them the sights of London. Yet another visitor to London at this time was J. W. Blakesley, who reported to W. H. Thompson that during his stay he had 'seen Hallam, Heath, Martineau, Garden, Tennyson, Brookfield, Thackeray and Arthur Buller, the three last of whom seemed exceedingly inclined to profligacy. . .[Garden] was going with them to some divan where a female – of course naked – danced for the edification of the company. – Tennyson had his sister with him, to whom Tennant was doing the amiable in a very open way for a mystic. She is really a very fine looking person, although of a wild sort of countenance, something like what Alfred would be if he were a woman, and washed.' Blakesley, who had just been ordained himself, seems to have been feeling a little out of touch with the more ribald of his fellow-Apostles, for his letter continues by suggesting to Thompson that the members of the Society resident at Cambridge 'ought to be a little less fond of dirt in their conversation, which during the latter part of last term abounded with so many allusions to the propagation of the species, that as a modest man, a clergyman, and a fellow of [the C]ollege I frequently found myself blushing'.[28]

For his part, Tennyson seems to have pretty well divested himself of the melancholia that had overcome him after his father's death, and he took an active part in the Apostolic goings-on of this time. In August 1833 Stephen Spring Rice reported to Blakesley from London that

'Alfred came to Cambridge the day the examinations were over[,] stayed there a week[,] came to town with Frederick, Monteith[,] Morton and myself, lost a portmanteau "full of Dantes and dressing gowns" by the way, went on here in a regular Cambridge debauchery style and ended by going into Scotland with Monteith.'

'Hallam is in town,' Spring Rice went on to say, 'and to leave it in ten days for the continent where he is going for six weeks with the governor, much to his disgust as he says that "too much contact between the governor and the governed is the worst possible thing."' 'Hallam either is or has been in Germany with his father,' Francis Garden reported to Milnes about a month later. 'He was most absurdly gay last season, – a mood and habit so unsuited to his character, that I can't believe the tendency will last long.'[29]

In fact Hallam had died before Garden wrote this letter. His complaint had troubled him at intervals for several years: at Vienna it recurred, and his father left him alone at the hotel on the afternoon of 15 September, since Arthur did not feel well enough to accompany him on his daily walk. When Henry Hallam returned he found his son still sitting in the chair as he had left him, but dead. The autopsy revealed a massive cerebral haemorrhage, probably caused by a vascular malformation that might have killed him at any time.

Blakesley, travelling on the Continent, chanced across some English acquaintances who had been in Vienna at the time and who told him the news in all its distasteful details. 'It seems,' Blakesley wrote to his family, 'that the rascals at the place took advantage of the circumstances under which the father was placed to extort money from [him] to an incredible extent – as much as £200; – under pretence that it was necessary to move the corpse to this place and that; – it was taken I believe to more than one place of burial without Mr H's consent, and there rejected by the Catholic priests on the grounds of heresy, and all this merely got up to furnish an excuse for extortion; for the police, on the English ambassador interfering, denied any knowledge of the matter.'[30]

The news reached the Tennysons in early October, and in time Apostolic letters of condolence came to Alfred – inevitably, from the pious Francis Garden, an attempt at religious consolation, and from Robert Monteith an outburst of the sense of loss that was felt within the group. 'He was so much a centre round which we moved,' wrote Monteith, 'that now there seems a possibility of many connections being all but dissolved. Since Hallam's death I almost feel like an old man looking back on many friendships as something bygone – I beseech you do not let us permit this, you may even dislike the interference of common friendship for a time, but you will be glad at length to gather together all the different means by which you may feel not entirely in a different world from that in which you knew and loved Hallam.'[31]

'It seems, indeed, a loud and terrible stroke from the reality of things upon the fairy building of our youth,' wrote Henry Alford to another Apostle. But Hallam's death, so far from weakening the Apostolic circle, gave it a special kind of unity. In the decades that followed many distinguished and amiable young men became Apostles, came to know the older members and to be regarded by them with affection and sometimes deep interest. Yet these later Apostles were members of the Apostolic set in some different sense: an indefinable but quite distinct gap separated those who merely belonged to the Society and those who 'knew and loved Hallam'.[32]

In the few scattered writings that Arthur Hallam left behind one can trace the outlines of a developing theory that seems directly related to the spirit of the Society. The Apostolic idea of opinion or belief as merely the superstructure of personality was certainly adopted by Hallam, and it seems to have been of value to him in finding a way out of the emotional crisis he experienced in 1829.

In that crisis he suffered from an acute sense of disparity between feeling and thought. 'An intellective thing | I seem, of inward spring | Devoid, a coreless rind,' he wrote in one of those poems he wished his father had not seen; he told Milnes that he felt the answer lay 'in the pure atmosphere of Feeling', although the word seemed inadequate for his meaning; and in another poem he wrote of an antithesis between feeling and speech: 'Make me to feel, not talk of, sovranty, | And harmonize my spirit with my God!' The central problem was one of religious doubt, though he also told Milnes that 'the basest passions have roused themselves in the dark caverns of my nature, and swept like storm-winds over me'. His first conclusions from this experience seem to have been negative, for the paper he read the Society in December 1829 probably dealt with his rejection of traditional orthodoxy. But tentatively affirmative ideas seem to underlie his essay, 'On Sympathy', read to the Society in December 1830. In a complex argument based on a Hartleian analysis of human development (through the principle of the association of ideas), Hallam traces the origins of the feeling of sympathy or love to infantile experience and demonstrates its central role in the development of moral consciousness. While his argument seems narrowly empirical, it also seems to be working towards a metaphysical conclusion, and in a significant sentence he admits the difficulty of explaining his position to the Apostles: 'Some of you, perhaps, may be disposed to set me down as a mystic, for what I am about to say; just as some of you may have despised me as a mechanist, or a materialist, on account of what I have said already.' Faced with such a subtle and demanding paper, the Apostles seem to have been rather puzzled. In voting on the question that closed the meeting, 'Is that Theory just which derives the Moral Sentiments from the principle of Association?' three Apostles agreed with Hallam, two disagreed, and five (including Blakesley) found themselves unable to make up their minds.[33]

Hallam's next paper (14 May 1831) dealt with an equally intimidating question: 'Did the Epicureans do more than the Stoics for the advancement of that portion of mental philosophy, which relates to the origin of our moral sentiments?' This paper was expanded into a longer essay, 'On Cicero', with which Hallam won the Trinity College prize for the best English essay of the year, and here the direction of his thinking becomes clearer.

Hallam's analysis of Cicero's thought is specifically Apostolic. The question 'concerning the merits of Ciceronian philosophy,' he states, 'naturally resolves itself into two parts. In what temper of mind, it should first be asked, did Cicero come to form and deliver his opinions? And, secondly, what those opinions were? Now the first of these is, beyond comparison, the most interesting and important. A man, it has been well said, "is always other and more than his opinions." To understand something of the predispositions in any mind, is to occupy a height of vantage, from which we may more clearly perceive the true bearings of his thoughts, than was possible for a spectator on the level... The inward life of a great man, the sum total of his impressions, customs, sentiments, gradual processes of thought, rapid suggestions, and the like, contains a far greater truth, both in extent and in magnitude, than all the fixed and positive forms of belief that occupy the front-row of his understanding.'

In seeking to explain Cicero's 'temper of mind' or 'inward life' Hallam identifies four 'predisposing influences' on him. Cicero was a Roman and must be viewed in the context of 'Roman life, and the peculiar tendencies of its national feeling'; he was 'a Roman statesman', much involved with politics; he was 'a Roman gentleman' and susceptible to class feelings; he was 'a Roman orator' and subject to the influence that oratory has on its practitioners. This fourth characteristic Hallam regards as one of the 'strong previous disadvantages' under which Cicero 'laboured. . .in his approach to the sanctuary of Wisdom'. Oratory is 'the bringing of one man's mind to bear upon another man's will'; it is to be distinguished from eloquence (the vivid expression of unadorned truth) and in its most debased form becomes mere rhetoric, of the sort that the Apostles deplored in Thomas Sunderland. 'Where understanding is more active in production than feeling,' Hallam claims, 'the predominance of rhetoric. . .over true oratory is the certain result.' He finds Cicero 'altogether wanting' in the 'loftier powers of imagination' as opposed to those of mere intellectual skill, and he explains the inadequacy that he finds in Cicero's thought in terms of a disparity between Cicero's words and his moral feelings. 'When we pass from the eloquent moralities of Cicero to examine the foundations of his ethical system, we find a sudden blank and deficiency,' he says. 'His praises of friendship, as one of the duties as well as ornaments of life, never seem to have suggested to his thoughts any resemblance of that solemn idea which alone solves the enigma of our feelings, and while it supplies a meaning to conscience, explains the destination of man.' Cicero's problem seems to have been that he did not understand 'the sublime principle of love', as taught by Plato.

Realizing that his reader may be more than a little confused by this time, Hallam admits, 'My meaning perhaps requires to be explained more in detail', and then outlines a theory by which the feelings that we call human love are seen to find their fulfilment in orthodox religious faith. 'Love, in its simplest ethical sense, as a word of the same import with sympathy, is the desire which one sentient being feels for another's gratification, and consequent aversion to another's pain,' he states. 'This is the broad and deep foundation of our moral nature.' The sympathetic emotions, regrettably, 'often succumb to other passions' that are 'nourished by the changing accidents of sensation', but properly cultivated they serve to connect 'the world of the senses' with spiritual reality and thus can have 'the effect of a regeneration to the soul'. This was well understood by Plato. 'Hence his constant presentation of morality under the aspect of beauty', and hence his praise of homosexual love at a time when 'social prejudices. . .depressed woman below her natural station', so that men were seen as the only fit objects of 'this highest and purest manly love'. But while Plato sensed 'the ulterior destiny' of the passion of love, it was left to Hebraic literature to throw 'a strong light. . .upon recesses of the human heart, unknown to Grecian or Roman genius'. The extension of human love to an unknowable God is an impossibility; hence 'the Christian faith is the necessary complement of a sound ethical system', for it shows the way that human, physical love can find its completion in the love of God. 'Ignorant by his position of this fact, untaught by imagination and meditative feeling', poor Cicero looked in exactly the wrong direction for 'a foundation for his moral system'. 'He left the heart for the head, sentiment for reason', and hence failed to see the emotional basis of moral thought.[34]

Hallam's later writings contain some important elaborations on these ideas. In his attack on Rossetti he further expounds his Apostolic distinction between emotion and thought. 'The work of intellect,' he claims, 'is posterior to the work of feeling. The latter lies at the foundation of the Man; it is his proper self, the peculiar thing that characterizes him as an individual. No two men are alike in feeling, but conceptions of the understanding, when distinct, are precisely similar in all.' In his 'Theodicaea Novissima' he asserts that 'the nature of personal being' is unknown to us and that God alone understands 'the abysmal secrets of personality'. In yet another essay he suggests that love is 'at once the base and pyramidal point of the entire universe', and the idea of religion as answering those feelings evinced in human love appears elsewhere as 'erotic devotion', which he sees as the hallmark of Hebrew literature and the central principle of Christianity.[35]

Since the poetry Tennyson wrote about Hallam is sometimes thought to have homosexual overtones and since people are fond of speculating about the nature of their relationship, it may be as well to acknowledge that these theories of Hallam's could be seen, in part, as a rationalization of homosexual feelings. All the evidence, however, suggests that their friendship was not actively sexual at all. Like any other Eton schoolboy Hallam might well have known what homosexuality was, but he would certainly have regarded such behaviour with contempt. If, arguing from the supposed tendencies of Tennyson's feelings, we choose to regard the relationship as latently homosexual, then we may conjecture that such feelings could have been among those 'basest passions' that disturbed Hallam in mid-1829, and possibly the comments that he makes on Platonic love in the essay on Cicero should be read in this light. Those disturbing passions, we may note, rose from 'the dark caverns' of his nature, an image that seems related to such expressions as 'the abysmal secrets of personality' and 'the enigma of our feelings'. In Hallam's view the most significant and powerful of the feelings that emanate from these 'recesses of the human heart' are those of love; while these feelings are all too often subjugated to the sexual passions, properly understood (as Plato understood them) they are not sexual but moral and find their ultimate meaning in religious terms. For Hallam, then, homosexual feelings would have been merely part of the larger problem of reconciling his experience of human love with the orthodox faith that he wished to profess. His 'grapplings with Atheism', the 'spectres of the mind' he faced before he 'came at length | To find a stronger faith his own', had to do with discovering a link between his deepest emotions and the vision of Providential love that he saw as central to his faith. His conclusions, interestingly enough, are close to those of Maurice, who also argued that our experience of earthly, human relations is basic to our understanding of God's love. In his exploration of the connection between feeling and belief Hallam seems to have been deeply influenced by the spirit of the Society. However fragmentary and incomplete his exposition of his ideas, we can trace in his writings something of the intellectual and emotional development he underwent as a member of the Society, and can sense something of what the Society meant to him.[36]

Of what Hallam meant to the Apostles we have a surer witness. It seems impossible to improve on Tennyson's nostalgic evocation of the days when the Society was under the sway of Hallam's spiritual leadership, and this chapter in the history of the Apostles may be most fittingly closed with his well-known words:

I past beside the reverend walls
In which of old I wore the gown;
I roved at random through the town,
And saw the tumult of the halls;

And heard once more in college fanes
The storm their high-built organs make,
And thunder-music, rolling, shake
The prophet blazoned on the panes;

And caught once more the distant shout,
The measured pulse of racing oars
Among the willows; paced the shores
And many a bridge, and all about

The same gray flats again, and felt
  The same, but not the same; and last
  Up that long walk of limes I past
To see the rooms in which he dwelt.

Another name was on the door:
  I lingered; all within was noise
  Of songs, and clapping hands, and boys
That crashed the glass and beat the floor;

Where once we held debate, a band
  Of youthful friends, on mind and art,
  And labour, and the changing mart,
And all the framework of the land;

When one would aim an arrow fair,
  But send it slackly from the string;
  And one would pierce an outer ring,
And one an inner, here and there;

And last the master-bowman, he
  Would cleave the mark. A willing ear
  We lent him. Who, but hung to hear
The rapt oration flowing free

From point to point, with power and grace
  And music in the bounds of law,
  To those conclusions when we saw
The God within him light his face,

And seem to lift the form, and glow
  In azure orbits heavenly-wise;
  And over those ethereal eyes
The bar of Michael Angelo.[37]

CHAPTER 10

THE ROUND TABLE IN THE THIRTIES AND FORTIES

When Arthur Hallam died the Apostolic set was undergoing a process of gradual change that continued undisturbed by even this event. As the members of Hallam's circle graduated and began taking their first steps towards the various professions and careers that would eventually be their life work, the character of the group was altered. Some Apostles came close to vanishing from the knowledge of the group; some did vanish entirely; some acquired added significance as old alliances were strengthened and new ones formed and as the development of their individual careers changed their lives and their relationships with one another. Nor was it merely a matter of individual change. A series of events and issues impinged on the group in the thirties and forties; in many cases their mutual relationships were affected by the way they responded to the political, social and religious currents of their time.

They came increasingly to rely on correspondence to stay abreast of developments within the group. Always informative and entertaining, their letters become the key to the group's history throughout this period. There are many gaps in the record, since many of the letters have perished or survive only in the decorously edited versions one finds in official Victorian biographies. But there are quite enough for an account of the Apostles and their activities to be given, for the most part, in their own words.

When Hallam died in late 1833 the Apostles were widely dispersed, but several were, for various reasons, thrown together at Cambridge. John Sterling had forsaken his programme of self-education at Bonn and had returned to read for his degree and to attend the divinity lectures in the company of an Apostle even less suited for ordination than himself – James Spedding, who had made several unsuccessful attempts to win a fellowship at Trinity and was now casting about rather aimlessly for something to do. John Kemble was hard at work preparing his lectures on the history of the English language, in the hopes of launching an academic career, although he had not entirely forsaken the idea of entering the Church. At this time the Society numbered only four undergraduates among its active members – Kenneth Macaulay, Savile Morton, Stephen Spring Rice and Henry Lushington. W. H. Thompson, Henry Alford and G. S. Venables had graduated and were still competing for the fellowships they were eventually to win. Douglas Heath, Charles Merivale and J. W. Blakesley had won theirs, and the latter two had been appointed to teaching posts at their respective colleges. Late 1833 found Blakesley holidaying on the Continent, where he received a chatty letter, full of Cambridge gossip, from Thompson.

'You will be glad to hear,' wrote Thompson, 'that [John] Heath has been made lecturer on Whewell's side...Christopher Wordsworth shares the classics with Evans, who is reported to have visions of connubial bliss disturbing his tutorial quietness. It must have been some such visitation which the other day reconciled him to standing a good quarter of an hour in the heaviest rain, under the most leafless tree I ever remember to have seen...With regard to a much more important Society I have but little to say. We are grievously thinned by the departure of Spedding and our two Scotch friends [Monteith and Garden]: nor have we as yet struck out any new roots to make up for the loss of our most flourishing branches, and the expected loss of others. We are talking seriously of Helps, who is getting licked into something which in loose and popular language may be called shape.' The Apostles also had their eye on William Coningham, a young cousin of Sterling's who was then in his first year, for Thompson goes on to say, 'Sterling as you would probably expect is here, reading Homer and Euclid for his degree. He seems in splendid condition – to judge from his spirits in society. His cousin seems made of excellent stuff, as far as his human qualities are concerned: whether he has in him any lurking veins of Apostolical metal we have scarcely had time to discover. He is reading with me, and has certainly a most Apostolical contempt for the moralities of Euripides, joined to a not unapostolical inability to construe them.' In the event, Arthur Helps was elected and Coningham was not. The only other elections of this academic year were John Heath and Edmund Lushington, both of whom were elder brothers of already elected Apostles and both of whom were already well launched in academic careers – indeed, John Heath had been a Fellow of Trinity since 1831. These elections filled the last places at the

Round Table, for no later Apostle could be said to have belonged to Arthur Hallam's circle.

'Touching the rest of the Brotherhood,' Thompson continued, '– Spedding is in Town taking lessons in drawing and astonishing his master by his success[.] Suspicions are afloat that he has discovered painting pictures to be a more amusing occupation than writing sermons: at any rate he has for some time been in the habit of making companions between Truth and Beauty, less to the advantage of the former than most candidates for holy orders would think justifiable. – Trench has I believe left [H. J.] Rose – not in consequence of any disagreement of opinion, but because Rose has exchanged livings with Archdeacon Lyell and Trench does not like the new situation to which he would have to remove. He has been to visit Donne and has preached in several of the neighbouring pulpits much to the astonishment of their usual occupants, and of their hungry flocks: who it seems had been so long accustomed to an air-diet as to find some difficulty in swallowing the gobbets of strong meat flung among them with so vigorous a hand. Donne describes his visits to his brother clergymen to have been as if Elijah had paid a morning call to Jezebel's private chaplain. – I have told you already a most startling number of facts, more remarkable I fear for their truth than their interest: but it would be sending coals to Newcastle to talk about truth and Beauty to a man who has been in Germany and is in Italy – the one the repository of all visible[,] the other of all invisible excellence. You will conclude from this that I am not yet cured of the Englishman's prejudice that nothing is to be learnt worth knowing unless a man shall travel for it. As however there is little chance of my having leisure (for a long time at least) for this Peripatetic method of arriving at truth, I have resolved to try how far Transcendentation may be learnt on this side the Channel, and have proceeded so far towards the understanding of Kant as to have ordered a German book and to have determined on ordering a German Grammar and Dictionary. . .You will observe from the direction of this letter that we imagine you to be by this time in Rome: where you have probably met Garden and Monteith. I believe you may also expect to see Milnes shortly. He is to pass through Cambridge, on his way thither, in a few days – You will of course long since have heard of Arthur Hallam's melancholy death. Alfred Tennyson passed through the other day on his return I believe from the funeral: which you [?would] hear was to take place in England. He seemed less overcome than one would have expected: though, when he first arrived, he was very low – He left among us some magnificent poems and fragments of poems. Among the rest a monologue or soliloquy of one Simeon Stylites: or as he calls himself Simeon of the Pillar: a poem which we hold to be a wonderful disclosure of that mixture of self-loathing self-complacence and self-sacrifice which caused our fore-fathers to do penance when alive and to be canonized when dead. It is to be feared however that the men of this generation will hold it to be somewhat too unwholesome; the description of his sufferings being too minute for any but those whom the knowledge of the Art holds above the subject. . .I find I have not answered your enquiries about George Farish. He is in Town professing as usual to read Law, and practising as usual the smoking of cigars. It is a great pity that he cannot be persuaded to choose some profession (as the Medical for instance) more suited to his habits and more likely to bring his peculiar gifts into play – Spring Rice I believe intends writing to you soon. He is reading as hard or harder than one might expect from a young gentleman with such good Trowsers. Sterling who has just been here desires to be remembered to you as does also Kemble: though with certain imprecations (I suppose for your not writing to him) which regard for your cloth induces me to suppress.'[1]

R. J. Tennant was one of those who joined the group at Cambridge in the following year, and he provided Tennyson with an account of one of their social functions. 'Last Saturday, we had an Apostolic dinner, when we had the honour among other things of drinking your health, as having *once been* one of us,' wrote Tennant. 'Edmund Lushington and I went away tolerably early, but most of them stayed till past two: John Heath volunteered a song, Kemble got into a passion about nothing but quickly jumped out again, Blakesley was afraid the Proctors might come in, and Thompson poured huge quantities of salt upon Douglas Heath's head.'[2]

'Kemble,' Tennant continued, 'has just received a Diploma from the Royal Society of Antiquities at Copenhagen which is one of the highest marks of distinction that could have been conferred upon him.' Kemble's philological studies had greatly impressed those few scholars qualified to understand his work, but they had not helped him to a position at Cambridge, as he had hoped. The series of lectures he gave was far too difficult for most of his auditors, and his social position at Trinity was uncomfortable, for he had been admitted to the Combination Room as if he were a Fellow of the College and yet he did not feel he was treated as one. The situation was not helped by his tendency to get drunk and quarrel with people. His decision to pursue his studies in Germany, where he was appreciated by such eminent scholars as Jacob Grimm, was probably received with relief at Trinity. 'Little Jacky is gone to Göttingen to eat roots with Grimm,' Blakesley reported to Thompson in late 1834, and the Apostles seem to have heard little more of Kemble until 1836, when they learned that he had married the daughter of a German professor. 'I did look for him never to marry,' Donne confessed to Blakesley: 'but the shock of surprise was much milder than if it had been told me that Spedding or H. Romilly had sacrificed themselves to the good of posterity.' In the same year Kemble returned to England and became the editor of the newly founded *British and Foreign Review.* Characteristically, he had high hopes for reforming British society and strong opinions as to how it should be done. '[A]ll reform is misplaced,' he told Donne, 'which does not begin by reforming our system of *education*, from the lowest to the highest and from the dame school to the University. I do thank God that I for one escaped the soulkilling and ruinous effects of a University education: I hated and despised them, and I owe them nothing. Yet if accident should ever set me up on a pedestal and raise me to a name, they will claim me. Education must be taken out of the hands of the parsons, till the parsons are educated for their task of educating others. The *clerisy* of the land must no longer be the parsonry of the land.' Kemble recruited some Apostolic support for the journal and continued working away at it very successfully until 1844, when it abruptly ended and put him once more at a loose end. But during this period he seems to have lost touch with the Apostolic group as a whole, although he remained close to Donne.[3]

A number of the Apostles found themselves isolated from the group by the demands of their careers, among them the fastidious and sharp-tongued W. H. Thompson, who became a schoolmaster at Leicester in 1836, much to his distress, 'Every succeeding day reveals more of the sterility of the Leicester mind,' he wrote in great distaste to Blakesley. 'I doubt very much whether it be possible for boys to be taught by one much less stupid than themselves – unless indeed he make up for possessing an ordinary share of understanding by a most extraordinary one of benevolence; that is, of love for his species *as such*. For any amiable quality beyond this, – it were as easy to love Plato's plucked chicken as an average Leicester boy – The only motive one has for giving oneself trouble with them is the fear lest they should grow up like their parents.'[4]

Blakesley counselled him to bear his lot 'with tolerable philosophy, – as a man does gout or a voyage to India, – by the help of considering that your state is not a permanent one'. In the following year Thompson was relieved to hear that he had been chosen to succeed Edmund Lushington as an Assistant Tutor at Trinity, although he had reservations about having to take holy orders, as he told Blakesley with rueful humour: 'If I am not orthodox enough now, what can I expect to be after a residence in Trinity with you and Heath? 'Tis good striking when the iron happens to be hot. Don't flatter yourself that you are the last heretic that is to get into orders. The days of economies are not yet over. – This is all very unprincipled but I am convinced the weather is at fault. Who can help feeling relaxed by these suns and showers? Moses himself would have felt pantheistic in such weather. In that great dry desert no wonder he was such a monotheist. So was I while the east winds lasted. – And so am I now, for that matter, only one gets a habit of speaking in parables to the wise.' On the other hand, he was entirely of one mind on the subject of leaving Leicester: 'Now it is all settled I begin to be heartily glad at the prospect of getting rid of these people. They are an evil and filthy generation: and who knows whether I might not have been made like unto them by a longer sojourn. Perhaps, some fine day, one might have caught oneself intermarrying with the daughters of the people of the land, and so defiling the purity of apostolic descent.'[5]

It was with considerable pleasure that Thompson passed on to Milnes a story illustrative of Apostolic reactions to provincial society. 'Speaking of Arthur Buller,' he wrote, 'I find his fame rife in these parts, both on other accounts, and by reason of a famous speech he is reported to have made to a pompous dowager of the neighbourhood, who was dilating greatly on the blessings which under Providence she had been conferring on the poor of her village, through the instrumentality of blanket societies – "I should be sorry to say anything to discourage so apparently excellent an undertaking – but *are* you aware, Mrs Potchin, that it was societies of this nature which were the *immediate* cause of the French Revolution?" '[6]

Throughout this period James Spedding remained a prominent member of the Apostolic group, and his letters are especially valuable as examples of the lively exchange of views and gossip that went on within this circle of friends. His habitual self-mockery and lightness of tone also offer a refreshing contrast to the enormous seriousness with which so many of the Apostles took themselves. Not that Spedding was any less concerned about social or moral issues, but he was by nature incapable of the egotistic rhetoric and Wertherism of Kemble and Sterling. He shared most Apostolic attitudes, for example their disdain for worldliness, but his treatment of this subject (in a letter to Thompson) is distinctive, not least in his consciousness that mere disdain must be a temporary attitude. 'By the by,' he asked Thompson, 'what is your opinion about worldly prosperity? There was an Englishman who went to see Vesuvius, and as soon as the great beast began to spit fire and spout flame, he stuck his hands in his sides, cocked his hat on one side, and looking calmly up exclaimed "You're a humbug!" And truly till I can find out whether worldly prosperity increases or diminishes a man's happiness (upon the whole) I shall be almost inclined to think worldly prosperity a humbug.'[7]

James Spedding was thought by both Alfred Tennyson and Edward FitzGerald to have been the wisest man they had ever known, a reputation doubtless gained by the calm, dispassionate, invariably graceful way he faced both the adversities and triumphs of life. That this manner was by no means the whole man is attested by his close friend, Sir Henry Taylor, who wrote that Spedding 'was always master of himself and of his emotions; but underlying a somewhat melancholy composure and aspect there were depths of tenderness known only to those who knew his whole nature and his inward life'. In this context Taylor mentions Spedding's response to the deaths of those he loved, the first of whom was an unnamed schoolfellow at Bury. The Apostles stood in awe of Spedding's ability to reconcile himself to death. 'To me,' he once wrote, 'there are no companions more welcome, cordial, consolatory or cheerful than my dead friends.'[8]

This attitude is nowhere more strikingly evident than in a letter he wrote on the occasion of Edward Spedding's death:

My dear Thompson

This letter will find you I hope comfortably established in Blakesley's rooms, according to the directions I gave to Tennant. I am sorry that it is not likely to add to your comfort – if you have seen Tennant you will be prepared to hear that my brother Edward died early on Friday morning after above a month of severe suffering; leaving a ghastly vacancy in my prospects, not to be filled up. However, what is past, – the profit and the pleasure which I have gathered out of long and pleasant years of brotherly society – this at least is safe, and is so much to be thankful for. Why should I be the sorrier because I have so long been graced with a source of comfort and of pride, which if I had never known I should now be as cheerful as when I last wrote to you?

The tone of Tennyson's poem 'To J. S.' becomes the easier to understand when one realizes how distasteful Spedding found the traditional modes of Christian consolation. 'When I returned yesterday from one of these black businesses with which I am familiar of late,' he wrote to Thompson after attending yet another funeral, 'I found an intimation that Garden and Monteith were at the Burlington till 3, on the wing for Scotland – But I was not in a humour either for the Blasphemer or the Calvinist. I suppose the first thing the good Garden would have done would have been to administer religious consolation after his own fashion – and I have already had some religious consolation from Blakesley, – which would have been amusing enough to any one not the object of it.'[9]

After his unsuccessful attempt to win a Trinity fellowship Spedding spent about three years at his father's home in Cumberland, where on occasion he entertained friends, such as Thompson, Tennyson and FitzGerald, but more usually did very little at all, being quite uncertain what he wanted from life. 'For myself,' he confided to Thompson, 'I am unsettled in all my prospects and plans. I am in fact doing nothing – but I flatter myself I am pausing on the brink, to take a good look at the different ways of life which are open to me before I take the fatal plunge. I must have some character or other to sustain; or else I shall run in danger of being contented with my lot; which I take it is the next way to be damned. I think of getting handbills stuck up in all populous places or an advertisement in the Times to this effect

> We are requested here to state
> That there is shortly TO BE LET
> Ready for INSTANT OCCUPATION
> In a cheerful situation,
> At some distance from the SCHOOL,
> Airy, quiet, clean, and cool:
> Very healthy: aspect good:
> And eligible neighbourhood:
> Unfurnished: never used: A HEAD, En
> -quire of the owner, that's [Jam]es Spedding.'[10]

Not the least endearing of Spedding's qualities was the liveliness and interest of his letter-writing. Even when he had little more than the slightest of gossip to pass on, he was never less than entertaining, as an extract from a typical letter may show:

Douglas Heath and Pickering left a week ago. Where they are now I do not know, but probably in the rain. Douglas brought me a few Alfredian MSS. of great price, but small quantity – Alfred himself described his poems as proceeding 'very pagewise'. The Thoughts of a Suicide is as a vast trunk on the shore – it wants both the beginning and the end (I mean the copy I have got) – vast and costly both in design and material, but the expression in many places obscure to me and sometimes I think inaccurate. The poet himself seems to have been in great favour at Kitlands [the Heaths' home]. My nephew [his brother John's new son] thrives uncommon; he is never unwell, and quite contented with the show of things – passing phenomena detain his mind without disquieting it – he now knows better than to vomit; but pisses occasionally on the tablecloth, and sometimes in my Father's face. But time will correct this, and as he travels further from the East he will learn to piss in a chamberpot. Tennant, you have perhaps heard, has made up his mind to go into the Church; and who shall say that the Church is in danger? He asked my advice on the subject – I certainly did not urge him to take the step: for I thought and think it a hazardous speculation. Anyone can see the evil of a young man not adopting a profession; the evil of adopting an unfit one every body cannot see: yet I shrewdly suspect that as many mistakes are made on the one side as on the other: as many men spoiled for the service of mankind by having to do what they cannot do heartily, as by the indolence and inertia which comes from having nothing to do at all. I am myself undetermined as ever, a very bad state to be in, as nobody knows better than myself: but I am unwilling to take upon me any business which, while I should do it badly, would yet prevent me from doing anything else. I was on the point of making a resolution the other day while I was on the top of the Telegraph to trust in God and my organisation, and take the first active Duty which offered, whatever it might be. I had not been off the coach for half an hour before I was offered to be recommended as a tutor to a young nobleman who wanted to travel on the Continent for a twelvemonth, before coming to Cambridge! This should teach us not to make resolutions![11]

Spedding eventually accepted Sir Henry Taylor's offer of a job in the Colonial Office at £150 a year. According to Taylor, Spedding 'was in a difficulty at the time about the choice of a profession, and feeling that a life without business and occupation of some kind was dangerous, was glad to accept this employment as one which might answer the purpose well enough, if he proved suited to it, and if not might be relinquished without difficulty and exchanged for some other'. Spedding proved to be an excellent civil servant but complained a good deal about the amount of work he had to do. In time he regretted his decision to join the Colonial Office, but he lacked the resolution to leave. 'He laments,' Blakesley told Thompson, 'that he did not go to the bar. He is convinced that Nature meant him to be an unsuccessful barrister. He would begin to write a book in order to be able conscientiously to resign the Colonial Department, but that he cannot trust himself to doing anything else than lie in bed and smoke cigars.' In 1841 Spedding finally resigned, and although he was offered the Under-Secretaryship of State (at £2,000 a year) on Sir James Stephen's retirement in 1847, he could not be persuaded to accept, for he claimed he was unfit for the post. His friends were annoyed, but he merely remarked, in response, that 'it was fortunate *he* was by when the decision was taken'. He remained in London and became engrossed in research on Sir Francis Bacon, the task that was to occupy him for over thirty years, until his monumental edition of Bacon was completed.[12]

It must have been annoying for the young James Spedding to witness the self-assurance with which some of his Apostolic friends found themselves places in the professions he himself was unwilling to join. Chief among these was John Sterling, as assertive in his new opinions as he had been in his old and much inclined to effect conversions among his friends. 'Sterling trusts you will pay him a visit at Hirstmonseux [*sic*],' Spedding informed Thompson. 'If you wish to be persuaded to take orders I advise you to go directly: Sterling is very strong on that subject. He made an assault on me at Farish's, but without effect. He seems to think that no man can have any moral effect on society therefore under a moral obligation) to profess orthodox opinions *as they are, by the orthodox in this generation, expounded*, – as long as he can expound them to himself, *either in that or any other manner*, so as to satisfy his reason. At least this is the best way I can state what appeared to me to be his persuasion: of course I have misunderstood and misrepresented it. Whatever might be his real argument I think it could hardly do for me. I must develop a much clearersighted moral sense and a much stronger spiritual strength than I can as yet boast of, before I can safely give up the poor strength of sincerity and an honest mouth. In the mean time by way of giving myself a last chance and justifying the pretensions of my organisation I have possessed myself of the Aids to Reflection, and am in deliberate progress through them – but I sadly fear without any increased disposition to admire and accept. I shall give them however a fair trial; and if it does not succeed I can only decline the struggle, give myself up for a reprobate past regeneration, and assume that I am after all in the right.'[13]

'I hope you were as much annoyed as I was at my not being able to see you when you were in London and its neighbourhood,' Sterling wrote to Blakesley as he was about to take up his post at Herstmonceux and just after Maurice's *Eustace Conway* had been published. 'I designed going to Blackheath [where Blakesley's family had their home] – but having hired a lunatic Cook who was in charge of my house I was obliged to come down hither sooner than I should otherwise have left town and so was prevented. . .I have since heard of you but not very minutely from John Heath and also from Trench who spent last week here. The latter wrote from this to to give up his Colchester curacy on account of his health and is on the look out for another in a milder climate. . .Trench will be for the present at his Father's, where his wife I fancy will speedily produce another arrow for the Trenchian quiver. You will believe that his visit gave me great pleasure and I hope it did me some good. His views of the Pastoral office are highly interesting and valuable and I do not think any Clergyman could converse with him without deriving benefit. We had of course much talk about Coleridge, Irving and so forth – and I was rejoiced to find him as little inclined as you or I to believe in the Divine origin of gibberish. We also prated (or as Heath would say – *prote*) considerably of Eustace Conway – which I have read twice through and he partly once. Hare also has read it and we 3 tripodically determined the book to be a good one – worth reading – and almost worth buying. I hope you will go through it and let me know your judgment. I trust you will agree with me that no reflecting and serious minded man can read it without having his views enlarged and his principles deepened – besides learning much with regard to our own time which it especially behooves us to know. It gave me more pleasure than anything that has occurred to me for a long time to find how much the Heaths and Thompson liked it. I have heard from the author. . .He writes as wisely and more quietly than in the book. It seems to me that the having known him and Coleridge and some others and read their books and had the thoughts presented to us in various ways which have been floating for a few years in the circles we both of us are familiar with – adds prodigiously to the seriousness of our responsibility in times of perturbation and destruction like these. For immense as is the evil that exists I am daily more and more convinced that by God's blessing immense good is possible if even a very few energetic men would seriously take in hand to strengthen their own faith and that of those around them. This persuasion makes me even more desirous than I should otherwise be to know what you and our common friends are doing and meditating.

It will be a great kindness to me if you will write to me and tell me how fares the Church at Cambridge – and especially what the little flock of honest believers in the Reality of the Invisible are doing for themselves and for others. Everyone who believes in Christianity must at all times be in the world as a missionary amid savages – above all in these times – when, if ever, the Daemon, and one of no mean faculties too, has entered into the swine, and made him that fierce and beastly Swine-Fiend whose Gospel is preached by the present Parisian playwrights and romancers.' After a little more in this vein Sterling interrupts himself to remark, 'I am not yet ordained and you will perhaps think I have begun to preach prematurely.'[14]

Whatever others thought of it, Sterling's religious enthusiasm was certainly to the taste of J. C. Hare, who was delighted by the way Sterling threw himself into his new job. The young A. P. Stanley, fresh from Rugby and the moral influence of Thomas Arnold, visited Herstmonceux for a few months before going up to Oxford and was quite overcome by the intense piety that prevailed there. But Sterling's career as an active clergyman was shortlived, for the energy he put into his new duties helped to weaken his always precarious health. After only a few months at Herstmonceux he decided to leave, thought at first of settling in Cambridge, but realized the arrangement would be too expensive and chose to move to London. 'Sterling has established himself and his family in Bayswater, and gives tea parties to the wiser minds,' Spedding reported to Thompson in 1835. By this time Sterling had met Carlyle, whose views were to have their effect on his impressionable mind. He began, with his usual hopefulness, a full-scale study of German theology, but this was to have no more concrete result than his increasing disaffection from traditional Christianity.[15]

With their natural tendency to modernist views it was natural that the Apostles should be drawn into the religious controversies of the day. In 1835 Maurice published a pamphlet, *Subscription No Bondage*, in which he tried to take an independent, conciliatory stand on the issue of the religious tests then demanded at Oxford and Cambridge. In effect, Maurice supported the liberal view of the matter, but without immediately appearing to do so. He claimed that persons of any or no religion might subscribe to the Thirty-Nine Articles on entering the universities, for by so doing they were merely assenting to the Articles as the 'conditions of thought' of their education, that is, as the conditions of thought imposed on them by the fact that their teachers believed what is expressed in the Articles, whether they themselves did or not. Since anyone wishing such an education might subscribe to the Articles in this sense, subscription is plainly no bondage.

The reaction of Maurice's Apostolic friends to this extraordinary argument was mixed. *Subscription No Bondage* arrived at James Spedding's home while he was writing a letter to Blakesley about a recent visit from Tennyson and FitzGerald; he broke off to read the pamphlet and then resumed his letter in some agitation: 'If I write incoherently, excuse me – and attribute it to the "conditions of thought" which have been "imposed" on me. My dear Blakesley, what is to be done? This is a stranger theory than any thing in Greek. If the 39 articles would clear up this mystery too – if they would explain the coexistence in the same mind of these two Principles – the Principle of Bad Logic and of Good Logic – or reconcile them into harmony with each other and with the original laws of human thought – I would not only consent to be taught by them as conditions of thought – I would even subscribe them. What do other people say? Is there anybody that is not struck dumb? Say and what do the Oxford Dons say? Will they accept their champion? Pray God they may, that the measure of their follies may be full. Of course I speak only of that part of the pamphlet which concerns the question of Subscription or no Subscription – The rest is for Faith, but I am afraid not for me. It is as the light, I am as the darkness.'[16]

Actually, it does not appear that Newman and Pusey, although they read the pamphlet in proof, were much bothered by the questionable nature of Maurice's support for their position. But the Apostles took the matter quite seriously. Blakesley tried to defend the pamphlet to Spedding and wrote about it to Thompson, who in turn asked Spedding for a further, more considered opinion. 'Surely it is a production about which there can be only one opinion,' rejoined Spedding; 'or, to speak more correctly, about which there must be exactly two: one entertained by the author himself, the other by all his readers without exception. Mine is, that it meets nobody, that it proves nothing, and, generally, that it is beside itself.' Spedding professed himself 'lost and utterly bewildered' to know what Maurice could be thinking of. If the Thirty-Nine Articles are only 'a prospectus of the theological opinions maintained and recommended by the University', then the 'simplest and best way would be to present every student at Matriculation with a copy of the 39, headed with a notice that such were the theological opinions of his future teachers – and therefore, that, whatever he might think of the opinions, he must not after such fair warning, quarrel with tutors and lecturers for holding and teaching them'. 'If there must be a ceremony,' Spedding concluded reflectively, 'let him [the student] kiss a rod (by way of type) or anything else that might happen to be turned towards him.' But his devastating attack on Maurice's argument ends with an important qualification: 'I ought by the by to add that, in spite of my perplexity touching his intellectual organisation, my reverence for the earnestness and simplicity of Maurice's character is encreased rather than diminished by "Sub. no. Bon." '[17]

In 1836 Maurice was appointed to the chaplaincy of Guy's Hospital in London, and in the next year he began to publish his 'Letters to a Quaker', the first version of one of his most important books, *The Kingdom of Christ* (1839, 1842). In this work Maurice examined the teachings of the various groups that make up Christianity and tried to show how each contains an important element of religious truth, how the religious 'systems' derived from these teachings have falsified them by claiming to be in possession of the whole truth, and how the positive aspects of these rival views can be seen to be complementary to one another and to find their natural fulfilment, for English people, in the Church of England. But by the Church of England he meant the Church as he would have it be, not as it was; of the parties that then divided the Church he optimistically remarked, 'we may find that there is a divine harmony, of which the living principle in each of these systems forms one note, of which the systems themselves are a disturbance and a violation'. Maurice's views were directly related to his own experience: he argued that the individual's first experience of spiritual relationships, for better or worse, is derived from his experience of the family, and that 'human relationships are not artificial types of something divine, but are actually the means and the only means, through which man ascends to any knowledge of the divine'. The mission of the Church is to assist in the development of the universal society or universal family that Christ has planned for man, and to struggle against the contending forces that have hitherto prevented the family, the nation and humanity from achieving the divine goal of spiritual unity that has been set for them.[18]

According to W. H. Thompson, 'the Apostolic mind' was equally preoccupied with the 'Letters to a Quaker', as they appeared, and with a somewhat more popular serial of the time, *Pickwick Papers.* Trench saw Maurice's writings as 'more calculated to help us out of our present difficulties than any thing that has yet been written'. Thompson and Blakesley thought highly of the 'Letters', and Blakesley planned to recommend them to Spring Rice as an antidote to his growing 'High Churchism'. But not all the Apostles were quite so impressed. 'At length I have read Maurice's "Kingdom of Christ" in its collected form,' Donne wrote to Blakesley in 1839, '– much of so much as I understand of it is admirable[,] some things I scratch my head at, and at some shake it altogether. His idea of a church History at the end of the second volume is a first rate piece of critical philosophy – Howbeit with certain reminiscences of Church history present with me I cannot altogether trace the catholic unity of Christendom so smoothly as he would point it out – We must imitate Sir Roger de Coverley's method of showing off his family pictures, and when we come in front of a cracked reputation, give a short cough, and pass on to another subject – It is at least a comfortable hypothesis that from the very first a continued series of men have greased one another's heads and fingers successively and that the last comers have the "genuine article" as Rowland and Son express themselves no less surely than the earliest.'[19]

The Apostles were exceptional, even among educated people, in their awareness of the currents of thought that were then undercutting traditional orthodoxy. The rationalistic demythologizing of D. F. Strauss's *Leben Jesu* attracted their horrified fascination long before Strauss's name became a by-word for infidelity with the British public. 'Edmund sends his kind remembrances,' Henry Lushington wrote to Richard Milnes in 1837. 'Notwithstanding your good wishes for his orthodoxy, he is deep in Strauss, having got to the end of one volume not less thick than impious, and being preserved from the abyss of scepticism only by the accident of having left the second at Cambridge. His fate cannot therefore be deferred beyond February: my ignorance of German, which however I intend to remove, may preserve me a little longer.'[20]

'[D]iscussions of Strauss. . .rage around me,' Robert Monteith wrote to Milnes from his home at Carstairs, near Glasgow, where he was being visited by Edmund Lushington and other Cambridge friends. 'Now I envy a man that is *convinced* – about anything – on any side. Otherwise one is a poor lobster with[out] a shell, that had better hide out of [the] way of the world's jar. What difference whether your shell shall be black or blue, so you have one to resist and bite with?' Edmund Lushington had recently left Cambridge 'with disgust only mitigated by his natural indisgustibility' (according to George Venables), and had become Professor of Greek at Glasgow University, so that Monteith saw him often. 'Lushington gave me some pleasant days here,' Monteith told Milnes after one of these visits, '– great talk about all the secret trouble of theology – they are mere mental perplexities with him – his lymphatic, xanthous temperament never permits these things to be really grievous to him. It is curious enquiry, as about Greek roots, and his intellectual ambition to be a man of insights and a truth-proclaimer may be mortified – but he pineth not at heart, and will die of gout like his fathers for 4 generations hale and happy and fresh of spirit, all riddles unread, and God's statutes unexpounded.' As for Monteith himself, his desire for religious certitude was to lead him, in time, to convert to Roman Catholicism.[21]

Thanks to Blakesley, the Apostles also became involved in academic politics at Cambridge. In 1840 he persuaded his former student, Lord Lyttelton, to become a candidate for the office of High Steward of the University. Lyttelton had graduated as Senior Classic only two years before and was just twenty-three years old, but he was popular at Cambridge and especially at Trinity, and Blakesley hoped that with this somewhat unlikely candidate he might break the stranglehold the Tories held on the most exalted positions in the University. The hope was frustrated, for Lyttelton was roundly defeated by Lord Lyndhurst, the Tory candidate. But the campaign that raged in both Cambridge and London caused much excitement, and some amusement at the predicament of such supporters of Lyttelton as Thomas Thorp, Tutor of Trinity College and Archdeacon of Bristol, who committed himself to Lyttelton's side before Lyndhurst had declared himself a candidate. 'I discreetly declined all service in the Committee room at London,' Spedding told Thompson, '– by which I suppose I escaped many vomitings but by [W.D.] Christie's account lost much fun. Kemble was the busiest man in the London Committee, and his grandiosity appears to have been worthy of his best days. Blakesley was the main spring of the activities at Cambridge; – where I found a new word in household use – which has been created or revealed since my time solely, I believe, with reference to him – "I polyprag; thou polypraggest; he polyprags: etc." Anecdotes, entertaining and illustrative, are very plentiful; and shew that the business has been badly managed at both ends. Thorpe [*sic*] had been miserable ever since he found himself embarked in the Lyttelton cause, and the Bishop of Gloucester against him. Every day, as often as he heard of a vote refused which had been counted on, he would come to the Committee room and entreat them to give up the contest. One day he was observed to be in better spirits, and more active in his duties – the cause of which appeared soon after when he delivered over to Blakesley among other documents connected with the election, as if to be filed up with them, a note of which I will treat you with a copy –

Saturd[a]y Nov. 3

Dear and Venerable Sir

I must begin by making a sad confession, that I rashly promised to vote for Lord Lyndhurst, before I knew of any intention to propose your young friend of excellent character, Lord Lyttelton, and without having sufficiently considered the objections to Lord Lyndhurst's character. It is now too late to change: but I cannot refrain from furnishing you with information which my support of Lord Lyndhurst has enabled me to collect – viz: that the number of promises is not nearly so great as they represent; and that I believe, and they believe, Lord Lyttelton will win – This will console me among other things for voting on this occasion against one whom I love and respect so much as you, Sir, my former Tutor.

You will at once understand why I do not sign my name, and call myself

A Friend in the Enemy's Camp.

P.S. It is with great grief that I am obliged to add that a friend of mine has today seen Lord Lyndhurst enter (proh pudor!) a house of ill fame. This will probably make me change my vote. You shall hear again from your sincere friend.

'Can these things be justified?' Spedding asks. Thompson also heard Blakesley's views on the behaviour of 'some of the Peel-fearing Lyndhurst-hating supporters of Lyttleton in the late affair'. 'The only comfort,' wrote Blakesley, 'is that the offenders have drawn down on their heads universal contempt without in the slightest degree saving themselves from the anger they dreaded in high places. It is reported that the Bishop of Gloucester is preparing a bullspizzle to be applied to Thorp's naked posteriors at the next visitation, and certainly, if this be the case, the Dean of Bristol will not interpose to save the victim.'[22]

'What is the state of Apostledom in Cambridge – Has anything occurred to divert the great Apostolic mind from solving the universal riddle[?]' Thompson asked Blakesley in a letter of the mid-thirties. During this period the Society at Cambridge had lost much of its earlier vitality. Beginning with such Apostles as Charles Merivale and

Arthur Helps, there had been a tendency to elect merely clubbable types, and the Society had degenerated accordingly. Nearly all the members of Hallam's circle had resigned from active membership by 1835, and only two of their immediate successors – W. F. Pollock and W. D. Christie – became well known to the older Apostolic set.

By the early forties, however, the Society was led by Tom Taylor, a man of many parts, although he is chiefly remembered today as a popular dramatist and writer for *Punch*, and in these years the Society gained several noteworthy members – Henry and Edmund Lushington's younger brother Franklin, Arthur Hallam's younger brother Henry, Henry Maine and William Johnson (later Cory). By this time the older members seem to have re-established their contacts with the Society at Cambridge: they kept a friendly eye on it and were sometimes influential in its affairs. When Donne's young cousin Henry Johnson went up to Cambridge, for example, Donne commended him to Blakesley's attention and two years later wrote again to ask Blakesley to advise Johnson on how to become an Apostle. The advice seems to have been effective, for Henry Johnson was elected in 1842 and treated Donne to some Apostolic gossip of that time. 'Tom Taylor,' he wrote, '. . .is ensnared again by theatrical interests – the sin that most easily besets him. He has been turning people's heads and hearts at Canterbury in the light comedy department, and after narrowly escaping the police had to beg his way back to his fellowship and pupils as he best might. [H]owever he will be as transcendental as ever in aesthetic debates when we meet next term. . .Merivale has been translating some of the [L]otuseaters into Latin verses of the 4th century, and assuring Venables that he has just accidentally discovered them amid a heap of old MSS. and detected Tennyson in barefaced plagiarism: but as he went so far as to serve the May Queen the same he was of course detected in his turn.' 'I was much pleased,' Venables reported to Milnes at about this time, 'by hearing that young Hallam represented in the Apostles the character of a "supralapsarian Erastian." [W]hat it means Heaven knows, but sic fortis Etruria crevit – by talking so we became wise men.' And Henry Lushington told Milnes that 'Venables reports rather well of the rising Cambridge generation. I daresay they think themselves as clever as we were. Who can place limits to youthful vanity?'[23]

During this period the annual dinner of the Society took on increasing importance as a link between older and younger members. These dinners had nothing of the high-mindedness that often characterized Apostolic debates and were mainly devoted to drinking and speeches, especially the speeches of the Chairman (always one of the older members) and Vice-Chairman (the most recently elected member of the Society). 'We were 24,' Spedding reported to Milnes after the dinner of 1837, '– Charles Buller in the chair, who drew favourable comparisons between us and other public bodies – but committed an irregularity in recognizing (for the first time I believe in Apostolic solemnities) the existence of the Royal Family.' Some idea of the fare on these occasions appears from a letter to Milnes from Blakesley, who writes, 'I deprecate such an expense as you speak of. I think so numerous a party as we shall be might have a first rate dinner at Blackwall for something under £1.10.0 [apiece], and I think our first dinner there did not cost us so much. Let us only have Whitebait, Moselle, Sherry, Champagne and Claret, all excellent of their kind, and I think most other delicacies come under the category of indifference.' The obligation upon the Chairman to be amusing and witty could seem an onerous one, even for someone so well qualified for the task as W. B. Donne, who told Trench in 1851, 'I must be in London in June as I am to be, I fancy, Chairman at the Pan Apostolicon. This is Spedding and Thompson's doing for which may Lucifer requite them. I cannot say unluckily that "I am unaccustomed," etc., since it has been my evil lot to be Chairman sundry times: but I had rather address a Norwich mob than the "Apostles," not that I mean to compare them, but the latter are so formidable.'[24]

The Apostles never complain of being under an obligation to be entertaining in the letters they wrote each other, yet their letters are consistently entertaining, and it could be argued that this was an important factor in the group's continued existence. As the members of the group grew older the Society naturally came to have a different meaning for them. Major developments in their lives were less and less likely to be directly related to discussions with their fellow-Apostles, and the idea of a concerted attack upon public opinion had long since been forsaken. The purely social aspect of the group came to be increasingly important, and this is reflected in the obvious enjoyment they took in their correspondence. In content, their letters were often little more than amiable gossip, but in style they maintained the wit, good humour and sense of intellectual companionship that had always characterized Apostolic discussions.

'Trench, you probably know, has added a man-child to the already overpeopled world,' Donne wrote Blakesley in 1837. 'It is fortunate that some of the apostles are fellows of colleges. They do not openly contradict Malthus – and set at least a good outward example to the rising generation. I think, if I may judge from the spirit of his last letter, that our friend makes rather wry faces at this squaring of his product – there is a sort of grumbling reliance on providence that argues something besides content – I shall send him half-congratulations only when I write; reserving the other half for the next occasion.'[25]

'Early next month a younger brother of the Apostolic Adelphi – the Bullers – is coming to reside in Mattishall, having taken Churches in the neighbourhood,' Donne wrote in the following year, '– A Buller in orders is I believe a sort of theological nondescript, which it will enlarge your knowledge of human nature to contemplate. Whether in the approaching subversion of all things it is intended to make him a radical archbishop, or whether his family think it advisable to have a friend, or a spy in the enemies quarters, or that he is inferior to his frères ainés in talents, (argal more fitted to the church,) are questions which time may one day resolve. I had been hoping his presence might attract at least Arthur Buller to the heart of the Iceni, but in the meantime he and his brother are gone to Canada to heal the Rebellion – a remedy I suppose of the same kind and efficacy as the rust of Achilles Sword.'[26]

'About ten days back,' Thompson told Blakesley in October 1838, 'I was surprised by an apparition of Garden in the character of Benedick – white gloves and all. He had been married the same day and the next morning I dined with the happy couple at the Bull – where regardless of the omen they had – not slept – to judge from the lassitude of one party, and the illdisguised satisfaction of the other. "The saints shall rejoice in their beds." They were on their way to Scotland. You are aware that Garden is to be Hare's curate. Mrs G. has been handsome, perhaps is – and is clearly clever – but I thought a little slang. This she may have contracted from her husband.'[27]

In 1839 Henry Lushington was prevented by his tendency to seasickness from accompanying his brother and other friends on a sailing cruise on Monteith's yacht, the *Orion*, 'wherein [Lushington told Milnes] they have been pitching about and among the Hebrides in storm and sunshine, generally the former, for some weeks of glorious peajacket hilarity. The original curse is as strongly manifested, I think, in the case of seasickness as in any other fleshly evil – so exceedingly annoying, and so utterly unnecessary a visitation, a thing that might so well have been spared from the world without a single regret: warning from no sin, bringing out no goodness or kindliness whatever; but rather exasperating selfishness into ferocity.'[28]

In 1842 Henry Lushington visited Italy and met several members of the group. R. J. Tennant had married and settled at Florence as the English Chaplain. 'Do you know Mrs Tennant?' Lushington asked Milnes. 'I liked her, and think Tennant on the whole a happy man, now that his health is restored – certainly much happier disguised as an orthodox clergyman than he used to be in his true shape of a God-doubting metaphysician.' In the same letter he reports that he has seen Frederick Tennyson and Savile Morton, both of whom were flourishing, and that he was greatly disappointed by the failure of Mount Vesuvius to erupt when he was there to see it – 'it will only smoke as hard as Alfred Tennyson,' he complained: 'wasting itself, as he does himself in cigars'.[29]

Ironically, Tennant was to die of consumption a few months later, and in the same year Tennyson broke the 'ten years' silence' with a two-volume set of poems, including his much-revised versions of many poems that he had published in 1830 and 1832. '[T]he worst of the man is,' Kemble wrote to Donne, 'that he rubs and scrubs and polishes till he gets half the bloom off. I hate to miss a favourite line; and yet one never sees in print a poem which one has known for years without missing a dozen, when Alfred is allowed to have his own way. I know that the villain has sublimed away some of the Gardener's Daughter, for which may he be circumcised!' A further volume of Trench's poetry appeared at about the same time, and Kemble goes on to praise it, though with a serious reservation: 'But why the d(Lord forgive me! it's Sunday, on which day none may curse and swear but the Profession) will he always insist on giving us such a screed o' doctrine? He certainly will never dwindle down into a Pollok or Montgomery, but he will end in being as dull as the tailpiece of the Homily on Original Sin.'[30]

Tennyson was passing through a difficult period in these years, and a letter from Henry Lushington to Milnes records something of his way of life, at a time when Tennyson had been submitting his nervous ailments to hydropathic therapy at a hospital near Cheltenham. 'Alfred is here,' Lushington wrote from London: 'having come to be here in the usual way. He came up to town from Cheltenham for a day or two: he staid in my rooms – then vacant – for a week or more: he came down here one afternoon with and by permission of Morton: bringing with him his "things" for a day or so: and he is now entering the fifth week of his sojourn, with (I hope) every prospect of indefinite prolongation thereof. He certainly seems to have derived some benefit from the water treatment, or its concomitants: yet he has been very unwell during the last two days. Indeed if one of the *earlier* set of Apostles were to heal him for the time ever so completely, he could not continue well as long as he paid so little attention to their words of healing: "Arise *and walk.*" How can a man of such great natural strength of body live so indolently, and be well?'[31]

Finally, a single, typical letter from Henry Lushington, one that admirably captures the light, witty, graceful style that made Apostolic correspondence so charming, even when its content was perfectly insubstantial:

My dear Milnes

If you have of late paid much attention to the course of public events, you will have observed that the Government, profuse of plausible inutilities, has invented a thing called Winter Assizes – a thing sounding as if it would be of some good to somebody, but as far as I have hitherto learnt, producing no effect except that of driving the whole *profession* wild; which indeed may to some persons appear in the light of a benefit. Upon me it has the comparatively mild effect, of making it desirable that I should be at Maidstone early next week. – So that I should have little more than time to go – if I did go – to your parish church. I fear therefore that I must decline your invitation for the present.

As to Venables – I received your letter while he was in the agonies of tying a shawl round his mouth, preparatory to being turned off in the coach for Cambridge. I handed it over to him. He read it with the face of a man who thinks he is too late already, and if his gnashing of teeth expressed any answer of any kind, I did not ascertain what this answer was. Conjecturally I should say his thought was what an infernal bore it was – and how exactly in accordance with the general and indeed universal course of things – to receive an agreeable offer which it was hardly in his power to accept. I speak however, as I have said, conjecturally. He said no articulate word, good or bad, and rushed down 4 flights of stairs with the speed and countenance of a demon. And since that time I have not seen him, or heard from him. He was to have reappeared today but has not.

Ever, my dear Milnes, yours truly

HL.[32]

CHAPTER 11

THE STERLING CLUB

One of the most valuable accounts of student life in Victorian Britain was written by an American, Charles Astor Bristed, whose *Five Years in an English University* (1852) gives a breezy, detailed and amusingly frank account of his experiences at Cambridge in the early eighteen-forties. One way or another, Bristed came to know most of the prominent students of his time, usually by inviting himself to their rooms to 'chat quietly over endless cups of tea – or even potations more generous'. A fellow-student has revealed that this habit caused Bristed to be 'thought an awful bore at this time', but according to Bristed himself he was welcome wherever he went and especially among the Apostles, to whom he attributes 'a very considerable influence on the literary train of thought in the University of Cambridge, and on the opinions of the English literary public'. While Bristed thought that everything that happened to him was important, his belief in the Apostles' national significance is noteworthy, and his explanation of their influence (for the benefit of his American readers) is an interesting if somewhat erroneous one.

'There is an association founded by the contemporaries of the late John Sterling, and called from him the *Sterling Club*,' Bristed says. 'It comprises among its members men distinguished in various and somewhat different walks of life: theologians, like Maurice of King's College, London, and Stanley, Arnold's biographer; poets like Tennyson and Milnes; novelists like Thackeray; some universal geniuses. They are mostly Cambridge men, Stanley and some few Oxonians, Thomas Carlyle, I believe, the only non-university man among them. By way of school or nursery to this club, there was a club at Cambridge of Undergraduates, popularly called *the Apostles*. . .Some of them took high Honours, more generally in Classics than in Mathematics; some of them did not compete for Honours at all; but they all had a certain fondness for literary and metaphysical pursuits in common, and none of them were *solely* reading men. They were always on the look-out for eligible members to supply the place of those who had left the University and stepped into the regular club, and were very ingenious in making the acquaintance of men that were in any respect lions, and drawing them out to ascertain if they were apostolic material. Sometimes they were very successful in catching celebrities just as they began to develop themselves. At one time, for four years in succession, the University Scholar was an apostle; but shrewd people remarked that in three cases the lucky man had been elected into the club *after* it was pretty certain that he would be University Scholar. These men did not make any parade of mystery, or aim at notoriety by any device to attract attention; they did not have special chambers for meeting, with skeletons in the corner, and assemble in them with the secrecy of conspirators; nor did they wear breastpins with initials of bad Greek sentences or other symbolic nonsense on them, as our young Collegians do.'

Bristed goes on to say that, while their 'immediate and tangible influence in the University amounted to just nothing', their 'association together had a great mutual effect on the formation of their minds and characters, and thus indirectly on the whole body of men'. Moreover, 'the parent club taken in connexion with its embryo' made up what Bristed calls 'a most innocent and effective *camaraderie*'. He explains that the members of the two societies control among them 'many avenues of approach to the public' and thus are enabled 'to benefit one another and help on one another's reputation very much'.

'Thus when a member of the club publishes,' he says, 'one of the fraternity has a footing in the Edinburgh, another in the Quarterly, a third in Fraser, a fourth in Blackwood, and so on – among them all there is a pretty good chance that his beauties will not be hid, or the reading community allowed to overlook his merits.' While Bristed allows that this is fairly done, for (in his own phrase) there is 'no putting on the butter of adulation with the knife of profusion', he is not entirely uncritical. In his view, 'It is not possible for any clique, however excellent and liberal its individual component members, to be without some *shop* and cant of its own. The cant of these men was inveighing against cant. . .[T]hey all affected much *earnestness* and a hearty dislike of sham and formula, which rendered them far from popular with the *High and Dry* in literature, politics, or religion. The younger members at the University were eyed with terror by grave, plodding Johnians, as something foreign, German, radical, altogether monstrous

– they hardly pretended to know what. About the Society proper – the Sterling Club – some immense mares' nests were discovered at different times, and I am sorry to say that some Evangelical newspapers let loose a great deal of trash on the subject once or twice – indeed they talked as much nonsense as the Puseyites.'[1]

While Bristed was mistaken in his belief that there was a direct relationship between the Society and the Sterling Club, his recognition of their combined influence was astute, and he was not alone in thinking the Sterling Club to be some sort of conspiracy by a clique of intellectuals. Nor is this view of the Sterling Club entirely wrong. From our vantage-point in time we can see that the club was an event of some significance in the development of the Victorian intelligentsia and in that persistent Victorian battle, the conflict of modernists and traditionalists. When the Sterling Club began, however, it was with no such intentions in mind, though there is reason to believe that Sterling himself might have been secretly pleased by the outcome, had he survived to witness it.

The foundation of the Sterling Club in 1838 owed much to the curious position that Sterling found himself in after leaving his curacy at Herstmonceux. The ill-health that bedevilled him prevented his making any concerted effort towards a new career and forced him to spend most of his winters abroad. Much of his time was spent in the study of theology, but his views were as unsettled as his life. Though he still regarded himself as a clergyman, he never took priest's orders, and he seems to have been increasingly attracted to journalism as an alternative to the Church. By the spring of 1838 he found himself with two sets of friends, corresponding to the two sides of his mind. On the one hand were such friends as Hare, Trench and Maurice, who had come to terms with the Established Church, even if their position within it left them open to attack. On the other hand were such friends as Thomas Carlyle and John Stuart Mill, whose sceptical attitude to Christian orthodoxy had become increasingly congenial to him. His indecision was reflected in his letters to Mill: early in 1838 he felt that he must refuse Mill's invitation to contribute to the *Westminster Review*, since the connection would 'offend and grieve mightily' certain of his friends, yet within a few months he was planning an article that was designed to have precisely the effect he had earlier feared.[2]

Since Sterling was well aware of the antagonism between his two sets of friends, it seems likely that the club he proposed and helped to establish had as one aim the bringing together of these opposed groups in a social context which might, like the Society itself, encourage them to understand one another better. But this was hardly his dominant motive, nor did he set out to achieve anything so ambitious as a society for the reconciliation of orthodoxy and scepticism. His professed and probably his principal intention was merely to bring together his many different friends for the sake of the social atmosphere that such a varied and talented group would provide.

In June 1838 he told Hare of his plans. 'I am,' he wrote, 'trying to set up a club after the fashion of Johnson's to dine together in London once a month. – My object is to be sure of finding several of my friends, when I may be occasionally in town, without having to hunt for them separately. I should wish to vote you in, and others living at a distance, so as to make the most of your occasional visits to London.'[3]

Carlyle was also approached at this time and, though he initially pleaded his dyspeptic aversion to dining out, was prevailed upon to join by mid-July, when Sterling had arranged a preliminary dinner 'to settle on a name and some other matters'. J. S. Mill was invited to this dinner and told that the other members to date were Hare, Carlyle, J. F. Elliott, William Bingham Baring and seven Apostles – Blakesley, Spedding, Milnes, Douglas Heath, Monteith, Venables (introduced to Mill by Sterling, 'as a poet and thinker as well as a scholar') and Thompson ('the most accomplished metaphysician among Englishmen that *I* know'). At this dinner, held at the Piazza Coffeehouse in Covent Garden, no suitable name could be found, but James Spedding was selected to act as Secretary and to arrange the dinners, though he protested that he was entirely disqualified for the task and threatened to order nothing but mutton.[4]

A search for suitable members was soon rewarded, though hopes of recruiting Samuel Rogers and Henry Crabb Robinson were frustrated and though Maurice and a few others put up unexpected resistance for some time. W. B. Donne was among those who thoroughly approved of the idea. 'Greatly to my surprise, and pleasure, and increase of self-admiration,' he told Blakesley, 'I received an invitation to become a member of Sterling's Deipnosophists from Spedding – and as I answered immediately "Yea", I conclude I was among the great men chosen by acclamation.'[5]

The invitation Spedding sent Donne provides a useful description of the Sterling Club on the eve of its foundation and helps to explain its popularity:

Sterling has been endeavouring to get up a Club which is to exist for the purpose of dining together once a month. The dinner is to be cheap; the attendance not compulsory; the day and the place fixed; and the members chosen unanimously, from the witty, the worthy, the wise, and the inspired – and it is hoped that the Society will sooner or later combine within itself as much of the wit, worth, wisdom and inspiration of the age, as can live together in an apostolic harmony. Being able to agree upon no name at all, we christened ourselves for the present Anonymous. Being unable to fix upon a place, it was left to me to make enquiries, and I have fixed for the present upon Wills' Coffee House, which stands conveniently near to my rooms.

The Society consists at present of the following members –

Bingham Baring (Hon. W.)
Blakesley
Boxall W. (Painter)
Carlyle T. (French Revolution)
Colville – (Trinity man of my standing)
Mr Dunne (Old Platonic clergyman – friend of Sterling – *refused Bishoprick*)
Eastlake (C. L. – Painter)
Elliot – (capital fellow, Emigration Agent General – married but tells bawdy stories)
Copley Fielding – (Painter)
Hare – Rev. J. C.
Douglas Heath (Apostle)
H. Lushington (Apostle)
Lord Lyttelton (Clever young man – with a mind of his own – Senior Medalist)
Macarthy (Roman Catholic)
Malden (History of Rome in L[ibrary of] U[seful] K[nowledge])
Mill (John)
Milnes R. M. (Apostle)
Monteith (R. – Apostle – candidate for Glasgow – splendid fellow)
Spedding (Secretary and orderer of dinner)
Sterling
A. Tennyson
Thompson (Revd. W. H. – Apostle)
Venables (G. S. Apostle)
Wood (Samuel – Newmanite)
Worsley (Vice-Chancellor of Cambridge)

In addition to these it was proposed last meeting to invite the following gents to become members –

W. B. Donne
George Cornewall Lewis
Stafford OBrien
Sir F. Palgrave
Rio
Thirlwall
Allan Cunningham
Alexander Ellice
R. Trench
Sir Edmund Head
Richard Cavendish

The meetings are to happen on the last Tuesday in each month. The dinner to cost only 7 shillings a head. No forfeits for non attendance; but notice of intention to attend to be given the day before. Members may be proposed and elected next Tuesday without notice and by acclamation. But no elections to take place afterwards except by ballot (a single black-ball to exclude) – except notice have been given the previous meeting – and except in January and the 5 following months. – How say you – will you be of us?[6]

By the time of the first regular meeting, held on 8 August 1838, the Sterling Club comprised a remarkable collection of eminent and gifted men. There were over forty members at that time, and they represented an extraordinarily wide variety of interests, attitudes and backgrounds. For the next ten years the club flourished, with as many as eighty members, including such unlikely dinner companions as W. H. Brook-field, William Whewell, W. M. Thackeray, Bishop Samuel Wilberforce (and his two brothers), Henry Manning and A. P. Stanley. Apparently only a dozen or so of this large membership might be expected to attend any single dinner, but the group was sufficiently large and varied to provide interesting company whatever the attendance, even in the exceptional case that occurred in early 1843, when Blakesley and the portrait-painter William Boxall seem to have been the only members present for the monthly dinner. 'Two is not enough,' Lord Lyttelton wrote, commiserating with Blakesley on the event, 'but B[oxall] must be as good for such a purpose as any the Club could furnish.'[7]

Soon after its foundation the club acquired the name that was to cause such offence when it came to public notice ten years later. The change seems to have occurred at the club's second meeting, a dinner of some fifteen members, held in late August 1838. 'We had agreed to revise the name and statutes on that occasion,' Sterling reported to

Hare; 'and one of the changes was to call the club *the Sterling*: but I did not think it necessary to make a speech on the occasion, the word being happily equivocal.' '[A] person who was present,' Hare wrote later, 'has told me that, after some discussion on the point. . .it was resolved that the members present should write down their suggestions, and throw them into a hat. When the one which was adopted was drawn out, it was received. . .with general satisfaction. Its double meaning seemed to render it happily appropriate. For people on such occasions are fond of taking a name which implies a certain playful assumption of superiority; as Johnson's club did in calling itself *the Club*; the institution of which was soon followed by another under the mock-heroic name of *the King of Clubs*.'[8]

The new club seems to have been successful from the first and to have won approval even from those most likely to look askance at Sterling's eclecticism in forming friendships. After his first visit Trench told Donne that he 'liked the taste of its quality very much', and this was evidently an admission, for he added, 'you know there are animals in it clean and unclean – Editors of Westminster Reviews, and such like'. If Sterling hoped to moderate his orthodox friends' hostility to non-believers, he seems to have been largely successful, for (as Hare later assured his fellow-clergymen) orthodox members found the club congenial, interesting and in no way threatening.[9]

'[T]here was never the slightest intention of giving the club any peculiar colour,' Hare claimed in his later defence of the club. 'It was merely meant to be a meeting of personal friends, of all shades of opinion, and to include any artists or literary men, who might wish to join it. This character it has preserved throughout. The state of Sterling's health, which confined him to warm climates, seldom allowed him to attend the meetings. Nor have I, as my avocations keep me mostly in the country, dined there a dozen times in as many years. But when I have been able to do so, I have generally found the conversation very pleasant and instructive; as it is especially useful for those who are called in any way to teach and preach to their brethren, to see the workings of various modes of thought, and to hear the opinions which are prevailing and exercising an influence in the world. Nor have I ever heard a word on any moral or religious subject, at which it was possible to take offence. The restraint which good breeding imposes on all gentlemen in the presence of a clergyman, would have represt this, if there had not been still higher motives. If there are some persons among the members, whose views on the highest subjects are supposed not to be all that we could desire, they are at least men who have employed their high intellectual gifts diligently and energetically for the moral and social good of mankind; and so far as my acquaintance with them enables me to form a judgement, I have found a confirmation of the conclusion which has been imprest upon me by my observation of my friends, that high intellectual gifts are mostly accompanied with noble or beautiful features of character.'[10]

While the Sterling Club was in no sense a parent organization to the Society (as Bristed had concluded), this mistaken opinion was a natural one, for Apostles were prominent among the club's supporters from the first, and a good number of younger Apostles joined in the succeeding ten years. One might say that the club began as a kind of informal extension of the Society, bringing together people who might otherwise never have associated with one another and who almost certainly would have attracted the attention of the Apostles, had they been Cambridge men. Yet the Apostles never made up more than a quarter of the club's membership, and in its ten-year history the membership became so large and varied that any connection with the Society could hardly have been of the first importance.[11]

Nonetheless the Sterling Club never entirely lost some of the ideals of the Apostles who were its principal founders. Something not unlike the Apostolic spirit was attributed to it by several observers, including an apologist for Bishop Samuel Wilberforce, who noted that its only unifying principle, besides 'mental culture', was 'a certain supposed genuineness of character and freedom from conventionality'. Richard Monckton Milnes defined its purpose as 'the bringing together of earnest men, who might not otherwise come into contact, and in the variety of whose opinions each might learn to appreciate and to honour the belief of others, *without* weakening his own'. Some element of serious purpose may thus be ascribed to the Sterling Club, and indeed without some such purpose it is doubtful that it would have succeeded as it did. But earnestness was hardly the characteristic mode of expression among its members, as the following announcement of a monthly dinner may suggest:

Mr Green's fresh paint makes him unapproachable, whereby all the statutes* of the Club are nullified. The Secretary is gone over to Rome (though only for the winter), and the Club is thus left without law or government. Under these circumstances a Rump-steak Commission has been appointed to look to the Republick; it consists of all who choose to dine at Mr —'s, Covent Garden, at seven o'clock next Tuesday. Steaks,

Stout, and Ale *ad lib.* for 5*s.* 6*d.* a head: those who drink wine do so on their own responsibility.

*These are but two: –

I. The Club shall dine at Mr Green's.

II. On giving Mr Green notice.[12]

It seems likely that this highly informal and slightly unusual dinner club might have remained merely a pleasant feature of intellectual life in London and have attracted little or no attention from the general public. But Sterling's rejection of orthodox Christianity was, in time, to be made the subject of furious controversy, and no organization founded by him and bearing his name could expect to escape without censure amid the bitter theological disputes of the Victorian age.

During 1839 Sterling's growing sympathy with heterodoxy seems to have been the subject of rumours among his acquaintances of the Sterling Club, and these rumours were largely confirmed by the article on Carlyle that he published in the *Westminster Review* towards the end of the year. Although his relationship with Maurice and Trench became strained, he was certainly not rejected socially at this time. Trench's account of a dinner at the Sterling Club suggests that, if Sterling was argumentative, he was far from offensive. 'I arrived here in good time for "the Sterling" on Tuesday evening,' Trench told his wife in a letter of 1840. 'I was obliged to take my departure immediately after, and was laid up for the evening with a sick headache, and so (having looked forward to the meeting with pleasure) learned in a small way the vanity of human expectations. It went off by all accounts very pleasantly, ending in a grand single combat between Sterling and Robert Wilberforce on the meaning of Christianity, which I understand was not without its profit; the latter having most truth, but Sterling being certainly the heaviest hitter, and the greatest master of the dialectic fence.'[13]

But Sterling confessed to more sympathetic ears the bitterness that he came to feel for the Church of England and its defenders. In 1843, having entered into a correspondence with Emerson, Sterling wrote, 'But you perhaps – though having your own difficulties, – hardly know the utter loneliness of a Rational Soul in this England. Except Carlyle, I do not know one man who sees and lives in the idea of a God not exclusively Christian: two or three lads perhaps; but every grown man of nobler spirit is either theoretical and lukewarm, or swathed up in obsolete sectarianism.' Sterling and Maurice had fallen into fierce argument with one another – a breach of the Apostolic spirit for which Maurice never forgave himself – and their long friendship had been broken.[14]

The following year Sterling died, at the age of thirty-eight, and while his friendships with Maurice and other orthodox men were restored during his long final illness, these friends were disturbed to learn that he had once again illustrated his divided loyalties by appointing the free-thinker Francis Newman as guardian of his son and Maurice as guardian of his daughters. Moreover, he 'committed the care of his literary Character and printed Writings' to an equally ill-matched pair, Hare and Carlyle. 'After some consultation on it,' Carlyle later wrote, 'and survey of the difficulties and delicate considerations involved in it, Archdeacon Hare and I agreed that the whole task, of selecting what Writings were to be reprinted, and of drawing-up a Biography to introduce them, should be left to him alone.' As Hare admitted to his old friend William Whewell, the biography gave him more anxiety than any other work he had ever written. He would never have undertaken the task if it were not for the alternative, that it would be written by someone who (in Hare's opinion) would stress exactly the wrong things. However, he reflected, 'the lesson of his whole life ought to be most profitable, if I can but bring it out rightly'. But how was this delicate task to be accomplished? As he told Caroline Fox, he was 'almost forced to publish more than he would wish in order to leave Mill and Carlyle no pretext for an opposition portrait'.[15]

Perhaps brevity and lightness of touch might have allowed a biographer of Sterling to spare the feelings of orthodox Victorians and to avoid the anger of Sterling's non-orthodox friends. But these literary virtues were never characteristic of Hare, whose ponderously annotated sermons and apologetics for Christianity include 'the longest treatise calling itself a note in the English language'. Hare's memoir mulls over the development of Sterling's religious views at great length and with obvious pain, sparing himself and the orthodox reader nothing and making very heavy weather of what a more tactful writer might have hinted at or passed over. The result, as published four years after Sterling's death, did not give general satisfaction. As Carlyle wrote, Hare 'had been led, in editing a Work not free from ecclesiastical heresies, and especially in writing a Life very full of such, to dwell with preponderating emphasis on that part of his subject. . .as if religious heterodoxy had been the grand fact of Sterling's life, which even to the

Archdeacon's mind it could by no means seem to be'. The result was that Hare's work had precisely the results he most feared. J. S. Mill and Sterling's brother Anthony both contemplated writing a rival biography, and this task was eventually assumed by Carlyle, whose *Life of John Sterling* (1851) remains one of the finest biographies of the century and perhaps the most readily appreciated of Carlyle's works for the twentieth-century reader. And the immediate effects of Hare's anxious efforts were even less to his liking, for his book touched off a first-class row and religious witch-hunt that may seem amusing now but that had serious implications for its victims.[16]

The year 1848 was not a good time to publish an account of a heretic's life, if one wished to avoid public controversy. Traditionalists within the Church were increasingly uneasy about the popularity of liberal and sceptical religious ideas and increasingly ready to see a single subversive plot behind the tendencies that were soon to produce such works as J. A. Froude's *Nemesis of Faith* and Francis Newman's *Phases of Faith.* A great public outcry had arisen over the appointment of R. D. Hampden to the bishopric of Hereford, for Hampden had earlier been accused of heresy, which he was supposed to have contracted from his former associate, the notorious Joseph Blanco White. Maurice had been one of those who had publicly defended Hampden, and in the same year he had published a pamphlet taking the liberal side in the contentious issue of admitting Jews to Parliament. Moreover, Maurice and his friends had drawn adverse attention to themselves through the publication of *Politics for the People* (May–July 1848), a short-lived periodical having as its aim the conciliation of Chartism and other forms of working-class radicalism. Maurice, Trench, James Spedding, Arthur Helps and A. P. Stanley all contributed to this journal, but the articles that most shocked the traditionalists were the work of two younger men, J. M. Ludlow and Charles Kingsley. Perhaps the most offensive of all was Kingsley's admission to his working-class audience: 'We [clergymen] have used the Bible as if it was a mere special constable's handbook – an opium-dose for keeping beasts of burden patient while they were being overloaded – a mere book to keep the poor in order.' The Principal of King's College, London, where Maurice and Trench taught theology, had become concerned about Professor Maurice's associates and the tendency of his ideas. And Maurice, Trench and Kingsley were among those who had recently founded a school for governesses – Queen's College, London. It is not surprising that some members of the public became alarmed about the kind of influence these men might exert over the impressionable young minds in their care.[17]

The writers of the *English Review*, a High Church journal, had professed themselves 'no lovers of Archdeacon Hare's writings', but their reviews of works by Hare, Maurice and Trench had not, for all this, been markedly unsympathetic or harsh before 1848. But in the latter part of that year a volume of sermons by Maurice was contemptuously attacked as being contrary to the Ordination Service in its view of the priesthood. And the following issue bore a full broadside, a lengthy article portentously called 'On Tendencies towards the Subversion of Faith'. This article argued on the ground of guilt by association and attempted to smear Hare and his liberal associates by placing them in company with Sterling and Sterling in company with such enemies of the faith as Strauss and Blanco White. But even if the reviewer, William Palmer, was willing to stoop to such intellectually dishonest arguments, he was genuinely convinced that he had discovered some sort of key to a great plot against Christianity.[18]

'It was, doubtless, the boldness and speculativeness of his views,' he wrote, 'which gathered around him [Sterling] the friendship of a host of congenial minds, sympathizing in the general complexion of their philosophical and theological tendencies, though separated by strongly marked differences in points of detail. We only miss one name from the circle who ought to have held a conspicuous place there, we mean Blanco White. But the names of Hare, Bunsen, Carlyle, Coleridge, Emerson, Thirlwall, Maurice, Francis Newman, John Mill, Samuel Wilberforce, Arnold, and Trench, are familiar to all the readers of this work, as the friends and associates of Mr Sterling, – the subjects of his warmest admiration and deepest sympathies. . .His life reveals a link between writings and doctrines, which we mentally class together almost involuntarily, notwithstanding their differences in many points, but which we could hitherto only connect by their tendencies. In Sterling's life, however, these various systems are brought together as parts and offshoots of one great movement, each playing its part, and allied by secret ties of sympathy with the rest.'

Even Palmer had to admit that there was the widest divergence of actual doctrine among these men, but he claimed that they nonetheless represented a single school. As for the unifying principle of this subversive movement, he believed it 'to consist simply in the striving after intellectual liberty, a tendency to reject all which does not commend itself to the individual reason as right and true – a tendency to resist *authority* of whatever nature it may be, which interposes any restraint on the freedom of speculation'.[19]

In a fury against the *English Review's* misrepresentations of his connection with Sterling, Hare counter-attacked with a pamphlet bearing the uncompromising title *Thou Shalt Not Bear False Witness Against Thy Neighbour*. But the pamphlet contained some damaging admissions, including a statement by Maurice (in an appended letter) that the persons named by Palmer were indeed united in believing that 'the popular English religious systems cannot last'. Maurice of course always attached an entirely negative meaning to the idea of 'religious systems', but he seems never to have understood how to avoid misunderstanding of his subtle distinctions. A scurrilous Evangelical newspaper, the *Record*, having become aware of the controversy through Hare's pamphlet, at first tended to sympathize with him in his anger at the *English Review* but asked Maurice, in some alarm, whether belief in the Thirty-Nine Articles was one of the systems he opposed.[20]

Nothing brought together the High Churchmen and the Evangelicals like a chance to defend orthodoxy by attacking the heathenish tendencies of liberal theologians. Within a week the journalists who managed the *Record* had found time to read Hare's memoir of Sterling. They abruptly lost all sympathy with Sterling's friends, for reasons that they announced to their readers in no very moderate language: 'STERLING fell, lamentably fell, till. . .he rejected the miracles, rejected the Mosaic history of the Creation, rejected the Bible. He fell still deeper and deeper. . .until, having denied the Father, the Son, and the Holy Ghost, he adopted the blasphemous speculations of STRAUSS, and rolled headlong into the gulf of a dark, gloomy, and degrading Pantheism.'

From some source they had obtained information about the Sterling Club. Indignant at the discovery of an institution apparently founded in honour of such a man, the *Record* demanded an explanation in its most strident tones: 'It is time that we should know how we stand. Who then are the leading members of this STERLING CLUB? Infidels, Papists, Tractarians, Trimmers, Benthamites, speculators of every class, painters, poets, and humorists, are in the STERLING CLUB, all intermingled with Bishops, Archdeacons, College Fellows, and College Tutors. With shame we read the names of all the *three* WILBERFORCES in a club, whose common bond of union seems to consist, in reverence for STERLING as a bold speculator'.

Why, the *Record* wondered, would such eminent Churchmen associate with this motley group, one that included (apparently a sore point) 'the three most eminent writers in Punch!' But at least they knew what poor Maurice would be at. Recalling that he had once described the Articles as mere 'conditions of thought' (thus wholly misreading *Subscription No Bondage*), they described his spiritual position as one of 'extreme peril'.

One week later the Record returned to the fray, with some freshly accumulated mud in hand: 'In the wildness of his Pantheism, STERLING, we have heard, did not scruple to avow that he regarded CARLYLE as being as truly inspired as Isaiah!' Moreover, the printed list of Sterling Club meetings gives Christmas Day as the date of the last meeting for 1848! (This proved to be an error on the Secretary's part.) At first 'disposed to smile at the incongruous society with which these ecclesiastical names are intermingled', the *Record* now confessed to real concern: 'If asked what is the probable bond of union. . .in the STERLING Club, we answer at once, that we believe it consisted in aversion to what they call "Bibliolatry," or reverence to the Bible as the inspired word of God.' Within a few weeks the *Record* had learned that Bishop Thirlwall, as a young man, had translated a work by Schleiermacher. With this slim evidence, the *Record* was able to uncover a long-standing subversive plot against the Church of England, one connected with Strauss and the undermining of Christian faith by pantheism.

Needless to say, they were not permitted to proceed without a counter-attack, but they evaded this by the simple method of not staying to one point long enough to suffer defeat. For example, in deploring the fact that '[m]itred bishops and venerable archdeacons were not afraid. . .to crowd round the Board with Benthamites, Infidels, Pantheists, waverers, and such like', they claimed that grace was not said at these dinners. Faced by an angry denial from Trench, the *Record* simply refused to believe him and claimed that in any case the real question was whether men who disbelieve in the plenary inspiration of the Bible shall be allowed to teach theology to 'our young men' at King's College and to 'the *governesses* of our daughters' at Queen's College. By this time the *Record* had no doubt as to how the conspiracy came about: 'The succession is from Coleridge to Maurice, and from Maurice to Sterling, and their "dark and winding paths of speculation,' ending in the denial of all creeds and the rejection of God himself." But there was a brand to be snatched from the burning, for they had heard that Bishop Samuel Wilberforce 'joined the club solely in a missionary spirit, and with the view of tempering the intellectual crudities of its members with some infusion of Christianity', and they adjured him to stand up as a true son of his father and denounce his fellow-diners.[21]

However extreme and ridiculous the *Record*'s attack may have been, it could not fail to have considerable effect. Those ambitious and politic prelates, Henry Manning and Samuel Wilberforce, found themselves in an unpleasant spot. In a letter to Wilberforce Manning examined the three courses he felt were open to them:

1. to change the name, 2. to dissolve, 3. to withdraw. The first is perhaps the least violent: but I am not quite at ease in continuing a member of a voluntary Society formed by and out of such loose materials. There may be no infidels in strict speech, but there is much that I do not wish to mix with by my free will and advance...

As to the second – i.e. dissolving. It is cumbrous, uncertain, involves others, and might provoke mischief.

The third is the course to which I incline most.[22]

John Allen, always earnest and quixotic in his beliefs, felt that 'if the name...causes offence to a single individual, it ought to be changed', and withdrew from the club when (at a meeting in March 1849) the majority of members disagreed with him. They argued that they should 'by yielding, be supposed to admit that we are detected conspirators, organized by Sterling for the attack and undermining of Christianity'. But this argument proved to no avail, for pressure mounted from outside, and (as Carlyle wrote in 1851) 'the name was again altered, to suit weak brethren, and the Club still subsists, in a sufficiently flourishing though happily once more a private condition'.[23]

As Bristed says, the members of the Sterling Club controlled 'many avenues of approach to the public', and they made their appeal to public opinion in a number of ways. J. C. Hare had been Archdeacon of Lewes since 1840 and had not avoided controversial issues in his annual charges to the clergy of the archdeaconry: his charge for 1849 contains a full account of the Sterling Club, as an answer to the wild rumours that had been set loose by the *Record*'s campaign. 'These misrepresentations and insinuations,' Hare wrote, 'have spread so widely, and have excited so much wonder among persons ignorant of the worthlessness of the channel which gave them currency, – I have seen expressions of that wonder from Scotland, and even from America, and India, – that it seems right to set forth a simple statement of the facts from which these calumnies have been extorted, lest some ecclesiastical antiquary in after ages, some Mr Maitland in the twenty-fifth century, should draw forth this story from the dust and mould of an ancient library, as a curious account of a formidable conspiracy against Christianity in the year 1849.'[24]

At the other extreme from Hare's earnest defence, but no less effective for that, was Thackeray's treatment of the subject in the pages of *Punch.* 'This is the newspaper room,' says the narrator of one of his sketches, who is introducing a young man to a London club, '– enter the Porter with the evening papers – what a rush the men make for them! Do you want to see one? Here is the *Standard* – nice article about the Starling Club – very pleasant, candid, gentleman-like notice – Club composed of clergymen, atheists, authors, and artists. Their chief conversation is blasphemy: they have statues of SOCRATES and MAHOMET on the centre-piece of the dinner-table, take every opportunity of being disrespectful to MOSES, and a dignified clergyman always proposes the Glorious, Pious, and Immortal Memory of CONFUCIUS. Grace is said backwards, and the Catechism treated with the most irreverent ribaldry by the comic authors and the general company. – Are these men to be allowed to meet, and their horrid orgies to continue? Have you had enough? – let us go into the other rooms.'[25]

CHAPTER 12

THE OLD ORDER AND THE NEW

The affair of the Sterling Club well exemplifies the influence of the Cambridge Apostles. This influence was as diffuse as the group itself: the demands of their individual careers continued to separate the members of the Apostolic set, and though certain friendships were deepened over the years, in most cases the ties of sentiment replaced those of active comradeship. Yet the Apostles' influence tended to a single end, for they shared the kind of critical intelligence that was encouraged by the Apostolic spirit. Whatever else they were, they were intellectuals, and intellectuals with a strongly liberal bias. They naturally associated with other liberal intellectuals, they encouraged the growth of liberal intellectual values in whatever ways they could, and they found themselves in conflict with people who held other values. As William Palmer was astute enough to recognize, Sterling and his associates represented a growing movement of those who threatened the known and accepted order of things because they opposed the restraints of traditional authority over intellectual liberty. Palmer, an intellectual himself and one of staunchly conservative views, would have been even more disturbed had he known that this group was in the process of forming important links with a younger generation who, as the 'new intelligentsia' of the eighteen-sixties, would achieve many of the results he feared. The Sterling Club was one sign of the changes to come – one of the many channels through which the influence of the Apostles worked to help bring about the new order.

In a brilliant essay Lord Annan has shown the important role played within the new intelligentsia by an 'intellectual aristocracy' that was dominated by the descendants of certain middle-class families whose religious opinions – Evangelical, Quaker or Unitarian – had in the late eighteenth century placed them at the periphery of established society and given them a common interest in philanthropy. Their children grew away from the particular beliefs of this generation but retained their parents' critical perspective on society. These families were noted for their intellectual gifts: the children became liberally inclined, socially conscious dons, scholars, clergymen and barristers and spread through the new professions of the civil service and journalism. By the sixties they and their children formed a major element within the intelligentsia. Such families as the Stephens, the Darwins, the Stracheys, the Trevelyans were connected by a complex network of intermarriage and interrelations of many kinds, and newcomers to this social class tended to form similar links with its established members. This generation of liberal intellectuals were further united by what Annan calls 'the new liberalism of franchise reform, women's education and university extension'. The issue of Irish Home Rule, he says, later divided them, and thereafter they went in several political directions. 'But in the sixties two objectives vital to their class and, as they rightly thought, vital to their country, united them. They worked tirelessly for intellectual freedom within the universities which, they thought, should admit anyone irrespective of his religious beliefs, and for the creation of a public service open to talent. If they can be said to have had a Bill of Rights it was the Trevelyan–Northcote report of 1853 on reform of the civil service and their Glorious Revolution was achieved in 1870–1 when entry to public service by privilege, purchase of army commissions and the religious tests were finally abolished.'[1]

The intellectual aristocracy formed an important element in the portion of the intelligentsia that was connected with the universities and hence with the social Establishment. The Victorian intelligentsia had a highly complex social structure: at one extreme it formed a bohemian subculture of the sort that is often meant when we speak of the intelligentsia today; at the other it penetrated the world of fashionable society, and between the two it was scattered throughout the professions, both established and new. The Sterling Club, with its indiscriminate mixture of prelates and journalists, painters and dons, provides a useful cross-section of that portion of the intelligentsia that lay between the extremes. But Sterling and his fellow-Apostles were unusual for their time in choosing to ignore the ideological barriers that protected the Establishment from outsiders. The Society and the Sterling Club both prefigured the new intelligentsia in drawing no significant line between those intellectuals who professed Anglican orthodoxy and those who did not, and it was precisely this attitude that so offended William Palmer and the journalists of the *Record*.

As Palmer and his associates in the Oxford Movement kept loudly asserting, the spread of liberal intellectual values meant the destruction of the Church's traditional role in society – a fact that is quite evident if we look back at the old order at Cambridge and the social mechanism it represented. In the old order, higher education was frankly acknowledged to be the mark or privilege of a class, and for those whose social position was most assured Cambridge acted as the merest of finishing schools. But it also served to stock the national Church by providing a channel to ordination and preferment for those who would otherwise have been unable to remain within the respectable classes, and through this process the Church also acquired great power over the intelligentsia and the educational system.

The nature of this social mechanism was well understood at the time. A would-be reformer of Oxford and Cambridge, writing in 1836, expressed the current idea of the system very clearly: 'the two national Universities,' he said, 'have a threefold character. They are to be considered, 1st, as seminaries of education for the young nobility and gentry of the realm; 2ndly, as nurseries for the Established Church, and for the learned professions; and 3rdly, as schools for the advancement and development of science, and the deeper researches of literature.' He pointed out that it was 'a very common error to consider the Universities in the light of large public schools, and to fancy that if they do no good, they can, at any rate, do no great harm'. But it was, he asserted, not correct to assume, as one might of a public school, that marked degeneration of the institution would inevitably be followed by a decrease in the number of students. 'If the Universities should at any time, from their low condition, cease to be beneficial to the country, they will always have sufficient wealth to purchase largely the power of yearly infusing mischief into the community. The large number of fellowships, scholarships, exhibitions, etc., which the Universities hold out to the competition of young men. . .will always procure for the Universities a sufficient number of students to enable them to keep up their station in the country, and to maintain a very wide influence on the intellectual and moral character of the people.'

'The pecuniary enticements which Oxford displays to the public,' this anonymous critic of the Universities went on to say, 'are about 450 livings, 24 headships of colleges, about 570 fellowships, many hundred scholarships and exhibitions, besides several lucrative University offices. And the bait which Cambridge holds out, is about 330 livings, 17 headships of colleges, about 420 fellowships, many hundred scholarships and exhibitions, 15 masterships of schools, and the various

University offices, – a few of which have a large emolument attached to them. These riches, which in most cases are open to competition, will, it is evident, draw yearly to the Universities a much larger number of students than can, with any *reasonable* hope, look forward to be benefited by them; and instead of decrease, there is every prospect of their numbers being annually augmented, as population increases and the arena of speculative contest becomes enlarged.'[12]

The force of this argument is increased when one considers the wider implications of the system he describes. It would not be true to say that the educational system of the country as a whole was thus controlled, but this was very nearly the case. Positions at nearly all the public schools were obtained by essentially the same means – successful academic competition at a university, followed by ordination. And the private schools were for the most part run by clergymen whose qualifications for the task lay in their own success at Oxford or Cambridge and who prepared their students for the same system. For some of these students the ability to turn out Greek verses might be a mere social frill, for others it might be the key to their future careers.

Cambridge undergraduates represented a very wide range of social privilege. Many of the sizars, and other students whose families could not pay for their education, came from the social class portrayed in Trollope's Rev. Josiah Crawley, perpetual curate of a rural living so poorly endowed that he subsisted in abject, if technically genteel, poverty. Samuel Butler has provided a graphic description of these undergraduates in the fifties, when they still frequented the 'labyrinth', a collection of 'dingy, tumble-down rooms' behind the old chapel of St John's. 'In the labyrinth there dwelt men of all ages,' he says, 'from mere lads to grey-haired old men who had entered late in life. They were rarely seen except in hall or chapel or at lecture, where their manners of feeding, praying and studying, were considered alike objectionable; no one knew whence they came, whither they went, nor what they did, for they never showed at cricket or the boats; they were a gloomy, seedy-looking *confrérie*, who had as little to glory in in clothes and manners as in the flesh itself.'

Butler points out that most of these students were destined for the Church by the fact of their social position. 'To most of them the fact of becoming clergymen would be the *entrée* into a social position from which they were at present kept out by barriers that they well knew to be impassable: ordination, therefore, opened fields for ambition which made it the central point in their thoughts', and an ardent

Evangelicism flourished among them. It will be remembered that the Society began on the fringes of this group, and though it soon moved upwards on the social scale, quite a few of its later members came from families with nothing in the way of money or social connections. Several of these Apostles sank into the abyss of obscure curacies and impoverished rural livings that awaited such students if they did not distinguish themselves academically. But most escaped this fate, for they belonged to the tiny minority of poor students whose academic gifts enabled them to win a higher social position. As Butler recalled, a few of those who dwelt in the labyrinth 'would at once emerge on its being found after their first examinations that they were likely to be ornaments to the college; these would win valuable scholarships that enabled them to live in some degree of comfort, and would amalgamate with the more studious of those who were in a better social position, but even these, with few exceptions, were long in shaking off the uncouthness they brought with them to the University, nor would their origin cease to be easily recognisable till they had become dons and tutors. I have seen some of these men attain high position in the world of politics or science, and yet retain a look of labyrinth and Johnian sizarship.'[3]

W. H. Thompson, the eldest of eleven children of a Yorkshire solicitor, entered Trinity as a sizar but quickly found the money to become a pensioner, an elevation in rank that would have been most important to him. The sizars of Trinity were no longer required to wait on the tables in Hall, but they sat at a separate table, and their dinner consisted (at least in theory) of the left-overs from the High Table, where the dons, noblemen and fellow-commoners sat. For a young man like Thompson, someone who had a living to make with only his brains to help him, the most desirable route to economic independence went by way of a fellowship at Trinity. He had first of all to win a scholarship, so that his food and tuition were provided for and so that he would be eligible to take the fellowship examinations when he graduated. Intense competition took its toll among such students: a friend of Thompson's recalled finding him wandering about in tears after learning that he had been placed fourth in the Classical Tripos. Such a student might take several years to win a fellowship, even supposing him to be successful, and during this time he would probably supplement his income by tutoring undergraduates: Sterling's cousin William Coningham was probably only one of Thompson's pupils. Those who won fellowships were assured of a modest but adequate income so long as they remained unmarried and took holy orders within seven years.

If they planned to use their fellowships to launch academic careers, they would almost certainly have to take orders in any case, since only a handful of positions at the University could be held by laymen. If they planned to teach outside the University they would find themselves in much the same spot: Thompson was lucky enough to begin his career by finding a teaching post that could be held by a layman, but he knew that ordination was essential for more desirable posts, and (as we have seen) he eventually submitted with some reluctance to the inevitable. He might have tried to establish himself in some other profession during the seven years at his disposal, but if he was unsuccessful and had no other means of support he might have to accept ordination after all. Connop Thirlwall was among those who felt obliged to take orders because they could find no better way to support themselves; it was typical of Thirlwall that he chose to seek out academic work on his return to Cambridge and did not sink into the sloth of a Combination-Room life. Someone else in his position might well have merely subsisted as a dependent of the College until a rural living came his way and he could, in Leslie Stephen's words, 'try how far his knowledge of the Greek drama or the planetary theory would qualify him to edify the agricultural labourer'. The wait for a suitable living could be long and unrewarding: the livings in the gift of the College were offered, as they became vacant, to each of the Fellows in order of seniority, but many of them were so poorly endowed as to be no better than the ill-paid curacies that the sizars of St John's could look forward to.[4]

This system could only be taken for granted so long as the Universities were seen as primarily the preserves of the Christian gentleman, and the Christian gentleman was understood to be no mere educational ideal but a distinct social being – an Anglican male with an established relation to the traditional ruling classes. But times were changing, and the system was under attack from several sides. One was the Oxford Movement: the Tractarians' idea of the high religious calling of the clergyman (and hence of the University don) was just as subversive of the old order as any of the liberal notions they attacked. Yet another was the Broad Church movement, a movement of the late forties that precisely parallels the rise of liberal intellectualism and is actually the manifestation of it within the Church. There had always been liberal elements within the Church, but in the earlier part of the century they were not generally regarded as being allied in opposition to the other parties that divided the Church. In part, the distinction was a political one: the Church was for the most part a conservative institution and those liberals who strayed into it were made to feel uncomfortable. The Whigs did their best to protect their followers among the clergy: when they were in power they were willing to give preferment to any liberal clergyman who had distinguished himself but whose views were not so markedly liberal as to touch off a religious witch-hunt. Sometimes they made mistakes, as in the case of R. D. Hampden, who does not seem to have understood the implications of his own liberal theories. But most of those they appointed were better able to defend themselves, although their views were often markedly in opposition to those of the majority. Quite typical was Thirlwall's first appearance before his fellow-bishops in the House of Lords, in 1841. He seized the opportunity to promote the very unfashionable idea of admitting Jews to Parliament, an idea that flew in the face of the traditional conception of England as a Christian country. 'My friend Bishop Thirlwall has made a capital *début* in favour of the Jews,' Richard Milnes reported. 'The whole Bench wept over him as a renegade brother, but he took it very easy.'[5]

The liberals were not only a barely tolerated minority within the Church but were divided among themselves. Though Hare, Thirlwall and the Apostles had their equivalents at Oxford in the so-called Oriel Noetics and in the disciples of the most famous of the Noetics, Thomas Arnold, they did not form a single social group nor a single movement. The Cambridge group tended to Coleridgean views, whereas Oxford liberalism had descended directly from eighteenth-century rationalism, and the two groups seem to have known little of each other. By the late forties, however, the liberal Churchmen were able to come into the open. They became more aggressive in putting forth their ideas and soon were recognized by themselves and their enemies as a distinct movement. The term 'Broad Church', coined by the Oxford contingent, was quite unacceptable to F. D. Maurice, who always maintained that he was not a member of any sect or party. Without questioning his sincerity, one may point out that he was simply wrong: his ideas and actions made him a natural rallying-point for liberals from both camps, and whether he liked it or not they regarded him as one of the principal leaders of the movement.

Maurice was addicted to a way of thinking so complex that the direction of his ideas was often obscured, even to him, by the labyrinthine religious theory by which he justified his actions. Nonetheless, that direction was persistently liberal, for Maurice was dominated by his early experiences as a social outsider and as a member of a family that carried the principle of social dissension in the name of religion to new heights of destructiveness. Maurice was obsessive in his search for spiritual unity within society and a determined enemy of the traditional causes of dissension. As he told J. C. Hare, he was unwilling to pursue conventional preferment within the Church because he did not feel like a conventional Churchman: his life-work as a clergyman, he said, lay 'with the outlying sheep more than with those within the fold. . .among all that are in distress and are in debt and are discontented – Quakers, Unitarians, Rationalists, Socialists, and whatever else a Churchman repudiates, and whatever repudiates him'. In *Subscription No Bondage* he had tried to show how the universities in their existing form could be opened to everyone; in *The Kingdom of Christ* he had tried to show how orthodox Anglicanism might be reinterpreted to meet the needs of all believers. The educational schemes in which he was to involve himself – Queens' College and the Working Men's College – were practical attempts to extend some of the privileges of the Establishment to those traditionally excluded from them. A similar impetus might even be said to underlie the theory of eternal punishment that was to win him such notoriety: though Maurice carefully avoided the heresy of universalism, he could not bear the idea of a God who perpetually excluded the damned, and he set out to construct one of his ingenious, perverse and infinitely subtle arguments to show that an orthodox person need not believe this to be true.[6]

The primary example of Maurice's influence is the Broad Church social movement that began with the foundation of Queens' College in 1847 and the publication of *Politics for the People* in 1848. This movement had the title of Christian Socialism bestowed upon it by Maurice in 1852, but it was scarcely a significant event in the history of socialism. Maurice had acquired a following of enthusiastic young disciples, whose unbounded reverence for 'the Prophet', as they called him, did not prevent their having very independent views of their own. Some of these followers had radical ideas and favoured direct political reform of the sort that Maurice had rejected in the twenties and thereafter, but as a whole the movement was committed to moral or educational reform, and (not surprisingly) its one distinct achievement was the foundation of the Working Men's College in 1854. Shortly before this event Maurice had courted and won public martyrdom by publishing his advanced views on eternal punishment, an act that led directly to his expulsion from his teaching position at King's College. Had he planned it, he could scarcely have found a better way of uniting the forces of liberalism behind him, and the success of the Working Men's College was due in no small measure to the energies released in this earlier struggle.[7]

While the Working Men's College began as an outgrowth of the Broad Church movement, as the most notable in a series of undertakings by a group of social reformers who were nearly all liberal Churchmen, it was by no means restricted to this group. The College drew its strength from the liberal intelligentsia in general, and this seems to have been Maurice's intention from the first. His son has pointed out the conspicuous absence of 'any kind of religious test' at the College. 'Had there been no other motive,' he says, 'all test as to the religious views of teachers or students would have been forbidden by the central principle on which my father's faith was based – that Christ was the head of every man, not only of those who believed in Him – and by his special desire to bridge the gulph between the working men and the "clerisy," as, following Coleridge, he habitually called the body of university men, artists, scientific men, and others who are capable of teaching. . .Much of the most valuable assistance that was given to the teaching of the college was given by men who could have accepted no common religious formula, and many of whom would have accepted none at all.' The College appealed to an extraordinarily wide range of the Victorian clerisy, for its teachers included John Ruskin, Lowes Dickinson, D. G. Rossetti, Frederic Harrison and (at a later date) such diverse figures as Burne Jones and Thomas Huxley, and some of these men were in fact outspoken opponents of the Broad Church movement.[8]

Maurice was forever being shocked to discover that his ideas had more radical implications for other people than they had for him. His professed goals were conservative, for he hoped to reinvigorate the traditional forms of faith and to demonstrate the vital role that the Church could play in modern education. But his ideas were a direct challenge to the traditions of the Establishment, for he perpetually tried to break down the barriers by which it excluded outsiders. An institution that provided the fundamentals of middle-class education for working men and that drew its teachers from the educated classes without consideration of their religious beliefs was a major break with tradition and one that suggested even more significant changes to come. As Principal of the College Maurice was hard-pressed to prevent the development of his ideas in directions he could not approve, but after his death they were inevitable. Today the Working Men's College is a thriving concern, whose students need be neither working-class nor men – a natural part of an educational system that professes to give no advantage to the adherents of any particular religion or the members of any social class.

Conservatives within the Church had tended to leave Maurice alone because they did not understand him, but by the late forties the drift of his thinking had become unmistakable, and they did their best to discredit him. At the same time he became something of a hero to others, many of whom were mainly interested in the liberal implications of his ideas. Young men at Cambridge, including some of the more important members of the Society, were among those greatly excited by the controversies and schemes of social reform in which Maurice played a central role. They eagerly discussed the knotty problems of theology raised in these controversies; they taught at the Working Men's College; they helped set up a similar college in Cambridge; many of them became clergymen in their turn and helped to establish the Broad Church movement as the dominant religious influence at Cambridge. For the next two decades Maurice exerted a considerable influence over a succession of such students, both as the founder and Principal of the Working Men's College and (from 1866) as Professor of Moral Philosophy at Cambridge.

To many of these young men Maurice's distinctive theories were far less important than the personal example he set them in the width of his social sympathies and in the intensity of his spiritual ardour, which they sometimes found quite overwhelming. The sort of impact he could have is suggested by a fragmentary (but self-explanatory) newspaper clipping that may be found in the archives of the Working Men's College. 'The appointment of the Radical Dean of Ely,' this clipping runs, 'caused some comment at the time. To a representative of the *Sunday Magazine* the Dean has been explaining how his sympathies were first aroused on behalf of the labouring classes, and what prompted him to his enthusiastic study of social questions. His interest in these matters he traces to the remarkable influence of Frederick Denison Maurice in his undergraduate days at Cambridge. In one of his lectures Maurice quoted a saying from Goethe's "Wilhelm Meister": – "As he closed his book (said the Dean) he looked up suddenly, his eyes burning with the light of inspiration, and with a voice trembling with emotion, said, returning upon the quoted sentence: 'Young men! *earnestness alone makes life eternity.*'" "The effect," said Dean Stubbs, "was indescribable. The words burned themselves into my soul, and became one of the watchwords of my life." '[9]

It is noteworthy that Maurice had not actually said anything that might be thought likely to encourage such an undergraduate as Stubbs to become a 'Radical Dean'. Though Maurice helped to bring about the new order, he was distinctly a member of the old, and he was admired as a leader of the liberal cause by young men whose idea of liberalism was often very different from his own. Among them were some of the leaders of the new intelligentsia, including the principal members of the Society, which was as usual well in the forefront of public opinion at Cambridge. These young men seem to have shared with Maurice little more than the belief that they must be earnest, that they must regard social outsiders sympathetically and that the traditions of their elders were open to question. In a succession of controversies, culminating in the great public debates over *The Origin of Species* and *Essays and Reviews*, the right of liberal intellectuals to publish and publicly discuss what they thought had been effectively established, and this was a right that John Sterling's generation had not felt they had. Among the young, and especially among the Apostles, the cult of liberal intellectualism had become the established faith.

From an account of the cult written in later life by one of its leaders, Henry Sidgwick, it is plain that Apostolic theology had undergone a radical transformation since the days when 'Maurice and that gallant band of Platonico-Wordsworthian-Coleridgean-anti-Utilitarians' had run the *Athenaeum*. Maurice's old antagonist John Stuart Mill had replaced Coleridge as the central contemporary writer for the Apostles. As Henry Sidgwick recalled it, his early beliefs centred on an 'ideal which, under the influence primarily of J. S. Mill, but partly of Comte seen through Mill's spectacles, gradually became dominant in my mind in the early sixties: – I say "in my mind," but. . .it was largely derived from intercourse with others of my generation, and. . .it seemed to me the only possible ideal for all adequately enlightened minds. It had two aspects, one social and the other philosophical or theological. What we aimed at from a social point of view was a complete revision of human relations, political, moral, and economic, in the light of science directed by comprehensive and impartial sympathy; and an unsparing reform of whatever, in the judgment of science, was pronounced to be not conducive to the general happiness.'

The Apostles of Sidgwick's time were, evidently, no less presumptuous in their youthful contempt for their opponents than were those of

Maurice's, but the Coleridgean idea of recognizing the human needs met by opposing opinions had given way to what Sidgwick called 'social science'. 'This social science,' he states, 'must of course have historical knowledge as its basis; but, being science, it must regard the unscientific beliefs, moral or political, of past ages as altogether wrong, – at least in respect of the method of their attainment, and the grounds on which they were accepted. History, in short, was conceived as supplying the material on which we had to work, but not the ideal which we aimed at realizing; except so far as history properly understood showed that the time had come for the scientific treatment of political and moral problems.'

Their attitude to religion was also significantly different from that promoted by Maurice and his followers among the Apostles. 'As regards theology,' Sidgwick says, 'those with whom I sympathized had no close agreement in conclusions, – their views varied from pure positivism to the "Neochristianity" of the Essayists and Reviewers: and my own opinions were for many years unsettled and widely fluctuating. What was fixed and unalterable and accepted by us all was the necessity and duty of examining the evidence for historical Christianity with strict scientific impartiality; placing ourselves as far as possible outside traditional sentiments and opinions, and endeavouring to weigh the pros and cons on all theological questions as a duly instructed rational being from another planet – or let us say from China – would naturally weigh them.'

This point of view was a natural extension of the earlier Apostles' interest in innovative religious ideas and their willingness to examine Christianity in the way that one might examine any other subject, but it would scarcely have been welcome among those older Apostles who had come to see 'scientific' scepticism as the enemy and who had made their peace with Christian orthodoxy. It is not at all clear that the older Apostles who patronized the Society at this time were fully aware of the opinions of their juniors, but the juniors were fully aware of theirs and in some cases regarded these ideas with considerable antagonism. Sidgwick's description of his beliefs was, in fact, written to explain how he had come to adopt a way of thought 'entirely alien' to the Broad Church tradition.[10]

This difference of ideology did not, however, prevent these two generations of intellectual liberals from consorting with one another. The Apostolic principle of sympathy with opposing opinions prevailed, as is strikingly evident in Sidgwick's treatment of Maurice on his return to Cambridge in the late sixties. When in 1865 Sidgwick had reluctantly resigned his active membership 'to relieve the weight of years that seemed to be pressing on the Society', he had set about establishing an alternative discussion group among the more senior members of the intellectual community at Cambridge. This group, eventually named the Grote Club after the Professor of Moral Philosophy who preceded Maurice, included several Apostles and others who might well have been elected to the Society, and its proceedings were very like the Society's. 'We used to meet once or twice a term at Grote's vicarage at Trumpington,' one of its members recalled, 'where he hospitably entertained us at dinner, after which the evening was devoted to the reading of a paper by one of us, and its subsequent discussion.' In the later sixties the club included Maurice and one of the most brilliant of the younger Apostles, the mathematician W. K. Clifford. 'If I might have verbatim reports of a dozen of the best conversations I have heard,' another member later wrote, 'I should choose two or three from among those evenings in which Sidgwick and Clifford were the chief speakers. Another would certainly be a conversation at tea before a Grote Club meeting. . .(I think it was early in 1868), in which practically no one spoke but Maurice and Sidgwick. Sidgwick devoted himself to drawing out Maurice's recollections of English social and political life in the thirties, forties, and fifties. Maurice's face shone out bright, with its singular holy radiance, as he responded to Sidgwick's inquiries and suggestions; and we others said afterwards that we owed all the delight of that evening to him. No one else among us knew enough to keep on again and again arousing the warm latent energy of the old man: for he always looked tired, and would relapse into silence after two or three minute's talk, however eager it had been, unless stimulated by someone who knew how to strike the right chord.'[11]

Although Maurice was physically exhausted he took a keen interest in the development of the liberal cause and especially in the movement for women's rights at the University. For him this issue was one aspect of the widespread reform of higher education that he favoured. The University was still dominated by the use of competitive examinations, and Maurice urged his disciple Charles Kingsley to publicize the need for reform. 'I do not know any man who has seriously thought of our present examination system,' he wrote to Kingsley, 'who does not feel that it is undermining the physical, intellectual and moral life of young men, and that it may do this with even more terrible effect for girls, if they are admitted, as of course they should be, to all the privileges of the other sex.' Henry Sidgwick and his friends were the key figures in promoting women's education at Cambridge: Maurice joined the association they formed in the late sixties and seems to have supported its work enthusiastically. Similarly, he took part in the movement to abolish religious tests at the University, having finally had to admit that subscription was bondage after all. The continuity of academic liberalism at Cambridge is further exemplified by the fact that this movement also had the support of Adam Sedgwick, the oldest and sole surviving member of the group of liberal dons that had included Hare and Thirlwall. Sedgwick had come up to the University in 1804, the year before Maurice was born, and he died the year after Maurice, in 1873.[12]

It should not be thought that this persistent tradition of intellectual liberalism aimed at any major change in class structure. As a social movement it merely sought to open certain privileges of the Establishment to general competition, rather than restricting them to those who were willing to make public professions of orthodox Anglicanism or those who had powerful connections among the ruling classes. The state of primary and secondary education being what it was, the number of lower-class candidates for these privileges was infinitesimal. But the liberals, with their willingness to associate for the purpose of intellectual discovery with like-minded people of whatever social rank or religious group, helped to establish a new scale of values in the educational system as a whole, and it is no accident that the rise of the new intelligentsia coincided with the creation of a universal compulsory educational system outside the Church's control. The liberal intellectuals themselves rarely sought direct political power and, when they did, were not very good at party politics. But through their work in many different professions they exerted a steady, pervasive pressure on Victorian public opinion, and in time the liberal tradition of social criticism was deeply influential.

Few of the surviving members of Arthur Hallam's set played so prominent a role in public affairs as did F. D. Maurice, but most of them became well-established senior figures in the social network that made up the liberal intellectual world. They were often helped along in their careers by other members of the group and by their wide acquaintanceship within this network, but in most cases they were more than qualified for the positions they won and held them with considerable distinction. Though their belief in the Apostolic spirit as an instrument of social reform had passed away with their youth, they were often successful in promoting such a spirit in those around them. Their opinions tended to appear less progressive as they grew older and were assimilated into the Establishment, yet they were highly sympathetic to the advanced views of younger people and tended to be on excellent terms with them. The Society was above all an instrument of education: in their various ways the Apostles were not without effect in transmitting to others what they themselves had learned and in seeking to moderate the fanaticism and intolerance of the age.

The long and successful career of J. W. Blakesley is a case in point. In 1839 at the age of thirty-one Blakesley had fallen in love with an eighteen-year-old, Margaret Holmes. In the following year they were engaged, but Blakesley had to wait another five years until the living of Ware in Hertfordshire came his way and he could resign his fellowship and marry. At Ware he settled down to the production of children – eleven in all – and letters to *The Times*, where as 'The Hertfordshire Incumbent' he became well known as a commentator on political events. According to a biographer, he found his parish 'in a state of ecclesiastical mutiny' and 'undertook the abatement of parochial feuds by a well-considered dinner-treatment. A judiciously arranged round table prevented rivalries for precedence; and the quiet courtesy of the hospitable incumbent produced a feeling of deference which gradually ripened into imitation of a reasonable and dispassionate temper.' Blakesley maintained his reputation as an accomplished scholar, but his chief interests lay in public affairs, and he established a steady correspondence with some of the more prominent liberal politicians of his time. In 1863 Palmerston awarded him a canonry at Canterbury; in 1872, on Gladstone's recommendation, he became Dean of Lincoln, and he held this post until his death in 1885. As a Churchman, Blakesley was scarcely a great spiritual leader: rather, he 'combined with undisputed orthodoxy, and strict observance of ecclesiastical decorum, the ready tact and business-like instinct of an accomplished layman'. The biographer who thus described him summarized his career as that of a 'dignified, enlightened, sincere, and unprejudiced divine' of a bygone school, and remarked, somewhat ambiguously, 'Though Mr Blakesley might have acquired a larger amount of fame and fortune in a more ambitious career, he was probably content with a tranquil, useful, and prosperous life.'[13]

Though Richard Milnes' later career might seem quite unlike Blakesley's, he too had a role to play in furthering Apostolic values. Milnes was above all a dilettante. As a youth he had been drawn to associate with the Apostles as one of the social experiences he longed to sample, and from them he learned no more than to be a rather Apostolic dilettante. Milnes took up politics as his ostensible profession, but he made his real mark as a host in London society. He went out of his way to know everyone and became famous for his breakfasts, at which he assembled the strangest assortment of guests, culled from the full range of his amazingly diverse acquaintanceship. When Milnes married in 1851, his old friend Thirlwall remarked to him, 'It is very likely – nay, certain – that you will still collect agreeable people about your wife's breakfast-table; but can I ever sit down there without the certainty that I shall meet with none but respectable persons? It may be an odd thing for a bishop to lament, but I cannot help it.' Milnes was not merely enjoying himself: in his own way he tried to contribute to social harmony and understanding, and many talented young people – among them the younger members of the Society – discovered in him an assiduous and influential patron. Milnes kept in touch with the Society throughout his life: he found jobs for the young Apostles, introduced them to London society, attended their meetings at Cambridge when he could, and almost always went to the annual dinner, even that of 1885, when he was within a few weeks of his death. He became a father figure to the younger Apostles – someone they could consult about the traditions of the Society when they fell out amongst themselves – and he used his very considerable social influence to benefit the Society and its members in whatever way he could.[14]

Some Apostles were not so fortunate in their careers and yet managed to contribute significantly to the culture of their times. John Kemble, for one, had a life of many disappointments and frustrations. The *British and Foreign Review* had come to a sudden end in 1844, and Kemble spent years casting about for another suitable job. Among the many positions he sought was that of Librarian to the University, but the post went to an older Apostle, Joseph Power. 'I am sorry for Kemble's defeat but not disappointed,' Donne wrote to Blakesley, 'for I never expected him to be nominated. There is so much in our friend to frighten a university from its propriety, that I should have been surprised at his success. He would, I believe, make an excellent librarian, but he would never look like one.' Kemble's marriage had not been a success, and his drinking habits had become notorious. When the Chair of Modern History at Cambridge was vacated by Professor Smyth's death, George Venables told Milnes that he expected Kemble to try for the position but thought himself better qualified: 'He knows a great deal which I don't,' Venables admitted; 'but I think I know some practical points better; and my head stands drinking better – After the first pint I think I should be the more trustworthy historian.' But Kemble's energy was unflagging. He pursued one great scheme after another until his sudden death from pneumonia in 1857 and, for all his eccentric behaviour, was able to make major advances in the fields of philology, history and archeology.'[15]

The many Apostles who won high reputations as scholars in their lifetime – Kemble, Donne, Trench, Blakesley, Spedding, Alford, Thompson, Merivale and Edmund Lushington – were as innovative in their scholarship as was the Society as a whole in its social thought. It is a notable fact that their contributions to knowledge were all in the humanities, specifically in philology and the literary and historical studies related to it. Although the Apostolic set contained a few talented mathematicians, no one truly gifted in the sciences was elected to the Society until the fifties, when they more than made up for the omission by electing James Clerk Maxwell. But even then the Society was not a channel for new ideas in science, which had its own intellectual and professional network, linked to the more scientifically inclined of the older group of Cambridge dons that had included Hare and Thirlwall.[16]

George Venables' later life provides yet another variation on the Apostolic pattern. Venables taught at Cambridge for some years, then moved to London, where he shared quarters with Henry Lushington and supported himself by writing for the *British and Foreign Review* and other journals while he attempted to establish a legal career. Eventually he became a highly respected figure at the Parliamentary Bar, but his most significant work continued to be in journalism. Venables threw himself wholeheartedly into the scheme that produced the *Saturday Review*: he wrote its first leading article when it was founded in 1855 and thereafter wrote two or three leaders a week until his final illness in 1888. He was regarded as 'a sort of spiritual and intellectual uncle or elder brother' by the Saturday Reviewers, who were led by certain of the Apostles of the late forties and who were typically Apostolic in assuming a superior, non-partisan attitude to the issues of the day. 'As a journalist he belonged to a small but important class', the *Saturday Review* pointed out on the occasion of his death. He was content to remain anonymous throughout his writing career, did not regard it as his means of livelihood, and did not use it to further the interests of any parliamentary or other party. 'To him journalism was itself public life. What he wrote was his contribution to the current affairs of his time', and if his many articles had a drawback it was 'that they demanded more attention than the common run of readers were always disposed to give; that they were written from so large a store of experience that their allusions were not always fully understood; that they resembled, in short, careful judgments rather than leading articles'. His grasp of contemporary political affairs was extraordinary, his judgement was excellent: had he not willingly chosen a life of relative obscurity he might (the *Saturday Review* claimed) have won a place among such 'contemporary historians' as Macaulay, Carlyle and Froude.[17]

But it seems there was another side to this Apostolic success story. Venables' cultivated exterior, his extensive social life, the insatiable round of work to which he submitted himself, were all masks to hide his deep unhappiness. A single overwhelming passion – his unrequited love for Henry Lushington – dominated his life. When Lushington left London in 1847 to work in Malta Venables was grief-stricken, for the change threatened to end this one-sided love affair for good. The relationship tormented him, and he was deeply jealous of other friends of Lushington, including Tennyson. Lushington's death in 1855 left him with nothing but bitter memories, and only in his very last years does he seem to have been at peace with himself.[18]

James Spedding's later life was also rather sad. By the sixties he had been at work on Bacon for over twenty years without seeing the end of his labours, and he threw his friend Sir Henry Taylor into a depression by confessing his feelings to him. Spedding told him that the project 'has lasted too long,' Taylor wrote, 'and that the delusion of its value has worn itself out, and that he no longer persuades himself that it signifies greatly whether he makes good the truth about Bacon or not; and that his eyes and his memory are no longer what they were, and both research and composition are irksome to him. All this he said in a cheerful tone, but it was profoundly mournful to me.' Spedding's reaction to old age is well captured in some light verse of his own composition:

The Antiquity of Man: – A Poem by Uncle James

I

When I was a freshman old age did appear
A reverend and beautiful thing;
For knowledge must gather as year follows year
And wisdom from knowledge should spring.

II

But I found the same years which supplied me with knowledge
Took the power to digest it away;
And let out all the store I had gathered at college
Through leaks that increased every day.

III

So I said it, and think not I said it in jest,
For you'll find it is true to a letter,
That the only thing old people ought to know best
Is that young people ought to know better.

Nonetheless he successfully completed his great task in 1874, seven years before his death in a London street accident.[19]

W. H. Thompson died in the Master's Lodge at Trinity College in 1886, after an outstanding academic career. He had earned the highest reputation as a teacher at Trinity: though he was shy, reserved and much given to making caustic quips at other people's expense, he was very successful at establishing close relationships with the young people he taught. As Master, he was a welcome relief from the arrogant William Whewell, though his popularity was somewhat qualified by very justifiable fear of his sharp tongue. My favourite of Thompson's legendary sarcasms is the tersely malevolent sentence with which he dismissed the academic pretensions of two successive Professors of Modern History, Charles Kingsley and J. R. Seeley. Kingsley had been notoriously ill-qualified for the post, and Seeley was much more highly regarded at Cambridge. And yet as Thompson left Seeley's inaugural lecture he was heard to murmur, 'Poor Kingsley, I never missed him before.' Persistent illness made Thompson an increasingly distant figure in the College, and after his death Charles Merivale regretfully reported to Venables that 'in his later years of seclusion he was only known. . .as a morose satirist – he being as we know nothing of the kind'.[20]

For someone who has admired the idealism, the energy, the enthusiasm of the Apostles in their first years of comradeship, the story of their gradual decline towards old age and death is not pleasant to dwell on. As they reach middle age, their letters increasingly descend to the commonplaces of business and social life, with only flashes of the old vitality and wit. As they reach old age, their ill-health and the loss of their friends become recurrent subjects. In 1879, having mentioned

Merivale's name in a letter to Blakesley, W. H. Thompson saw fit to remind his old friend that they, Merivale and Spedding were 'almost the only remnants of our old fraternal set – Arthur (Hallam's) Round Table', and this was not much of an exaggeration on Thompson's part. Tuberculosis had killed George Farish in 1836, R. J. Tennant in 1842, John Sterling in 1844, Charles Buller in 1848, Henry Lushington in 1855 and Stephen Spring Rice in 1865 – the latter three at the point when they had seemed about to rise into public prominence. Savile Morton – bohemian, womanizer, would-be artist and latterly foreign correspondent for the *Daily News* – was stabbed to death by a jealous husband in 1852. On the other hand, the equally disreputable Arthur Buller survived until 1869 and died with a knighthood and a highly successful legal and political career to his credit. By the time of Thompson's comment F. D. Maurice, Henry Alford, Kenneth Macaulay and Sir Arthur Helps had all died. Ten years later, he, Blakesley, Donne, Spedding, Trench, Milnes, Monteith, Garden, Venables, and John Heath were all gone. Tennyson, Merivale, and Edmund Lushington did not die until the early nineties, and the last of all, Douglas Heath, survived till 1897. 'I feel very much like Sir Bedevere,' he wrote to Hallam Tennyson in the course of supplying him with information for the memoir of his father, 'having survived, I believe, all my contemporaries of the old goodly company, and certainly finding round me new men, strange faces, other minds.' The old order had indeed passed away.[21]

Long before Douglas Heath's death the ideals held by the Apostles of Arthur Hallam's Round Table had become a firmly established tradition at Cambridge. Over the past century and a half the Society has suffered a number of crises, the most serious being phases of stagnation in which it seemed that the younger members lacked the will-power or desire to perpetuate the Apostolic spirit. Throughout the known history of the Society, however, that spirit has persisted and helped to shape the lives of a long succession of men who have played a greater or lesser role in the development of the British intelligentsia. As we have seen, the liberal views of F. D. Maurice's generation came to prevail at Cambridge and elsewhere within his lifetime and encouraged the growth of a new liberalism among the generation led by Henry Sidgwick. By Sidgwick's death in 1900 the Society had entered yet another phase of liberal opinion and was at the point of still greater change. The element of continuity within this process was well captured in some words spoken at a dinner of the Society – one of those annual gatherings of young and old Apostles at which the spirit of the Society is ritualistically praised and its traditions half-mockingly celebrated. The occasion was the dinner of 1908, the speaker was an Apostle of the 1870s, Donald MacAlister, and he was replying to a toast that had been proposed to 'the Scattered Brethren'. MacAlister assured those present that they might safely assume of every absent member, however distant, 'that his heart, untravelled, fondly turns to the hearth-rug in Cambridge' – the symbolic centre of the active members' weekly meetings. For it was there, MacAlister claimed, that each member of the Society 'learned to contemplate pure being...There with eyes undimmed, even by tobacco smoke, he beheld the vision of absolute truth...There he mastered the art of reconciling by a phrase the most divergent of hypotheses, the most fundamentally antagonistic of antinomies. There he grew accustomed to differ from his comrades in nothing but opinion. There, upborne by the ethereal atmosphere of free and audacious enquiry, he mewed his budding wings, and discovered to his delight that, towards midnight on a Saturday, he too could soar. Others might find the medium but a vacuum...But *he* was no chimaera, for he felt his reality and knew that he was alive.'

Oscar Browning, Henry Jackson, Walter Raleigh, J. M. E. McTaggart, G. E. Moore, Bertrand Russell, the Trevelyan brothers, the Strachey brothers, Maynard Keynes, Rupert Brooke – MacAlister's audience included representatives of each stage of the Society's history in the preceding half-century. Whatever their differences in ideology and perspective on life, all these men had shared in the experience that MacAlister described and could appreciate the truth underlying his rhetoric. For all of them, election to the Society had begun a vital stage in their personal development. For all of them, in MacAlister's words, Apostolic discussions had afforded a 'schooling of mind and heart' that was 'a lesson for life'. And this, as he said, was 'not merely a liberal education – it was an education in philosophic liberalism', an introduction both to liberal intellectual values and to the people who held them. Thus all had shared in the legacy of intellectual companionship handed down from Maurice, Hallam and their friends, and through this legacy all had taken their places in the tradition represented by the Cambridge Apostles.[22]

APPENDIX

Members of the Cambridge Conversazione Society, 1820–34

Since in the early years of the Society most members signed only their surnames in the record book, it has not been possible to identify all of them. The following list gives the names as they appear, in the order of their election, and where possible supplies:

further identification (and relation to other members, if any),

dates of active membership,

details of academic career (date of matriculation, college at the time of matriculation, degree, etc.),

profession, positions held, etc.,

date of death.

For further information see Venn, *Alumni Cantabrigiensis* – cited below, p. 225.

1 Tomlinson, George; [1820–30 May 1822; matric. 1819 (St John's), B.A. 1823; clergyman, Bishop of Gibraltar; d. 1863.]

2 Brice, [Edward Cowell, brother of no. 15; 1820–17 February 1821; matric. 1817 (St John's), B.A. 1821; clergyman; d. 1881.]

3 Thompson, Henry; [1820–13 April 1822; matric. 1818 (St John's), B.A. 1822; clergyman, author; d. 1878.]

4 Harford, [Henry Charles; 1820–19 April 1823; matric. 1819 (Caius), B.A. 1824; Capt. in Glos. Militia, J.P. for Glos.; d. 1879.]

5 Punnett, John; [1820–6 December 1823; matric. 1819 (Clare), B.A. (13th Wrangler) 1823, Fellow 1826; clergyman, author; d. 1863.]

6 Ainger, [Thomas; 1820–30 December 1820; matric. 1817 (St John's), B.A. 1821; clergyman, author; d. 1863.]

7 Henderson, [?Robert; 1820–23 February 1822; matric. 1818 (St John's), B.A. 1822; clergyman; d. 1875.]

8 Shaw, [?George; 1820–25 November 1820; matric. 1819 (Caius), M.B. 1824; physician; d. 1888.]

9 Wiseman, [Charles; 1820–20 December 1820; matric. 1817 (St John's), B.A. 1821; d. 1823.]

10 Battersby, [Richard; 1820–16 December 1820; matric. 1818 (St John's), B.A. 1822; clergyman; d. 1866.]

11 Furnival, [James; 1820–27 April 1822; matric. 1818 (Queens'), B.A. 1822; clergyman; d. ?1878.]

12 Simpson; [not identified; 1820–18 November 1820.]

13 Guest, [?Benjamin; 18 November 1820–8 December 1821; matric. 1818 (Queens'), B.A. 1822; clergyman; d. 1869.]

14 Browne; [not identified; 2 December 1820–12 May 1821.]

15 Brice, [?Henry Crane, brother of no. 2; 24 February 1821–1 March 1823; matric. 1821 (Christ's), B.A. 1825; clergyman; d. 1867.]

16 Festing, [George Charles Ruddock; 3 February 1821–10 March 1821; matric. 1818 (St John's), B.A. 1822; clergyman; d. 1857.]

17 Fennell, [?Samuel; 3 February 1821–7 March 1821; matric. 1817 (Queens'), B.A. (11th Wrangler) 1821, Fellow 1822; clergyman, teacher; d. 1843.]

18 Power, [Joseph, brother of no. 46; 17 February 1821–20 February 1822; matric. 1817 (Clare), B.A. (10th Wrangler) 1821, Fellow 1823; clergyman, scholar, University Librarian; d. 1868.]

19 Veas[e]y, [Alfred; 17 March 1821–5 May 1821; matric. 1817 (Peterhouse), B.A. 1821, Fellow 1824; ?clergyman; d. 1834.]

20 Roberts, [not identified; 3 November 1821–5 November 1825.]

21 Judge, Edward Conduitt; [17 November 1821–22 November 1823; matric. 1820 (Trinity), B.A. 1824; clergyman; d. 1875.]

22 Stock, [John Shapland; 1 December 1821–25 February 1826; matric. 1821 (Trinity), B.A. 1826; barrister; d. 1867.]

23 Simpson, [not identified; 9 February 1822–21 February 1824.]

24 Parke, [John; 16 March 1822–8 February 1823; matric. 1819 (Trinity), B.A. 1823.]

25 Outram, [Thomas Powys; 27 April 1822–22 May 1824; matric. 1821 (St John's), B.A. 1825; clergyman; d. 1853.]

26 Taylor, [?Alfred; 9 November 1822–seat declared vacant 8 February 1823; matric. 1820 (Trinity); d. 16 January 1823.]

27 Burdon, [?William Wharton; 7 December 1822–29 November 1823; matric. 1817 (Emmanuel), LL.B. 1824; M.P.]

28 Marriott, William Marriott Smith; [1 March 1823–11 October 1824; matric. 1819 (Trinity), B.A. 1825; clergyman; d. 1864.]

29 Darwin, [Erasmus Alvey; 3 May 1823–26 November 1823; matric. 1822 (Christ's), M.B. 1828; d. 1881.]

30 Maurice, [John Frederick Denison; 22 November 1823–3 March 1827; matric. 1823 (Trinity), took first in Civil Law Classes 1826–7 but did not graduate, matric. 1829 (Exeter College, Oxford), B.A. 1829; clergyman, theologian, author, teacher, Professor of English Literature and Modern History and Professor of Divinity at King's College, London,

Professor of Moral Philosophy at Cambridge, first Principal of Queen's College London, first Principal of the Working Men's College; d. 1872.]

31 Patton, [George, later Lord Glenalmond; 6 December 1823–15 May 1826; matric. 1822 (Trinity), B.A. 1826; Solicitor-General for Scotland, M.P., Lord Advocate, Lord Justice Clerk; d. 1869 by his own hand – an inquiry into irregularities associated with his election to the constituency of Bridgwater so preyed on his mind that he cut his throat and threw himself into the River Almond.]

32 Whitmore, Charles Shapland; [13 December 1823–25 November 1826; matric. 1823 (Trinity), B.A. 1827; barrister, judge of Southwark County Court; d. 1877.]

33 Boylan, [Richard Dillon; 14 February 1824–March 1826; matric. 1822 (Trinity).]

34 Carter, [?James; 27 March 1824–6 November 1824; matric. 1823 (Trinity); barrister, Chief Justice of the Supreme Court of New Brunswick, knighted for his services to Canada; d. 1878.]

35 Harrison; [not identified; 8 April 1824–6 November 1824.]

36 Romilly, [Edward, brother of no. 48; 6 November 1824–27 October 1827; matric. 1823 (Christ's), took first in Civil Law Classes 1826–7, LL.B. 1828; M.P., High Sheriff of Glamorgan; d. 1870.]

37 Bacon, [Francis; 13 November 1824–5 November 1825; matric. 1822 (Trinity), B.A. 1826; barrister, journalist, assistant editor of *The Times*; d. 1840.]

38 O'Brien, [William Smith, brother of no. 63; 27 November 1824–no date of resignation; matric. 1821 (Trinity), B.A. 1826; M.P., radical Irish politician; d. 1864.]

39 Gedge, [Sydney; 4 December 1824–5 November 1825; matric. 1820 (St Catherine's), B.A. (14th Wrangler, 7th Classic) 1824, Fellow 1825; clergyman, teacher; d. 1883.]

40 Kennedy, [Benjamin Hall; 4 December 1824–18 February 1826; matric. 1823 (St John's), B.A. (Senior Classic) 1827, Fellow 1825; clergyman, teacher, Headmaster of Shrewsbury, Regius Professor of Greek at Cambridge; d. 1889.]

41 Wilson, [John; 12 February 1825–2 December 1826; matric. 1823 (Trinity), B.A. 1827; barrister, ?editor of the *Globe* newspaper.]

42 Farish, [James, brother of no. 76; 5 March 1825–4 November 1826; matric. 1821 (Trinity), B.A. 1825, M.B. 1828; F.R.C.S.; d. 1853.]

43 Richardson; [not identified; ?1825–18 November 1826.]

44 Sterling, [John; 7 November 1825–1 December 1827; matric. 1824 (Trinity), B.A. 1834; clergyman, author; d. 1844.]

45 Baines, [Edward; 7 November 1825–18 November 1826; matric. 1820 (Christ's), B.A. (4th Classic) 1824, Fellow 1825; clergyman, teacher; d. 1882.]

46 Power, [Alfred, brother of no. 18; 26 November 1825–25 November 1826; matric. 1822 (Clare), B.A. (2nd Classic) 1826, Fellow of Downing 1826; barrister, Chief Poor Law Commissioner in Ireland, awarded K.C.B.; d. 1888.]

47 Malkin, [Frederick; 11 March 1826–27 October 1827; matric. 1819 (Trinity), B.A. (Senior Classic) 1824, Fellow 1825; scholar, author; d. 1830.]

48 Romilly, [Henry, brother of no. 36; 11 March 1826–9 February 1828; matric. 1824 (Christ's), B.A. 1828; merchant, author; d. 1884.]

49 Smith; [not identified; 29 April 1826–2 December 1826.]

50 Walpole, [Spencer Horatio; 11 November 1826–no date of resignation; matric. 1824 (Trinity), B.A. 1828; barrister, M.P., Home Secretary; d. 1898.]

51 Hall, [Richard; 27 November 1826–no date of resignation; matric. 1824 (Trinity), B.A. 1828; barrister; d. 1857.]

52 Kemble, [John Mitchell; 25 November 1826–23 December 1828; matric. 1825 (Trinity), B.A. 1830; scholar, author, editor of *British and Foreign Review*; d. 1857.]

53 Sunderland, [Thomas; 2 December 1826–27 February 1830; matric. 1830 [*sic*] (Trinity), B.A. 1830; d. 1867.]

54 Buller, [Charles, brother of no. 61; 2 December 1826–no date of resignation; matric. 1824 (Trinity), B.A. 1828; politician, M.P., President of the Poor Law Board; d. 1848.]

55 Talbot, [the Hon. James, later Lord Talbot de Malahide; 3 March 1827–5 May 1827; matric. 1823 (Trinity), B.A. (10th Classic) 1827; M.P., F.R.S.; d. 1883.]

56 Donne, [William Bodham; 17 March 1827–9 February 1828; matric. 1825 (Caius); author, dramatic critic, Librarian of London Library, Licenser of Plays; d. 1882.]

57 Wrangham, [George Walter; 12 May 1827–9 February 1828; matric. 1825 (Magdalene), B.A. 1828; clergyman; d. 1855.]

58 Trench, [Richard Chenevix; 12 May 1827–13 December 1828; matric. 1825 (Trinity), B.A. 1829; clergyman, scholar, author, Professor of Divinity at King's College London, Dean of Westminster, Archbishop of Dublin; d. 1886.]

59 Martineau, [Arthur; 10 November 1828–28 February 1829; matric. 1825 (Trinity), B.A. (3rd Classic) 1829, Fellow 1831; clergyman; d. 1872.]

60 Blakesley, [Joseph Williams; 24 November 1827–12 November 1831; matric. 1827 (Corpus), B.A. (21st Wrangler and 3rd Classic) 1831, Fellow of Trinity 1831; clergyman, scholar, Canon of Canterbury, Dean of Lincoln; d. 1885.]

61 Buller, [Arthur William, brother of no. 54; 16 February 1828–27

March 1830; matric. 1826 (Trinity), B.A. 1830; barrister, judge at Calcutta, M.P., knighted; d. 1869.]

62 Barnes, [Richard Nelson; 16 February 1828–27 March 1830; matric. 1826 (Pembroke), B.A. 1830; clergyman; d. 1889.]

63 O'Brien, [Edward, brother of no. 38; 22 March 1828–13 December 1828; matric. 1825 (Trinity), B.A. 1829; barrister, author; d. 1840.]

64 Horsman, [Edward; 17 May 1828–1 May 1830; matric. 1826 (Trinity); politician, M.P., Chief Secretary of State for Ireland; d. 1876.]

65 Cookesley, [William Gifford; 8 November 1828–no date of resignation; matric. 1821 (King's), B.A. 1826, Fellow 1824; clergyman, teacher; d. 1880.]

66 Tennant, [Robert John; 29 November 1828–12 February 1831; matric. 1827 (Trinity), B.A. 1831; clergyman; d. 1842.]

67 Spedding, J[ames; 29 November 1828–12 February 1831; matric. 1827 (Trinity), B.A. 1831; scholar; d. 1881.]

68 Hallam, [Arthur Henry; 9 May 1829–10 December 1831; matric. 1828 (Trinity), B.A. 1832; d. 1833.]

69 Morrison, [Alexander James William; 16 May 1829–10 December 1831; matric. 1828 (Trinity), B.A. 1832; clergyman, teacher; d. 1865.]

70 Tennyson, [Alfred, later Lord Tennyson; 31 October 1829–13 February 1830; matric. 1828 (Trinity), did not graduate; poet, Poet Laureate; d. 1892.]

71 Milnes, [Richard Monckton, later Lord Houghton; 31 October 1829–27 March 1830; matric. 1827 (Trinity), M.A. 1831, Hon. Fellow 1876; author, M.P.; d. 1885.]

72 Pickering, [Percival Andree; 14 November 1829–10 December 1831; matric. 1828 (Trinity), B.A. 1832, Fellow of St John's 1833; barrister; d. 1876.]

73 Monteith, [Robert (Joseph Ignatius); 6 March 1830–9 November 1833; matric. 1829 (Trinity), B.A. 1834; manufacturer; d. 1884.]

74 Garden, [Francis; 6 March 1830–9 November 1833; matric. 1829 (Trinity), B.A. 1833; clergyman, author; d. 1884.]

75 Alford, [Henry; 30 October 1830–18 May 1833; matric. 1828 (Trinity), B.A. (34th Wrangler and 8th Classic) 1832; clergyman, scholar, author, first editor of *Contemporary Review*, Dean of Canterbury; d. 1871.]

76 Farish, [George, brother of no. 42; 30 October 1830–16 February 1833; matric. 1828 (Queens'), B.A. 1832; d. 1836.]

77 Thompson, William Hepworth; [20 November 1830–31 October 1835; matric. 1828 (Trinity), B.A. (4th Classic) 1832, Fellow 1834; clergyman, scholar, teacher, Regius Professor of Greek at Cambridge, Master of Trinity; d. 1886.]

78 Heath, [Douglas Denon, brother of no. 86; 19 February 1831–9 May

1835; matric. 1828 (Trinity), B.A. (Senior Wrangler) 1832, Fellow 1832; barrister, author, judge; d. 1897.]

79 Macaulay, [Kenneth; 10 December 1831–no date of resignation; matric. 1831 (Jesus), B.A. 1835; barrister; d. 1867.]

80 Venables, [George Stovin; 3 March 1832–10 November 1832; matric. 1828 (Jesus), B.A. (5th Classic) 1832, Fellow 1835; barrister, journalist; d. 1888.]

81 Merivale, [Charles; 10 March 1832–1 March 1834; matric. 1826 (St John's), B.A. (4th Classic) 1830, Fellow 1833; clergyman, scholar, author, Dean of Ely; d. 1893.]

82 Morton, [Savile; 31 March 1832–no date of resignation; matric. 1830 (Trinity), B.A. 1834; painter, journalist; d. 1852.]

83 Spring Rice, [Stephen Edmund; 16 February 1833–9 May 1835; matric. 1832 (Trinity); d. 1865.]

84 Lushington, [Henry, brother of no. 87; 25 May 1833–no date of resignation; matric. 1829 (Trinity), B.A. (6th Classic) 1834, Fellow 1836; barrister, Chief Secretary to the Government of Malta; d. 1855.]

85 Helps, [Arthur; 30 November 1833–31 October 1835; matric. 1831 (Trinity), B.A. 1835; barrister, author, K.C.B.; d. 1875.]

86 Heath, John [Moore, brother of no. 78; 15 February 1834–9 May 1835; matric. 1826 (Trinity), B.A. (27th Wrangler) 1830, Fellow 1831; barrister, clergyman, teacher; d. 1882.]

87 Lushington, Edmund [Law, brother of no. 84; 1 March 1834–31 October 1835; matric. 1828 (Trinity), B.A. (Senior Classic) 1832, Fellow 1834; barrister, scholar, Professor of Greek at Glasgow; d. 1893.]

88 Wilkie, William Clarke; [15 November 1834–no date of resignation; matric. 1833 (Queens').]

89 Pollock, William Frederick; [15 November 1834–no date of resignation; matric. 1832 (Trinity), B.A. 1836; barrister, Queen's Remembrancer; d. 1888.]

NOTES

Information omitted

Where no place of publication is given, the book was published in London.

To avoid incessant repetition I have not cited J. A. Venn, *Alumni Cantabrigiensis: A Biographical List of All Known Students, Graduates and Holders of Office at the University of Cambridge, from the Earliest Time to 1900. Part II, from 1752 to 1900*, 6 vols. (Cambridge, 1940–54). This invaluable reference work, to which I am much indebted, contains many errors, generally of transcription: for example, J. W. Blakesley's father was a factor, not an actor. Where possible, I have checked the entries against the sources listed and have made silent corrections in the information given in my text and notes.

Alphabetical list of short titles

The following sources are cited so frequently that I have used short titles for them. The titles of other works are given in full on first citation and thereafter referred to by author (or editor) and short title.

Allen's diary. Unpublished undergraduate diary of John Allen, now in Trinity College Library, Cambridge.

'Annals of a Family'. [Lucilla Young Powell.] 'Annals of a Family Who were all led by a right way to the City of Habitation. Whose faith follow'. Typed transcript of unpublished account of the Maurice family, owned by Mr R. L. Bayne-Powell, who has kindly given a photocopy of the work to Cambridge University Library.

Autobiography of Merivale. *Autobiography and Letters of Charles Merivale, Dean of Ely*. Ed. Judith Anne Merivale. Oxford, 1898. Rev. edn (principally revised by omission of some material) appeared as *Autobiography of Dean Merivale, with Selections from his Correspondence*. 1899.

Autobiography of Taylor. Henry Taylor. *Autobiography, 1800–1875*. 2 vols. 1885.

Blakesley MSS. The papers of J. W. Blakesley, owned by Mrs C. G. Chenevix-Trench.

The Cambridge 'Apostles'. Frances M. Brookfield. *The Cambridge 'Apostles'*. 1906.

Essays and Tales. John Sterling. *Essays and Tales*. Ed. Julius Charles Hare. 2 vols. 1848.

Five Years in an English University. Charles Astor Bristed. *Five Years in an English University*. 2 vols. New York, 1852.

Houghton MSS. The papers of Richard Monckton Milnes, first Lord Houghton, Trinity College Library, Cambridge.

Johnson MSS. Family and other papers, including the papers of W. B. Donne, owned by Miss Mary Barham Johnson.

Keynes MSS. Letters of John Sterling to John Stuart Mill, Keynes MSS, King's College Library, Cambridge.

Laws and Transactions. *Laws and Transactions of the Union Society*. Cambridge, 1822– . I have normally cited the issue of 1834, since a copy is available in Cambridge University Library.

Life of Alford. [Frances Oke Alford.] *Life, Journals and Letters of Henry Alford, D.D., Late Dean of Canterbury*. London, Oxford and Cambridge, 1873.

Life of Hort. A. F. Hort. *Life and Letters of Fenton John Anthony Hort, D.D., D.C.L., LL.D., Sometime Hulsean Professor and Lady Margaret's Reader in Divinity in the University of Cambridge*. 2 vols. 1896.

Life of Maurice. Frederick Maurice. *The Life of Frederick Denison Maurice, Chiefly Told in his Own Letters*. 2 vols. Rev. edn. 1884.

Life of Milnes. T. Wemyss Reid. *The Life, Letters and Friendships of Richard Monckton Milnes, First Lord Houghton*. 2 vols. London, Paris and Melbourne, 1890.

Life of Sterling. Thomas Carlyle. *The Life of John Sterling*. 1851.

'Materials for a Life of A. T.' [Hallam Tennyson.] 'Materials for a Life of A T Collected for my Children'. 8 vols. The first, handwritten draft of this work, Tennyson Research Centre, Lincoln. Differs substantially from the printed version in the British Library and from the final version, *Tennyson: A Memoir* (see below); consists largely of transcripts, in Audrey Tennyson's hand, of letters since destroyed.

'Memoir of Michael Maurice'. Edmund Kell. 'Memoir of the Late Rev. Michael Maurice', *Christian Reformer*, N.S. XI (1855), 407–17.

Memorials of Two Sisters. *Memorials of Two Sisters*. [Ed. Mary Atkinson Maurice.] 1833. Reissued, with additional material, 1837 (3rd edn).

Minutes. Handwritten minutes of the Cambridge Union Society.

Motter MSS. Papers of the late T. H. Vail Motter, Princeton University Library.

Poems of Tennyson. The Poems of Tennyson. Ed. Christopher Ricks. 1969.
Records of a Girlhood. Francis Ann Kemble. *Records of a Girlhood.* 2nd edn. New York, 1883.
Sidgwick: A Memoir. A[rthur] and E[leanor] M[ildred] S[idgwick.] *Henry Sidgwick: A Memoir.* 1906.
Sowing. Leonard Woolf. *Sowing: An Autobiography of the Years 1880–1904.* 1960.
Tennyson: A Memoir. [Hallam Tennyson.] *Alfred Lord Tennyson: A Memoir.* 2 vols. 1897.
Tennyson MSS. Papers in the Tennyson Research Centre, Lincoln.
Thompson MSS. Papers of William Hepworth Thompson, Trinity College Library, Cambridge.
Trench: Letters and Memorials. Richard Chenevix Trench, Archbishop: Letters and Memorials. [Ed. Maria Trench.] 2 vols. 1888.
Vida del General Torrijos. Luisa Saenz de Viniegra de Torrijos. *Vida del General D. José María de Torrijos y Uriarte.* 2 vols. Madrid, 1860.
Writings of Hallam. T. H. Vail Motter. *The Writings of Arthur Hallam, Now First Collected and Edited.* New York and London, 1943.

Chapter 1 The spirit of the Society

1 The nickname may have derived from Cambridge slang, as is suggested in A. M. Terhune, *The Life of Edward FitzGerald, Translator of 'The Rubaiyat of Omar Khayyam'* (1947), 26. The most academically incompetent members of the graduating class, the little cluster of unfortunates whose names appeared at the very bottom of the Ordinary degree list (see p. 12), were termed the Apostles when there were twelve of them. But there were not always twelve, nor does it appear that the earliest members of the Society fell into this group.

Here and elsewhere I use the term 'student' to refer to all persons *in statu pupillari*, whether or not they were undergraduates. The many students who stayed on after taking their degree were an important element at Cambridge and were particularly well represented in the Society after its first few years.

2 See Gordon N. Ray, *Thackeray: The Uses of Adversity (1811–1846)* (New York, Toronto and London, 1955), 128–9; *The Letters and Private Papers of William Makepeace Thackeray*, ed. Gordon N. Ray (1945–6), I, 107–9; Allen's diary, partly quoted in the preceding work, 493–8; *Life of Alford*, 50.

3 But see B. H. Kennedy, 'Introductory Memoir', *Sermons Preached Mainly to Country Congregations, by the Late Rev. Edward Baines, M.A., Vicar of Yalding, Formerly Fellow and Tutor of Christ's College, Cambridge, and Examining Chaplain to the Bishop of Ely,*

ed. Alfred Barry (1883), xv–xvi: 'We met every other Saturday evening to read essays and discuss their subjects, religion and party politics being excluded topics; and for some years we published a magazine called the *Metropolitan*'. Kennedy (an active member in the mid-twenties) was nearly eighty when he wrote this, and his memory may be at fault: 'every other Saturday' probably should be 'every Saturday', and 'some years' certainly should be 'some months'. It is possible that discussion was restricted in the early years of the Society, though this was not the case by Arthur Hallam's time.

4 A further glimpse of the Society's record book is provided in F. J. A. Hort to John Ellerton, 10 July 1851, in *Life of Hort*, I, 198: 'The record book of proceedings is very amusing; think of Maurice voting that virtue in women proceeds more from fear than modesty! It is a good sign that there is always a large number of neutral votes. Some of [?Kemble]'s are ludicrous enough; *e.g.* on the question whether we ought to follow the text of Scripture or the discoveries of science as to the formation of the earth, etc. He votes the latter, adding a note that he considers the question of very little consequence, as he "does not believe in matter"!'

5 *Sowing*, 130.

6 *Sidgwick: A Memoir*, 403.

7 James Spedding to W. B. Donne, 1–4 February 1836, Johnson MSS. Mrs Brookfield renders 'the *dramatic propriety* of his views' as 'the *dramatic profanity* of his views' (*The Cambridge 'Apostles'*, 266).

8 F. W. Cornish, *Extracts from the Letters and Journals of William Cory, Author of 'Ionica'* (Oxford, 1897), 46.

9 *Sidgwick: A Memoir*, 34–5.

10 Note in Kemble's hand in the margin of his copy of Connop Thirlwall, *A Letter to the Rev. Thomas Turton, D.D., Regius Professor of Divinity in the University of Cambridge, and Dean of Peterborough, on the Admission of Dissenters to Academical Degrees* (Cambridge, 1834), 40–1, now in the London Library (Pamphlets 105). Kemble goes on to say, 'In nearly 40 years that the society has existed I can only name three members who have been careless of their privilege. I write this in 1847.' I don't know how Kemble came to misdate the foundation of the Society by ten years.

11 Arthur Helps, *Realmah* (1868), ch. 12.

12 A further extract from the marginal note identified above, n. 10.

13 [A. J. Butler,] review of *Sidgwick: A Memoir*, *Athenaeum*, no. 4092 (31 March 1906), 383–4. For the attribution to Butler, see A. Quiller-Couch, *Memoir of Arthur John Butler* (1917), 118.

14 The lack of secrecy before the eighteen-fifties is evident from many sources, among them *Five Years in an English University*, I, 167–8:

Bristed remarks that the Apostles 'did not make any parade of mystery, or aim at notoriety by any device to attract attention; they did not have special chambers for meeting, with skeletons in the corner, and assemble in them with the secrecy of conspirators; nor did they wear breastpins with initials of bad Greek sentences or other symbolic nonsense on them, as our young Collegians do. They did not attempt to throw any awful veil of secrecy over their proceedings; it was known that they met to read essays and hold discussions, with occasional interludes of supper. I have more than once seen the compositions which were prepared for these meetings: the authors did not seem to think that either the interests or dignity of their club suffered materially from letting an outsider so far behind the scenes.'

Some interesting light on the development of secrecy within the Society is cast by a letter to Lord Houghton in the Houghton MSS, written in 1863 or 1864 by J. J. Cowell, who had been elected to the Society in 1859: 'I was anxious to know whether in your time in Cambridge the Society was kept a secret, or whether the brothers openly talked of it. According to all the traditions in my time it was considered that the Society ought not to be talked about by its members and that much of its utility depended upon its being kept to a great extent secret. This seemed to me so obvious that I had always supposed it was the rule from the earliest times of the Society; until about two years ago some brothers started a new practice and told all about the Society to their friends and acquaintances at Cambridge... [T]he innovators maintain that they are only reverting to the primitive system which prevailed till 12 years ago...Would you tell me whether;

1st publicity or secrecy was the rule
2nd the rule varied and, if so
3rd when? and with what results.
4th Whether publicity or secrecy was the prevailing rule during the few years preceding 1847 and 1848 when the Society was so nearly coming to an end.

My reason for troubling you with these inquiries is this: I and some other brothers intend to address a Remonstrance to the Society on the subject and we wish to know before doing so what were the traditions of the Elders. We are going to remonstrate against their permitting the Apostolic books to be shown to the uninitiated; and against members telling their particular friends all about the Society's proceedings and promising to "get them in".'

In a review of *The Cambridge 'Apostles'* in *The Nation*, LXXXIV (28 February 1907), 205, an American Apostle (William Everett, an active member at about the time of the proposed remonstrance) wrote: 'For several years after its institution the society maintained no particular secrecy. It is a tradition that the various elections and rejections made it extremely unpopular.' This Apostle believed, erroneously, that the active membership had at one point 'dwindled to William Vernon Harcourt and James FitzJames Stephen, both men with infinite capacity for everything, especially making themselves disagreeable', and he claimed that the Society had become secret when 'they ceased to reside' – i.e. in 1851, a date that seems to be corroborated by Cowell's letter. But I am told there is no oath of secrecy as such, despite the *Life of Hort*, I, 171, in which Hort's son credits him with being 'mainly responsible for the wording of the oath which binds the members to a conspiracy of silence'. What Hort probably helped to write was the curse on Roby, for which see *The Autobiography of Bertrand Russell, 1872–1914* (1967), 221.

15 This liberal set seems to have originated in an informal discussion group, the 'Sunday morning philosophical breakfasts' of 1815, for which see Isaac Todhunter, *William Whewell, D.D., Master of Trinity College, Cambridge: An Account of his Writings, with Selections from his Literary and Scientific Correspondence* (1876), 3, 5–6; J. W. Clark, *Old Friends at Cambridge and Elsewhere* (1900), 21.

16 *Essays and Tales*, x–xiii.

17 Sir Frederick Pollock, *For my Grandson: Remembrances of an Ancient Victorian* (1933), 28.

18 *Poems of Tennyson*, 287; *Tennyson: A Memoir*, I, 68, n. 1.

19 'The Lord Bishop of Chester and the London University', *Athenaeum*, no. 26 (23 April 1828), 412–13. Sterling identifies himself as the author of this series of articles in a letter to James Dunn, 2 May 1828, National Library of Scotland.

20 'The Lord Bishop of Chester and the London University. Letter II', *Athenaeum*, no. 27 (30 April 1828), 426–7.

21 'Letter to the Bishop of Chester. No. III', *Athenaeum*, no. 29 (14 May 1828), 460–1.

22 See 'The Universities of Europe and America. Cambridge. – No. I', *Athenaeum*, no. 58 (3 December 1828), 911–12, and 'The Universities of Europe and America. Cambridge. – No. II', *Athenaeum*, no. 60 (17 December 1828), 943–4. The first of these articles, but not the second, is attributed to Maurice by C. J. Gray in the bibliography prefacing the revised edition of the *Life of Maurice*, but the second is plainly by the same hand. The first article contains a passage that may have been one source of inspiration for Tennyson's 'Lines on Cambridge of 1830'. After describing the 'old and reverend splendour' of Cambridge, Maurice remarks that 'the question which the sight of these colleges must suggest to every man is this: "In what degree does the actual mind of Cambridge correspond to the dignity of its monu-

ments, and to that ever-present glory which lives in all its walks, and breathes amid the dimness of those gray cloisters and jewel-windowed chapels?'

23 Thomas Turton, *Thoughts on the Admission of Persons Without Regard to their Religious Opinions to Certain Degrees in the Universities of England* (Cambridge and London, 1834), 23, 26; Thirlwall, *Letter to Turton*, 20, 35, 40. Thirlwall himself was never an Apostle, though he has often been called one; the mistake seems to have begun with Robert Lytton, *Julian Fane: A Memoir* (1871), 25, and is seemingly corroborated by *The Cambridge 'Apostles'*, 303, but Mrs Brookfield has here interpolated words of her own; her transcription of this letter (301–3) should be compared with mine, pp. 186–7.

Chapter 2 The Society in its first years

1 *Fraser's*, LXX (July 1864), 96; *Macmillan's*, XI (November 1864), 18–25. For Christie, see *DNB* (Richard Garnett); *Fraser's*, XXXIV (December 1846), 661–3; *Carlyle and the London Library: Account of its Foundation: Together with Unpublished Letters of Thomas Carlyle to W. D. Christie, C.B.*, ed. Frederic Harrison (1907); Christie's *Notes on Brazilian Questions* (London and Cambridge, 1865); Christie's letters to Milnes, Houghton MSS.

2 The estimate of 1824 was made by an American Apostle, William Everett, in a review of *The Cambridge 'Apostles'* in *The Nation*, LXXXIV (28 February 1907), 205.

3 See Venables' biographical preface to Henry Lushington, *The Italian War, 1848–9, and The Last Italian Poet: Three Essays* (Cambridge, 1859), xliii. For Tomlinson, see S.P.C.K., *Annual Report* (1831–63); Minutes and *Laws and Transactions*; British Library Add. MS. 40343, fols. 303, 313, 321 (letters on Tomlinson's appointment as tutor to Peel's family); Tomlinson's *Report of a Journey to the Levant, Addressed to his Grace the Archbishop of Canterbury, President of the Society for Promoting Christian Knowledge* [1841]; Scott MSS, St John's College Library, Cambridge (biographical material on graduates of St John's compiled by R. F. Scott and F. P. White, includes letters from Tomlinson's daughter describing her father's career and offering to sell a portrait of him by George Richmond to the Society. The offer was considered and declined on behalf of the Society by Walter Leaf and Sir Frederick Pollock, partly because the Society had no place to keep it and partly because Miss Tomlinson wanted much more than its market value).

4 Robert Monteith to Milnes, 4 September 1855, Houghton MSS. For Lushington's career and his view of Tomlinson, see his letters to Milnes,

Houghton MSS, and the biographical preface by Venables identified above, n. 3.

5 Gladstone to his father, 27 September (actually October) 1829, St Deinol's Library, Hawarden, Flintshire; Kemble to Donne, [?early 1833], Johnson MSS. This distrust was persistent: see *Five Years in an English University*, I, 170, and Roden Noel, 'The Cambridge "Apostles"', *New Review*, VIII (1893) 560, for similar reactions in the forties and fifties. Noel says that he once heard the Society 'mentioned with bated breath as the "Society for the Propagation of Atheism," from the fact that twelve students who belonged to it...were at one epoch all Freethinkers'.

6 For Thompson, see *DNB* (E. I. Carlyle); W. R. W. Stephens, *The Life and Letters of Edward A. Freeman, D.C.L., LL.D.* (1895), I, 22–36 – quotation from Thompson to Freeman, 2 September 1839, I, 24; Thompson's *The Life of Hannah More, with Notices of her Sisters* (1838), especially 338–41.

7 Thompson, *Life of Hannah More*, 148–9.

8 For Erasmus Darwin, see Francis Darwin, *The Life and Letters of Charles Darwin, Including an Autobiographical Chapter* (New York, 1898), I, 20–1; *Emma Darwin: A Century of Family Letters, 1792–1896*, ed. Henrietta Litchfield (1915), II, 146–9 – the phrase was borrowed from Alice Meynell's description of her father in *The Rhythm of Life and Other Essays* (1905), 15.

9 Darwin to F. W. Farrar, 5 March 1867, in Reginald Farrar, *The Life of Frederick William Farrar, Sometime Dean of Canterbury* (1904), 104. For Shrewsbury's reputation, see M. L. Clarke, *Classical Education in Britain, 1500–1900* (Cambridge, 1959), 76.

10 Kennedy to Butler, 4 November 1823, in Samuel Butler, *The Life and Letters of Dr Samuel Butler, Head-Master of Shrewsbury School 1798–1836, and Afterwards Bishop of Lichfield, in so far as They Illustrate the Scholastic, Religious, and Social Life of England, 1790–1840* (1896), I, 259.

11 Minutes, 24 February 1824; *Laws and Transactions* (1834), 30–6, 108.

12 Kennedy to Butler, 22 July 1827, in Butler, *Life of Dr Butler*, I, 330.

13 *Life of Maurice*, I, 49; Butler, *The Way of All Flesh* (1903), ch. 27, and see chs. 28, 43, 44, 86.

14 For Kennedy's career and character, see *DNB* (T. E. Page); F. D. How, *Six Great Headmasters: Hawtrey, Moberly, Kennedy, Vaughan, Temple, Bradley* (1904), 89–137; J. E. B. Mayor, 'Obituary: Dr Kennedy', *Classical Review*, III (1889), 226–7, 278–81; G. H. Hallam, 'Dr Kennedy', *Journal of Education* (1 May 1889), 239–41; W. E. Heitland, *Dr Kennedy at Shrewsbury* (pamphlet, reprinted from *The Eagle*, XV (June 1889), in Cambridge University Library) and *After*

Many Years: A Tale of Experiences and Impressions Gathered in the Course of an Obscure Life (Cambridge, 1926), 72–100; Kennedy's *Between Whiles, or, Wayside Amusements of a Waking Life* (1877). Shrewsbury's record under Kennedy was extraordinary; most of his students went to Cambridge, where their success was quite disproportionate to their numbers: 'of the boys who passed under his teaching in the Sixth Form, 42 gained a First in the Classical Tripos, of whom eleven were Senior Classics, nine held the second, and four the third place in the First Class. During the same period his pupils gained, at Oxford and Cambridge, eighteen Classical University Scholarships. . .and not less than twenty-three Porson Prizes. . .It should be remembered that these distinctions, unapproached except by Eton, were gained by a school whose numbers during a great part of Dr Kennedy's Headmastership were but little over 100. . .and that Shrewsbury, unlike Eton and Winchester, was a poor foundation, with no Entrance Scholarships to attract able boys. Able boys were indeed attracted to Shrewsbury, but the inducement which drew them there was the fame of its great teacher.' (G. H. Hallam, 'Dr. Kennedy', 240). The most thorough and revealing account of the methods used by Kennedy to achieve these results is that by Heitland in *After Many Years*; though Heitland chides Samuel Butler for being unkind in his portrait of Kennedy, he provides much fresh evidence to support Butler's view.

15 See *Laws and Transactions* (1834), 35–51, 107–8. By way of contrast, only three of the thirty-two Apostles elected during the Society's first four years were well-known Union figures (although one of the three, John Stock, survived into the next phase). When the Society was founded the authorities' interdict on Union debating (see p. 33) was still in force; in 1821, when debating resumed, John Punnett and James Furnival were Union officers and prominent speakers on the conservative side. Their views seem to have been shared by other founding members of the Society, for H. C. Harford spoke against 'the principles of the French Revolution' and against current schemes for 'promoting the education of the lower orders of Society', while Tomlinson and Punnett were the only speakers on one occasion to oppose Catholic Emancipation. Another Apostle, John Parke, appeared on the liberal side in the same debate; it may be significant that, although Parke was a contemporary of the Society's founders, he was not elected until nearly all of them had left Cambridge and the Society was passing out of its first phase. See *Laws and Transactions* (1834), 16–23.

16 For O'Brien, see *DNB* (G. F. R. Barker); *Annual Register* (1864), part II, 199–201; Robert Kee, *The Green Flag: A History of Irish Nationalism* (1972), 215–16, 247–50, 257–8, 262–3, 266–89.

17 *Autobiography of Merivale*, 81.

18 *Laws and Transactions* (1834), 29, 31, 34, 40–1, 43, 46.

19 *Essays and Tales*, I, viii–ix; *Life of Sterling*, part I, ch. 4.

20 See Peter Allen and Cleve Want, 'The Cambridge "Apostles" as Student Journalists: A Key to Authorship in the *Metropolitan Quarterly Magazine* (1825–26)', *Victorian Periodicals Newsletter*, VI (December 1973), 26–33. This article, based on an annotated copy at the Wilson Library, University of Minnesota, corrects several of the attributions to Maurice made in the bibliography prefacing the *Life of Maurice*.

21 See 'A Lecture on Wordsworth' and 'An Essay on the Poetic Character of Percy Bysshe Shelley, and on the Probable Tendency of his Writings', *Metropolitan Quarterly*, I, 457–79; II, 191–203. Maurice's contributions are notable for their insistent attacks on Benthamism, their defence of religion and literature as associated forces for good, and their contention that the age suffers from an egotistic malaise whose widespread symptoms are party feeling and narrow-mindedness.

22 In order of their election to the Society, the Burians were Edward Romilly, Sydney Gedge, Frederick Malkin, Henry Romilly, Kemble, Donne and James Spedding; Edward FitzGerald and Edward Spedding also attended Bury. The school's popularity with liberal families derived from the reputation of its Headmaster, Dr Benjamin Heath Malkin; see *Autobiography of Merivale*, 65. Malkin was a very unusual teacher: he emphasized independence of thought and width of interests and knowledge rather than scholastic merit of the more ordinary sort, and in the sixth form he gave no examinations but placed boys according to his general sense of their abilities. His judgement was acute: he recognized FitzGerald's extraordinary qualities, for example, and placed him fourth in the school in his final year. But his best students, including Kemble and Spedding (whom he placed at the head of the school), were sometimes unfitted by Bury for the narrowness of the Cambridge system. Spedding points this out and indirectly refers to the large proportion of Burians among the Apostles in a letter to J. W. Donaldson, 3 September 1850, in Donaldson, *A Retrospective Address Read at the Tercentenary Commemoration of King Edward's School...*, 77–89 – a pamphlet bound with two others as *Record of the Tercentenary of the Foundation of King Edward VIth's Free Grammar School, Bury St. Edmunds, on Friday, the 2nd of August, 1850* (Bury St Edmunds and London, 1850). For school-lists, see [S. H. A. Hervey,] *Biographical List of Boys Educated at King Edward VI. Free Grammar School, Bury St Edmunds, from 1550 to 1900*, Suffolk Green Books, No. XIII, (Bury St Edmunds, 1908).

23 The first three meetings of this year, for which see *Laws and Tran-*

sactions (1834), 46, provide good examples of the Apostles' role in the Union. In the first meeting, Thomas Macaulay returned to the scenes of his former glories and was joined by Sunderland, Sterling, Edward Romilly and Kemble in upholding the cause of Catholic Emancipation. The debate was continued the following week, with Kemble, Trench, Buller and Kennedy among the speakers. In the third meeting, Stock, Sterling, Buller, Kemble and Romilly formed the liberal battery (against two Tories) in debating the question, 'Is an Hereditary Aristocracy beneficial to Society?'

24 A rebuke from Sir Robert Peel – 'if the Honourable member for Liskeard will cease for a moment from making a buffoon of himself' – is said to have taught Buller 'to curb his humour in Parliament' (G. M. Wrong, *Charles Buller and Responsible Government* (Oxford, 1926), 57). But he jested privately to the end, for the will he drew up two weeks before his death includes the entry, 'My Adam Smith and J. Mills Political Economy to Thomas Carlyle with the hope that he will improve thereby' (from a copy kindly loaned me by Mr S. H. Grylls).

25 Blakesley to Milnes, 15 November [1830], Houghton MSS.

26 *Ibid.*

27 Maurice's later views appear in a letter he wrote to a fellow-member of Gladstone's essay club, T. D. Acland (13 February 1834, in *Life of Maurice*, I, 162): 'Of Bulwer and such as he, I know not what to say. I remember him at Cambridge taking the tone of a high aristocratical Whig and scoffing at the Benthamites, at the same time that Read, now the editor of the "Morning Post," was talking Radicalism. I have heard of a poor creature in St Luke's in a lucid moment snatching a lady by the arm who was visiting the asylum with the exclamation, "Have you thanked God for your reason today?" and then relapsing into fury. Surely one of these men in a lucid interval might say to either of us, "Have you thanked God to-day for having passed through a debating society with any portion of your souls undestroyed?" and at least to one of us, "Have you meddled with periodicals, and have you thanked God that you still think, love, go to church and find any one to love you?"'

Chapter 3 Thomas Sunderland and the Cambridge Union

1 Transcript of Rev. Richard Gwillym to D. Pugh, 18 June [1867], Houghton MSS; *Laws and Transactions* (1834), 44–5, which however omits the final vote on the occasion of Sunderland's first speech; it was 91–16 (Minutes for 7 November 1826); letter to *The Times*, signed

'Once a President of the Cambridge Union' (?Blakesley), 6 November 1866, p. 6, col. 4.

2 Sterling to Blakesley, 2 February 1828, Blakesley MSS.

3 Kemble to Donne, postmarked 13 January 1829, Johnson MSS.

4 See pp. 41, 52. For 'A Character', see *Poems of Tennyson*, 218–19.

5 *Life of Milnes*, II, 160; 'The Universities of Europe and America. Cambridge. – No. III', *Athenaeum*, no. 64 (14 June 1829), 18 – by 'E.B.' of Christ's College.

6 Milnes to his mother, postmarked 7 November 1827, Houghton MSS; for a rather different transcription of this letter, see *Life of Milnes*, I, 50–1. See also *Laws and Transactions* (1834), 49.

7 Milnes to his father, 6 November [1828], Houghton MSS; Milnes to his father, postmarked 19 February 1829, *ibid.*

8 Hallam to Gladstone, 8 November 1828, British Library Add. MS 44352, fols. 88–9.

9 See W. W. Farr to Gladstone, 6 May 1829, British Library Add. MS 44352, fol. 119; Hallam to Milnes, 21 July [1829], Houghton MSS; *The Gladstone Diaries*, ed. M. R. D. Foot (Oxford, 1968), I, 270–1.

10 *Laws and Transactions* (1834), 48–9; Trench to Milnes, 17 July 1828, Houghton MSS.

11 *Laws and Transactions* (1834), 55; Minutes for 25 November and 2 December 1828.

12 Milnes to his father, postmarked 8 December 1828, Houghton MSS; *Laws and Transactions* (1834), 54.

13 Milnes to his father, postmarked 19 February 1829, Houghton MSS; *Laws and Transactions* (1834), 56.

14 Milnes to his mother, 10 March 1829, Houghton MSS; *Laws and Transactions* (1834), 57.

15 Milnes to his father, 6 November [1828], Houghton MSS; Arthur Buller to Milnes, n.d., *ibid.* Buller refers to his homosexual relation to another student, apparently Richard John St Aubyn, and concludes with a proposition to Milnes himself.

16 Milnes to his father, postmarked 19 February 1829, Houghton MSS; Milnes to his mother, 2 February 1829, *ibid.*

17 J. S. Mill, *Autobiography* (1873), ch. 5; Milnes to his mother, postmarked 27 February 1829, Houghton MSS. See Sterling to Blakesley, 8 February 1829, Blakesley MSS: 'The speech which I made about Wordsworth and Byron had many faults but chiefly that of being too short. The fact is that I ought to have stipulated for being allowed to speak during at least five hours. On the second evening of the Debate there were two or three unhappy performers of nonsense of whom I remember little, – but Mill. . .made an admirable speech in defence of Wordsworth. . .I wish you had heard it. Except in Wordsworth and

Coleridge – and Maurice's conversation – I have never seen or heard any thing like the same quantity of acute and profound poetical criticism. Late in the evening I replied in a speech of half-an-hour, and was obliged from want of time to omit the greater part of what I should have liked to have said. The whole question is involved to my mind (I speak not for others at present) in this; the power of Wordsworth is based upon the strength that of Byron on the weakness of the human mind. Nor is this inconsistent with the fact that much of good and true is expressed in the poetry of the peer. Were it not thus he could interest or excite no one, – for an utter negation of good repels – renders impossible all sympathy.'

18 *Laws and Transactions* (1834), 59–60, which rather surprisingly shows Sunderland to have been a neutral speaker in the latter debate. See also Milnes to his mother, 8 November 1829, in *Life of Milnes*, I, 73.

19 Reprinted in *The Cambridge Union Society: Inaugural Proceedings*, [ed. G. C. Whiteley,] (London and Cambridge, 1866), 64.

20 *Reminiscences and Opinions of Sir Francis Hastings Doyle, 1813–1885*, 2nd edn (1886), 108–13; *Oxford Union Society*, pamphlet, Cambridge University Library, entry for 26 November 1829; J. M. Gaskell to W. W. Farr, 8 December 1829, John Rylands Library, Manchester.

21 Sunderland to Milnes, n.d., Houghton MSS.

22 Kemble to Trench, 1 April 1830, in *Trench: Letters and Memorials*, I, 58.

23 Trench to Kemble, 7 May 1830, *Trench: Letters and Memorials*, I, 63.

24 Milnes to his father, postmarked 13 March 1830, Houghton MSS; Milnes to his father, 11 February 1830, *ibid.*; Milnes to his parents, 25 February [1830], *ibid.*

25 Milnes to his parents, 25 February [1830], Houghton MSS. The prophecy was an accurate one, for his inability to follow a party line was one factor in barring Milnes from the political eminence which he nonetheless continued to want. A thorough and excellent treatment of the difficulties he encountered in his Parliamentary career is provided in James Pope-Hennessy, *Monckton Milnes: The Years of Promise, 1809–1851* (1949), and *Monckton Milnes: The Flight of Youth, 1851–1885* (1951).

26 'The Union Debating Society', poem, Cambridge University Library; S. A. O'Brien to Milnes, 3 November 1830, Houghton MSS; Spedding to Blakesley, 10 June 1835, Blakesley MSS.

27 *Laws and Transactions* (1834), 69–72; L. R. Cogan to Blakesley, 24 August 1832 and transcript of Blakesley's reply (refusing), 26 August 1832, Blakesley MSS. Allen's diary (entry for 16 March 1831) shows that Sunderland also spoke at the Fifty at this time.

28 Sunderland to Milnes, postmarked 25 July 1831, Houghton MSS.

29 Transcript of G.H.E. [error for G.H.C.] Sunderland to D. Pugh, 11 June [1867], Houghton MSS. Sunderland also became a convert to Roman Catholicism: see transcript of Rev. Richard Gwillym to D. Pugh, 18 June [1867], *ibid.*

30 Blakesley to Trench, 24 January 1830, in *Trench: Letters and Memorials*, I, 48.

Chapter 4 Maurice: the making of a Victorian prophet

1 Hallam to Gladstone, [23 June 1830], British Library Add. MS. 44352, fols. 158–9.

2 *Essays and Tales*, I, xiv; Donne to Blakesley, postmarked 22 August 1829, Blakesley MSS; Blakesley to Donne, 2 September 1829, Johnson MSS.

3 Milnes to Aubrey de Vere, 25 May 1837, in *Life of Milnes*, I, 197; for Maurice's attitude to the dinners, see *Life of Maurice*, I, 547–8; for his influence on Hort, see *Life of Hort*, I, 196, which quotes Maurice as saying that his connection with the Apostles 'had moulded his character and determined the whole course of his life'.

4 Donne to Kemble, 2 February 1838, Johnson MSS.

5 Thompson to Blakesley, 5 June 1879, Blakesley MSS – quoted p. 217.

6 See *Life of Maurice*, I, 7; 'Memoir of Michael Maurice', 407–8; *DNB*, s.v. 'Kippis, Andrew', 'Rees, Abraham', 'Savage, Samuel Morton'; Herbert MacLachlan, *English Education under the Test Acts, Being the History of the Non-Conformist Academies, 1662–1880*, University of Manchester Historical Series, no. 59 (Manchester, 1931), 246 ff.

7 Edmund Kell to the editor, in 'Correspondence: The Late Rev. Michael Maurice', *Christian Reformer*, N.S. XI (1855), 561; 'Memoir of Michael Maurice', 414; *Life of Maurice*, I, 6; John Williams, *Memoirs of the Late Reverend Thomas Belsham, Including a Brief Notice of his Published Works and Copious Extracts from his Diary, Letters, etc.* (1833), 445.

8 'Memoir of Michael Maurice', 408; *Life of Maurice*, I, 8–9; 'Annals of a Family', 2–4.

9 *Memorials of Two Sisters* (1833), 3.

10 *Life of Maurice*, I, 19–20, 37; 'Memoir of Michael Maurice', 411.

11 [Emma Corsbie Haldane,] *Memoir of Joseph Hardcastle, Esq., First Treasurer of the London Missionary Society: A Record of the Past for his Descendants* (1860 [actually 1869]), Preface, 7; 'Annals of a Family', 7.

12 'Annals of a Family', 8; [Emma Lydia Maurice,] *The Converted Unitarian: A Short Memoir of E— E—, A Patient Sufferer who Entered into Rest, August 13, 1825* (Philadelphia, n.d.) – the American

edition of a work written by Emma in 1829 and originally published as *Patience in Tribulation, or Memoirs of E. E.* (see *Memorials of Two Sisters* (1833), 6).

13 *Monthly Repository*, IX (1814), 639, which shows that the Maurice family had also suffered the death, eight days before Edmund's, of Mrs Maurice's sister, Elizabeth Goodeve, who lived nearby at Clifton and whose son was a boyhood friend of Frederick Maurice; 'Annals of a Family', 19–20.

14 The former account, a tradition in the Hardcastle family, I owe to Miss Félicité Hardcastle; the latter, a tradition in the Maurice family, to 'Annals of a Family', 22–4.

15 'Annals of a Family', 26, 32; *Memorials of Two Sisters* (1833), 5.

16 *Memorials of Two Sisters* (1837), 22.

17 *Life of Maurice*, I, 22–3; 'Annals of a Family', 27. The child, Joseph Alfred Hardcastle, grew up to become a prominent member of the Society in the eighteen-thirties.

18 Emma Maurice, *The Converted Unitarian*, 80; *Life of Maurice*, I, 25–6, 28–9; 'Annals of a Family', 45.

19 Maurice to his son Frederick, 17 January 1866, Cambridge University Library, Add. MS 7792.

20 'Annals of a Family', 16; *Memorials of Two Sisters* (1837), 178.

21 *Memorials of Two Sisters* (1837), 179–80.

22 *Memorials of Two Sisters* (1833), 24–7; *ibid.* (1837), 182.

23 *Memorials of Two Sisters* (1833), 61, 212.

24 *Memorials of Two Sisters* (1837), 12, 94; *Life of Maurice*, I, 11; Michael Maurice, 'Account of the Late Mr John Bawn of Frenchay', *Christian Reformer*, VIII (1822), 256–61, 333–9, 'Memoir of Michael Maurice', 409–10.

25 'Annals of a Family', 55–9, 69, 72, 118–19; 'Correspondence: The Late Rev. Michael Maurice', *Christian Reformer*, N.S. XI (1855), 521–2, 560–2 – J. P. Gell and Edmund Kell to the editor on Michael Maurice's conversion.

26 J. M. Ludlow, 'Some of the Christian Socialists of 1848 and the Following Years', *Economic Review*, III (1893), 489.

27 A further extract from his letter to his son Frederick, identified above, n. 19.

28 *Ibid.*

29 'Annals of a Family', 39–42; of the many pamphlets on the subject, the most informative is *Unitarianism Untenable and the Believer in the Deity and Atonement of Christ Vindicated from the Charge of Enthusiasm*, 3rd edn (1818).

30 Second among the Society's founders was Edward Cowell Brice, son of a prominent Bristol merchant who lived in Frenchay, where the

Maurice family had settled in 1814. His younger brother, Henry Crane Brice, was also an Apostle, and both became clergymen in the Bristol area. The third of the founders, Henry Thompson, became the curate of Wrington, which was Hannah More's parish and, like Frenchay, in the immediate vicinity of Bristol. Thompson wrote a biography of Hannah More and held strong Evangelical views. The fourth founder was Henry Charles Harford, who later married into the Brice family and settled at Frenchay and whose family was closely associated with Hannah More and William Wilberforce.

31 Kemble to Donne, [1828], Johnson MSS.

32 *Sidgwick: A Memoir*, 403 – quoted, p. 4.

33 *Sowing*, 115–16. From Woolf's ironic account of 'the method' (113–14), it appears to have been original only in their willingness to apply it to a reluctant subject.

Chapter 5 Maurice: the rise of Apostolic theology

1 *Life of Maurice*, I, 15–16, 39–40, 178.

2 *Laws and Transactions* (1834), 33. *Laws and Transactions* (1823) shows that Maurice became a member in the Michaelmas term of 1823; there are no minutes for meetings before that of 11 November 1823, and they do not record his election that term, so that he must have been elected at the first meeting of the year, on 4 November.

3 *Life of Maurice*, I, 49; *Laws and Transactions* (1834), 108. The successful candidate was Edmond Beales, of later Hyde-Park fame.

4 *Life of Maurice*, I, 176, 56.

5 Maurice to his mother, 23 October 1823, c. early November 1823, 28 April 1826, in *Life of Maurice*, I, 48, 50, 71. Macaulay's article appeared in the *Edinburgh Review* for February 1826, and it may have been one influence in bringing about Maurice's second and last appearance as a speaker at the Cambridge Union, on 9 May 1826, when he proposed and opened a debate on the question whether London University 'should possess any exclusive privileges or endowments'. Given the liberal bias of student opinion at the time, the question was hardly controversial: only Maurice and Macaulay's younger brother John spoke, and they won easily by a vote of 54 to 10 – see *Laws and Transactions* (1834), 44.

Maurice's refusal to submit to the religious test demanded of Cambridge graduates is recalled, in a manner that throws some valuable light on Maurice's character, in James Collett Ebden to Charles Kingsley, 19 April 1871, *Life of Maurice*, I, 72–3: 'I was the senior and managing tutor of Trinity Hall when Maurice and John Sterling migrated to that College from Trinity. They both stood very highly in my estimate of them, intellectually and morally. Sterling was the more publicly noticeable man, from his oratorical displays. Maurice, reserved and retired, cultivating a few select and attached friends. Of him I saw much more than the other. When he had kept the terms and exercises for the LL.B. degree, he withdrew to go on with legal studies in London, and, after being there a few months, wrote to me to ascertain what degree of consent and adherence to the doctrines and formularies of the Church of England he would have to profess, in order to [?gain] admission to the degree. I stated to him the required subscription to the 36th Canon. He then requested that his name might be taken from the books, for he was convinced that he could never conscientiously fulfil this requirement. I then suggested to him that, as he was still eighteen months under the five years' standing necessary to the degree, it might be well for him to pause in his determination; that further search and thought might lead him to different conclusions; and that, without any mean or sordid motive, he might well hesitate before renouncing the advantages of a complete University course. His answer was prompt... He directed that the step of cancelling his name on the College books should be taken instantly, for whatever his opinions might eventually be, he would not hazard their being influenced by any considerations of worldly interest.'

6 Trench to Kemble, August 1828, in *Trench: Letters and Memorials*, I, 10; Sterling to Blakesley, 8 February 1829, Blakesley MSS; Blakesley to Donne, 2 September 1829, Johnson MSS; Henry Stebbing, 'The *Athenaeum* in 1828–30', *Athenaeum*, no. 2621 (19 January 1878), 89.

7 *The Gladstone Diaries*, ed. Foot, I, 270–1; see p. 46.

8 'Sketches of Contemporary Authors. No. II. – Mr Jeffrey and the Edinburgh Review', *Athenaeum*, no. 4 (23 January 1828), 49; 'Sketches of Contemporary Authors. No. VIII. – Percy Bysshe Shelley', *Athenaeum*, no. 13 (7 March 1828), 193.

9 'Sketches of Contemporary Authors. No. III. – Mr Southey', *Athenaeum*, no. 5 (29 January 1828), 65.

10 'Sketches of Contemporary Authors. No. I', *Athenaeum*, no. 3 (16 January 1828), 33.

11 'Sketches of Contemporary Authors. No. V. – Mr Wordsworth', *Athenaeum*, no. 8 (19 February 1828), 114.

12 'Sketches of Contemporary Authors. No. IX. – Sir Walter Scott', *Athenaeum*, no. 14 (11 March 1828), 217–18.

13 *Life of Maurice*, I, 178.

14 'The State of Society in England. (Fragments from the Travels of Theodore Elbert, a young Swede.) No. III', *Athenaeum*, no. 31 (28 May 1828), 487. Sterling goes on to mention Thomas Chalmers as being 'in another way' one of the unregarded prophets of the time.

15 'State of Literature in England. The Three Reviews', *Literary Chronicle*, no. 1 (31 May 1828), 10; 'On the Policy of a Union between the University of London and King's College', *Literary Chronicle*, no. 8 (19 July 1838), 113 – both articles appear to be by Maurice. The *Literary Chronicle and Weekly Review*, N.S. (31 May–26 July 1828) exists in a single uncatalogued copy at the Bodleian (Hope 4°86) – a fact for which I am indebted to W. D. Paden's useful article, 'Twenty New Poems Attributed to Tennyson, Praed and Landor', *Victorian Studies*, IV (1961), 195–218, 291–314.

16 'Coleridge's Poems', *Literary Chronicle*, no. 5 (28 June 1828), 68; 'Guesses at Truth', *Athenaeum*, no. 42 (13 August 1828), 656–7 – the latter article is attributed to Maurice by C. J. Gray in the bibliography appended to the revised edition of the *Life of Maurice*.

17 'Characters. – No. 1. The Sectarian', *Literary Chronicle*, no. 5 (28 June 1828), 73–4. The similarity of this characterization to the treatment of sectarianism in the fiction of E. M. Forster strikingly exemplifies the continuity of Apostolic thought.

18 *Life of Maurice*, I, 178.

19 *Life of Maurice*, I, 89–90.

20 *Eustace Conway, or, The Brother and Sister* (1834), I, 21; III, 270.

21 *Eustace Conway*, III, 271–4.

22 The records of this society survive as British Library Add. MS 44809; it lasted from October 1829 to June 1832 and differed in several significant ways from the Society, most notably in excluding the subject of religion from discussions. Maurice was elected on 15 May 1830, when the club was already encountering serious difficulties; unlike other members, he attended regularly and prepared his essays on time; shortly after being elected to the presidency he read an essay on the study of history that was cheered at its conclusion and unanimously supported when it came to the vote. Tennyson's poetry was twice discussed in this society (12 February and 21 May 1831, and on the second occasion the motion that 'Mr Tennyson's poems shewed considerable Genius' was accepted by a vote of 4–3 after heated discussion. Arthur Hallam attended one meeting of the club (11 June 1831) during a visit to Oxford with Frederick Tennyson (*The Gladstone Diaries*, ed. Foot, I, 363).

23 Maurice to his sister Priscilla, 4 January 1831, in *Life of Maurice*, I, 119.

24 Maurice to his mother [?29 October 1831], in *Life of Maurice*, I, 129.

25 Carlyle to Sterling, 9 June 1837, in *Letters of Thomas Carlyle to John Stuart Mill, John Sterling, and Robert Browning*, ed. Alexander Carlyle (1923), 202; *Memories of Old Friends: Being Extracts from the*

Journals and Letters of Caroline Fox of Penjerrick, Cornwall, from 1835 to 1871, ed. Horace N. Pym (1882), 169.

26 Gladstone to Maurice's son Frederick, *Life of Maurice*, II, 208.

Chapter 6 The mystics

1 Sterling to Trench, 24 July 1829, in *Trench: Letters and Memorials*, I, 28; Sterling to Blakesley, 25 November [1829], Blakesley MSS.

2 Sterling to Blakesley, 8 February 1829, Blakesley MSS.

3 *Records of a Girlhood*, 185–6.

4 Kemble to Donne, 4 September [1827], Johnson MSS.

5 *Life of Maurice*, I, 77; Francis Espinasse, *Literary Recollections and Sketches* (1893), 219.

6 Milnes to his mother, postmarked 7 November 1827, Houghton MSS; Kemble to Donne, postmarked 27 August 1827, Johnson MSS.

7 *Essays and Tales*, I, xxv; *Life of Sterling*, part I, ch. 8. The date of this first visit to Highgate was 23 August 1827, according to A. K. Tuell, *John Sterling: A Representative Victorian* (New York, 1941), 240. For Sterling's sense of his indebtedness to Coleridge and Maurice, see *Essays and Tales*, I, xiii–xv. A letter from Sterling to James Dunn, 2 May 1828, National Library of Scotland, contains an ominous reference to the aspect of Coleridge's work that was to become a preoccupation with Sterling: on the occasion of Sterling's second visit (1 May 1828) Coleridge promised to show him 'some MS. Letters' that 'relate to the true meaning of the inspiration of the Scriptures. He says that the first chapter of Genesis is a much later, and more valuable account of the Creation than that which begins at the fourth verse of the 2nd chapter.' – quoted by permission of the Trustees of the National Library of Scotland.

8 Sterling to Blakesley, 25 November [1829], Blakesley MSS.

9 Blakesley to Tennyson, 15 January 1830, 'Materials for a Life of A. T.', vol. I, fols. 94–7. The term 'mousing owl' is an interesting example of the Apostles' sense of their sufferings in an age of inferior minds; it refers to *Macbeth*, II, iv, 11–13: 'On Tuesday last | A falcon, tow'ring in her pride of place, | Was by a mousing owl hawk'd at and kill'd.'

10 'Unpublished Fragments. (From the Travels of Theodore Elbert, a young Swede.) No. II. – London', *Athenaeum*, no. 27 (30 April 1828), 423–4.

11 'The Streets of London. (A Fragment from the Travels of Theodore Elbert, a young Swede.)', *Athenaeum*, no. 43 (20 August 1828), 680–1.

12 For Sterling's influence see Trench to J. C. Hare, undated, in *Essays and Tales*, I, xxxiii.

13 *Poems of Tennyson*, 400; Blakesley to Milnes, 19 March 1838,

Houghton MSS.

14 Trench to Donne, postmarked 13 February 1829, Johnson MSS; Donne to Trench, 5 March [1829], *ibid.*

15 Blakesley to Donne, 2 September 1829, Johnson MSS.

16 Blakesley to Milnes, 15 November [1830], Houghton MSS.

17 [?E. Venables,] obituary of Blakesley, *Guardian*, LX (22 April 1885), 596; 'Were the Mosaic Institutions adapted to promote the happiness of the Jewish Nation', essay, watermarked 1828, Blakesley MSS; Blakesley to Donne, 2 May 1830, Johnson MSS.

18 The subject of Donne's essay is given in Trench to Donne, postmarked 13 February 1829, Johnson MSS.

19 Merivale to Thompson, 20 December 1878, in *Autobiography of Merivale*, 437.

20 *Autobiography of Merivale*, 72–3.

21 Fanny Kemble to H[arriet Leger], January 1828, *Records of a Girlhood*, 122.

22 Milnes to his mother, 2 February 1829, Houghton MSS.

23 *DNB* (William Hunt).

24 Kemble to Donne, 4 September [1827], Johnson MSS; Sterling to Trench, 21 November 1828, in *Trench: Letters and Memorials*, I, 17. For Maurice's influence, see Kemble to Trench, 1 April 1830, *ibid.* I, 57–8.

25 Blakesley to Donne, 2 September 1829, Johnson MSS; Donne to Blakesley, postmarked 22 August 1829, Blakesley MSS; Trench to Donne, 18 October 1829, Johnson MSS.

26 Kemble to Donne, 28 August [1829], Johnson MSS.

27 Kemble to Trench, 1 April 1830, in *Trench: Letters and Memorials*, I, 57; *Poems of Tennyson*, 257; Hallam to Robert Robertson, 14 March 1830, Motter MSS; Hallam to Donne, postmarked 13 February 1831, Johnson MSS.

28 Blakesley to Donne, 2 May 1830, Johnson MSS; Kemble to Donne, postmarked 24 March 1830, *ibid.*; Tennant to Donne, 19 March 1830, *ibid.* The cast-list for this production and the epilogue Milnes wrote for it are given in F. C. Burnand, *The 'A.D.C.': Being Personal Reminiscences of the University Amateur Dramatic Club, Cambridge* (1880), viii–x.

Chapter 7 The Spanish adventure

1 Trench to Donne, postmarked 23 June 1830, Johnson MSS.

2 *Ibid.*

3 Trench to Donne, 21–6 October 1830, Johnson MSS.

4 'Patriotic Songs of Spain', *Metropolitan Quarterly*, I, 349; Kemble to

Donne, 13 January 1829, Johnson MSS. The benefit fund for the Spaniards seems to have been administered with cheerful casualness, to judge from an undated note from Kemble to Blakesley in the Blakesley MSS: 'Dear Blakesley | That most excellent of men, the Secretary, has sent me in such a balance sheet of Receipt and Expenditure it rather floors my comprehension: by it our Expenses (*necessary*) for the year ending Easter 1827 amount to £480:0:0 while our receipts only came to £527:10:0, leaving a balance of £47:10:0 only. All the fund therefore from which we made such liberal donations to the Spaniards etc. including the purchase of books etc. etc., must have been either surplus from the last year, or we must have been drawing upon the fund for the present year. I hope the latter is not the case, for I have a sort of instinctive dread of a National debt, and cannot contemplate without shuddering the chance of a National (or rather, in this case, Social) Bankruptcy. The poor fund however looks very small and I know not what to do. My Cellar is at this moment in a state of destitution, or I would ask you to come and discuss this financial crisis over a bottle with me after Hall; but if you will descend to a cup of Tea, I will wait for you at home this Evening: in which case unless I see you *before*, I shall expect you *early*. Shall you be at the Union after Hall? | Yours very faithfully | J M Kemble.'

5 *Vida del General Torrijos*, I, 325–30.

6 Sterling to Mill, 31 March 1830, Keynes MSS.

7 See Kemble to Trench, 4 July 1830, in *Trench: Letters and Memorials*, I, 75–6; Trench to Donne, 7 July 1830, *ibid.* I, 76 (and Johnson MSS); Kemble and Trench to Donne, 26 August 1830, Johnson MSS.

8 Sterling to Blakesley, 6 June 1830, Blakesley MSS.

9 *Vida del General Torrijos*, I, 369–70; *Life of Sterling*, part I, ch. 10.

10 *Vida del General Torrijos*, I, 370–9, 385. The gold was worth about 17,000 francs or about £680, a fact I owe to the industry of Mr S. Elisha of the Reference Department, University of Toronto Library.

11 For Ojeda's rank, see Vicente Llorens, *Liberales y Romanticos: Una Emigración Española En Ingleterre (1823–1834)* (Mexico City, 1954), p. 97, n. 38 – a work which also provides a useful account of these events.

12 Donne to Blakesley, postmarked 1 September 1830, Blakesley MSS.

13 Kemble and Trench to Donne, 26 August 1830, Johnson MSS.

14 Fanny Kemble to H[arriet Leger], 9 March 1831, in *Records of a Girlhood*, 356; Kemble and Trench to Blakesley, 28 August 1830, reported in James Spedding to Donne, 21 September 1830, Johnson MSS.

15 *Vida del General Torrijos*, I, 379, 381; Llorens, *Liberales y Romanticos*, 108.

16 Trench to Donne, 21–6 October 1830, Johnson MSS; *Vida del General Torrijos*, I, 385–90.
17 Kemble and Trench to Blakesley, 28 August 1830, quoted in Blakesley to Donne, postmarked 24 September 1830, Johnson MSS.
18 Hallam to Donne, [?3 November 1830], Johnson MSS.
19 Sterling to Blakesley, 23 September 1830, Blakesley MSS.
20 Trench to Donne, 21–6 October 1830, Johnson MSS; *Vida del General Torrijos*, I, 390–1.
21 Kemble to Donne, 26 October 1830, quoted in Donne to Blakesley, 11 November [1830], Blakesley MSS.
22 Donne to Blakesley, [?8 November 1830], Blakesley MSS.
23 Donne to Blakesley, 11 November [1830], Blakesley MSS.
24 *Vida del General Torrijos*, I, 391–3, 402.
25 *Vida del General Torrijos*, I, 394, 397, 399–400, 403, 405.
26 *Vida del General Torrijos*, I, 405, 409–27; *Annual Register* (1831), 440–1.
27 Hallam to Donne, postmarked 13 February 1831, Johnson MSS.
28 Fanny Kemble to H[arriet Leger], 9 March 1831, in *Records of a Girlhood*, 355–6; Sterling to Trench, 31 March 1831, in *Trench: Letters and Memorials*, I, 85–6.
29 Donne to Blakesley, 14 May [1831], Blakesley MSS.
30 Kemble to Trench, 28 May 1831, in *Trench: Letters and Memorials*, I, 89.
31 *Vida del General Torrijos*, I, 437–547; 'The Execution of General Torrijos and Robert Boyd', *English Historical Review*, XX (1905), 766–7. If fifty-three set out from Gibraltar and only forty-nine were shot, it seems likely that the Royalist spies in Torrijos' party were four in number.
32 *Life of Sterling*, part I, ch. 13; Sterling to Mill, [March, 1832], Keynes MSS.
33 Sterling to Mill, 18 June 1832, Keynes MSS.

Chapter 8 The Society in the early thirties

1 Hallam to Trench, 2 December 1830, in *Trench: Letters and Memorials*, I, 84.
2 'Swing, at Cambridge', in [Henry Lushington and G. S. Venables,] *Joint Compositions* [1840], 13–25.
3 Sterling to Blakesley, 24 March 1831, Blakesley MSS.
4 Hallam to Trench, 6 March 1831, in *Trench: Letters and Memorials*, I, 85.
5 Trench to Kemble, 29 May 1831, in *Trench: Letters and Memorials*, I, 90.

6 Trench to Kemble, 16 July 1831, in *Trench: Letters and Memorials*, I, 96.

7 Trench to Maurice, 10 October 1831, in *Trench: Letters and Memorials*, I, 101. Trench's discipleship is evident from many passages in his correspondence with Donne (Johnson MSS), all carefully omitted from the *Letters and Memorials*.

8 *Life of Milnes*, I, 108–9; Trench to his brother Francis, 17 November 1831, in *Trench: Letters and Memorials*, I, 102; Spedding to Blakesley, [?1830], Blakesley MSS.

9 For a useful account of the movement, see Norman Cohn, 'The Saint-Simonian Portent', *Twentieth Century*, CLII (1952), 330–40, and Richard K. P. Pankhurst, 'Saint-Simonism in England', *ibid.* 499–512; CLIII (1953), 47–58.

10 Trench to Donne, 6 December 1831, Johnson MSS.

11 Trench to Donne, 11 December 1831, Johnson MSS.

12 *Poems of Tennyson*, 399–400; Hallam to Trench, 12 February 1832, in *Trench: Letters and Memorials*, I, 106.

13 Trench and Blakesley to Donne, 9 January 1832, Johnson MSS.

14 Hallam to W. H. Brookfield, postmarked 3 May 1832, Huntington Library; Donne to Blakesley, 31 July [1831], Blakesley MSS.

15 Sterling to Trench, 19 February 1832, in *Trench: Letters and Memorials*, I, 109–10, and *Essays and Tales*, xliii.

16 Sterling to Trench, 31 August 1832, in *Trench: Letters and Memorials*, I, 119, and *Essays and Tales*, xlvi; Sterling to Mill, 18 September 1832, Keynes MSS.

17 Sterling to Blakesley, 13 November 1832, 17 December 1832, 22 February 1833, Blakesley MSS. Sterling's reference is to ch. 12 of Scott's *The Monastery*.

18 Blakesley to Thompson, 14 September 1833, Blakesley MSS.

19 Hare's travel diary for 1833 (owned by Mr R. L. Bayne-Powell and made available to me through the kindness of Merrill Distad) has the following entry for 15 June 1833: 'It so happens also that Sterling one of my favourite pupils is here with his wife and two children. He is an admirable and most amiable person, full of enthusiasm and genius, and extravagantly grateful to me for the little kindness I shewed him while he was at Cambridge. He has exprest himself about me in print, in a manner which quite confounded me when I read the words. The thing I look back to with most satisfaction, as connected with my tutorial offices at Cambridge, is that he and his friend Maurice, two of the young men of the highest promise of the age, say that they have been under obligation to my lectures. I have been spending the day with him very pleasantly.' And see *Essays and Tales*, xlvii.

20 H. M. Butler to Hallam Tennyson, 15 November 1886, Tennyson MSS; *Poems of Tennyson*, 175–6.

21 Leslie Stephen, *Some Early Impressions* (1924), 23; Milnes to his mother, 10 March 1829, Houghton MSS; Lushington to Milnes, n.d., *ibid*. Versions of the 'v.g./v.q.' story appear in several sources; it seems to have been traditional in Cambridge gossip.

22 Francis Garden to Milnes, 11 November [?1834], Houghton MSS.

23 My information is drawn in part from Henry Sidgwick to Hallam Tennyson, 14 November 1894, Tennyson MSS, which gives a partial transcription of the Society's record book during the period of Hallam's membership. It should be noted that Thompson's is not an eye-witness account, since he was not elected to the Society until some months after Tennyson's resignation.

24 Douglas Heath to Hallam Tennyson, 9 October 1894, Tennyson MSS. Heath was quoting from 'The Epic', ll. 50–1; see *Poems of Tennyson*, 584.

25 Tennant to Tennyson, 8 June 1834, 'Materials for a Life of A. T'. vol. I, fol. 205; Hort to Tennyson, 14 May 1856, Tennyson MSS; Tennyson to Pollock, [1866], in W. F. Pollock, *Personal Remembrances* (1887), II, 151. The dinner of 1855 occurred on 20 June. It may be that Tennyson never actually attended one of the annual dinners: at least, I have been unable to discover any evidence that he did. In A. W. Brown's useful monograph *The Metaphysical Society: Victorian Minds in Crisis, 1869–1880* (New York, 1947), it is stated (p. 7) that Tennyson attended the dinner of 1880, but the source is *The Cambridge 'Apostles'*, which is misleading. Mrs Brookfield says (p. 249) that on Richard Milne's seventy-first birthday 'he assisted at an "Apostles'" dinner. There was still a group of College contemporaries to be toasted and talked over; Venables, Spedding, Tennyson and Trench were all four still alive.' Mrs Brookfield does not state that all four were present, but one might draw that conclusion. My copy of *The Cambridge 'Apostles'*, however, has marginal corrections corresponding to a review of the book in the *Athenaeum*, no. 4133 (12 January 1907), 39; the review was written by A. J. Butler (a fact for which I am indebted to Mr R. Welch of the *New Statesman*); and Butler (an Apostle of the mid-sixties) has several comments to make about these sentences. In his review he points out that the dinner was held three days before Milnes' birthday, that he presided rather than assisted, and that 'three of his contemporaries were present to support him'. Butler's marginal notes identify the three as Venables, Merivale and Blakesley, and this is borne out by Venables' journal entry for that day (Venables MSS, National Library of Wales), which mentions Blakesley and Merivale and would certainly have mentioned Tennyson if he had been there.

26 See Blakesley to Donne, 2 September 1829, Johnson MSS; Blakesley to Trench, 24 January 1830, in *Trench: Letters and Memorials*, I, 48–50; Blakesley to Tennyson, 15 January 1830, in 'Materials for a Life of A.T.', vol. I, fols. 93, 98. The name 'Leighton' has been heavily crossed out but is still legible, although the word was mistakenly read as 'Lightfoot' in a printed version of the 'Materials'. The reference is to William [Allport] Leighton (1805–1889) of St John's.

27 Allen's diary, entry for 12 September 1830; *Life of Alford*, 60–1, 65 (where there appears to be an error of transcription, since Alford became an Apostle in October, not April).

Chapter 9 Arthur Hallam

1 Alford to his fiancée, [1833], *Life of Alford*, 94.

2 Hallam to Gladstone, 8 November [1828], British Library Add. MS. 44352; Hallam to his sister Ellen, [3 December 1828], Christ Church College Library, Oxford.

3 For Milnes' comments on Hallam see his letters to his father, 6 November [1828]; to his father, postmarked 8 December 1828 ('I have a very deep respect for Hallam – Thirlwall is actually captivated with him – he really seems to know every thing from metaphysics to cookery – I dine with him, Thirlwall and Hare (what a parti quarré we shall be!) on Wednesday.'); to his father, postmarked 19 February 1829; to his mother, postmarked 27 February 1829; to his sister Harriette, postmarked 7 March 1829; to his mother, postmarked 12 June 1829; to his father, postmarked 23 October 1829; to his parents, 25 February [1830] – all in the Houghton MSS. For Hallam's views see Hallam to Gladstone, postmarked 28 February 1829, British Library Add. MS. 44352, in which he names his fellow-Etonian John Frere as his only 'close' friend in the 'metaphysical set' with whom he spent most of his time and dismisses Milnes as a 'kindhearted fellow, as well as a very clever one, but vain, and paradoxical'.

4 Hallam's *Timbuctoo* (*Writings of Hallam*, 37–44) is prefaced by a quotation from Wordsworth and accompanied by notes that identify Coleridge as one source of inspiration, refer to 'those few conversations which it is my delight to have held' with Coleridge, and provide an extensive quotation from 'that wonderful Poem', 'Mr Shelley's "Alastor" '.

5 Hallam to Robert Robertson, 6 July 1829, Motter MSS.

6 Hallam to Milnes, 21 July [1829], Houghton MSS.

7 Hallam to Milnes, 15 August [1829], Houghton MSS.

8 Hallam to Milnes, 1 September [1829], Houghton MSS.

9 Hallam to Milnes, 21 July [1829], Houghton MSS; Hallam to Milnes,

postmarked 14 October 1829, *ibid.*; Hallam to Gladstone, [14 September 1829], British Library Add. MS 44352.

10 Hallam to Robert Robertson, [?12] December 1829, Motter MSS.

11 Hallam to Robert Robertson, 14 March 1830, Motter MSS.

12 Hallam to Blakesley, [April 1830], Blakesley MSS. In Charles Tennyson's *Sonnets and Fugitive Pieces* (Cambridge, 1830) sonnet II begins 'When lovers' lips from kissing disunite | With sound as soft as mellow fruitage breaking, | They loath to quit what was so sweet in taking', and sonnet XLII describes 'bowers and dewy lawns unseen' as 'ringing all with thrushes on the left, | And finches on the right, to greet the sheen | Of the May-dawn' (these lines were later rewritten).

13 *Writings of Hallam*, 182–98; the quotation is from p. 190.

14 Hallam to Milnes, 22 August [1831], Houghton MSS; James Spedding to Blakesley, 10 September 1831, Blakesley MSS.

15 Hallam to Edward Spedding, 23 August [1831], Motter MSS.

16 For the complete poem see *Poems of Tennyson*, 349–50, and for an important analysis of it see F. E. L. Priestley, *Language and Structure in Tennyson's Poetry* (1973), 33–4.

17 Monteith to Milnes, 10 February 1831, Houghton MSS. Hallam's dominance over the Apostles is further illustrated in S. A. O'Brien to Milnes, [?2 March 1831] and 3 November 1830, *ibid.*

18 Hallam to Donne, 29 January [1832], Arents Collection, New York Public Library.

19 Hallam to Kemble, [14 June 1832], Beinecke Library, Yale.

20 Hallam to Emily Tennyson, postmarked 23 June 1832, Wellesley College Library; Edward Spedding to Donne, 27 June 1832, Johnson MSS; Edward Spedding to Blakesley, 11 July 1832, Blakesley MSS. For Tennyson's powers of mimicry, see Sir Charles Tennyson, *Alfred Tennyson*, rev. edn (1968), 75–6.

21 Hallam to Kemble, [July 1832], Motter MSS.

22 For the complete poem see *Poems of Tennyson*, 463–6.

23 Hallam to J. M. Gaskell, 8 September 1832, in *Records of an Eton Schoolboy*, ed. C. M. Gaskell (1883), 171.

24 Hallam to Tennyson, 13 September 1832, Tennyson MSS.

25 Hallam to Kemble, [18 October 1832], Motter MSS.

26 James Spedding to Thompson, 4 March 1833, Thompson MSS. In Kemble to Donne, [1833], Johnson MSS, Kemble writes from Cambridge, 'We had a delightful Anniversary on Saturday fortnight, and drank your health with Apostolic zeal. The London people have made themselves into a Society which they emulously have christened the "Fathers" but I am afraid it does not get on very well, its members being old, dull, and lazy: yea some of them have made themselves eunuchs for the Kingdom of God.'

27 Hallam to Milnes, 8 May [1832], Houghton MSS; Hallam to Emily Tennyson, 1 March [1833], Wellesley College Library; James Spedding to Thompson, 4 March 1833, Thompson MSS.

28 Blakesley to Thompson, 16 April 1833, Blakesley MSS: Blakesley names Savile Morton as the chief offender among the Apostles at Cambridge. Hallam to Emily Tennyson, [5 April 1833], Tennyson MSS, gives a pleasant picture of the two Tennysons' visit: 'Yesterday Mary, Alfred and I went to the Zoological Gardens where Mary made friends with several wild animals. Today we have seen the great Microscope and all the horrible lions and tigers which lie "perdus" in a drop of spring water. Poll [Mary] was much pleased and said it was "quite shocking" which I need not tell you means in Somersby language delightful. Today Alfred and Poll called on my mother and I took him up into my room leaving Poll to chat with my mother and Ellen in the drawing room. Then a walk in the park occurred, after which a dinner of salt fish and parsnips, in which the two male Heaths participated. Tomorrow we meditate grand things if the weather be fine – that is we shall take a boat to the Tower. Mary as you know has never been on the water, so it will be very pleasant to her.'

29 Spring Rice to Blakesley, 1 August [1833], Blakesley MSS; Garden to Milnes, 24 September [1833], Houghton MSS. Spring Rice ends his letter by saying that he had seen Hallam the day before, 'but I could not recollect what your message to him was, so I gave him some other which will do as well'.

30 Blakesley to his family, 4 November 1833, Blakesley MSS.

31 Garden and Monteith to Tennyson, 14 December 1833, 'Materials for a Life of A.T.', vol. 1, fols. 189–203. Garden's portion of this letter contains an interesting passage: 'Depend upon it, it is only in abstract questions that you can have strictly logical proof, and that in practical ones, conviction is wrought in a different way, but is not the less truly and rightly conviction for that. You rely, and fearlessly believe in a Mother's and a friend's affection, though you might by applying to these cases, the principles of doubt which I have heard you apply to Christianity, doubt the reality of these. Depend on it our Heavenly Father's love rests on surer ground still than these. Once open your eyes to it, and you will feel well assured that even in the sad affliction he has now sent you there is a love, which the concentrated contemplation you could give it throughout your immortality, would not enable you to grasp.'

32 Alford to Merivale, [1833], *Life of Alford*, 92. It might be thought that Arthur Hallam's younger brother Henry, who was a central figure among the Apostles of the early forties and like Arthur died suddenly in early life, would also belong to this inner circle, but he was thirteen

years younger than Arthur and hence belonged to an entirely different generation.

33 *Writings of Hallam*, 29; Hallam to Milnes, 21 July [1829], Houghton MSS; *Writings of Hallam*, 34; Hallam to Milnes, 1 September [1829], Houghton MSS; *Writings of Hallam*, 133–42 – the quotation is from p. 136.

34 *Writings of Hallam*, 144–5, 151–4, 157–61.

35 *Writings of Hallam*, 241, n. 2, 207, 210–11, 224–5, 269.

36 Hallam to Milnes, 1 September [1829], Houghton MSS; *Writings of Hallam*, 210–11, 157, 160; *In Memoriam*, XCVI; for Hallam's views on Providential love see Hallam to Gladstone, [14 September 1829], British Library Add. MS 44352 (the passage has been printed in John Morley's *Life of William Ewart Gladstone* (1903), I, 66–7).

37 *In Memoriam*, LXXXVII.

Chapter 10 The Round Table in the thirties and forties

1 Thompson to Blakesley, 11 November 1833, Blakesley MSS. Thompson was mistaken in thinking that Tennyson was returning from Hallam's funeral; it did not occur until 3 January 1834, and Tennyson did not attend. For a further account of Trench's visit to Donne, see Donne to Kemble, 24 October 1833, Johnson MSS; 'he preached two admirable sermons, full of zeal, truth and knowledge. Our folk who are weekly requested not to drink nor fornicate, and sometimes are told "to be obedient to the higher Powers," were delighted, and amazed at once. I carried him to see two of his brethren: but much to his grief, one, drest in a plush-shooting coat and leathers, asked him whether he had been at a Fancy Ball: and the other quoted Plays and talked slang – As if Elijah had made a call upon Queen Jezebel's private Chaplain.'

2 Tennant to Tennyson, October 1834, 'Materials for a Life of A.T.', vol. I, fol. 230. For one example of Hallam Tennyson's habit of omitting phrases and adding ones he himself invented, see the version of this letter that appears in *Tennyson: A Memoir*, I, 44.

3 Tennant to Tennyson, October 1834, 'Materials for a Life of A.T.', vol. I, fols. 230–1; Blakesley to Thompson, 15 September 1834, Blakesley MSS; Donne to Blakesley, 2 September 1836, *ibid.*; Kemble to Donne, 25 October [1836], Johnson MSS. Kemble describes the reception of his lectures in an undated letter to Donne in the Johnson MSS; his difficulties at Cambridge are evident from several sources, among them Joseph Romilly's diary and an undated letter from Kemble to Whewell in the Whewell MSS, Trinity College Library, Cambridge (Add MS c 89, letter 75). His most important treatment of his views of education

is his article on Cambridge in the *British and Foreign Review*, v (July 1837), 168–209. In his belief that the central problem was the Church's control over education he was entirely in line with the tradition of liberal intellectualism that I describe in ch. 12.

4 Thompson to Blakesley, 5 November 1836, Blakesley MSS.

5 Blakesley to Thompson, 13 September 1836, Blakesley MSS; Thompson to Blakesley, 27 April 1837, *ibid.*

6 Thompson to Milnes, 11 April 1837, Houghton MSS.

7 James Spedding to Thompson, 21 June 1832, Thompson MSS. His treatment of the St Simonians, in another of these letters to Thompson (4 November [1833]), is equally characteristic: 'The St Simonians have burst forth again,' he writes from London: 'and the Father holds fortnightly meetings in Burton Crescent, in whiskers and moustaches of great vigour, which (taken together with the character of the neighbourhood) leave little doubt of the speedy development of the free woman; who has become a Mother since the last accounts, and Mothers they say are not so common among that class. I have half a mind to buy a curly Wig and go to the next meeting incog.' Arthur Buller, Spedding goes on to say, 'thinks of dressing up as a woman and offering himself as candidate for the Motherhood'. The next two lines have been cut out of this letter.

8 See W. Aldis Wright, 'James Spedding', in *Tennyson and his Friends*, ed. Hallam Tennyson (1912), 435; *Memoir of Tennyson*, I, 38; *Autobiography of Taylor*, II, 213–14.

9 Spedding to Thompson, 27 August 1832, 8 September 1832, Thompson MSS. His uncle had died not long after his brother.

10 Spedding to Thompson, 1834, Thompson MSS. His friends were fond of making jokes about Spedding's head, which was balding and domelike; hence his reference to disguising himself with a curly wig in the letter quoted in n. 7, above.

11 Spedding to Thompson, 29 August [1834], Thompson MSS.

12 *Autobiography of Taylor*, I, 234–5, 238–9; Blakesley to Thompson, 20 September 1837, Blakesley MSS.

13 Spedding to Thompson, 29 August [1834], Thompson MSS.

14 Sterling to Blakesley, 16 May 1834, Blakesley MSS.

15 See R. E. Prothero and G. G. Bradley, *The Life and Correspondence of Arthur Penrhyn Stanley, D.D., Late Dean of Westminster* (1893), I, 112; Spedding to Thompson, 10 November 1835, Thompson MSS.

16 Spedding to Blakesley, 10 June 1835, Blakesley MSS.

17 See *Life of Maurice*, I, 182; Blakesley to Spedding, 2 August 1835, Blakesley MSS; Spedding to Thompson, 15 June 1835, Thompson MSS.

18 *The Kingdom of Christ, or, Hints to a Quaker Respecting the Prin-*

ciples, Constitution and Ordinances of the Catholic Church, ed. A. R. Vidler (1958), II, 322; I, 242.

19 Thompson to Milnes, 11 April 1837, Houghton MSS; Trench to Donne, 18 May 1837, Johnson MSS; Blakesley to Thompson, 20 September 1837, Blakesley MSS; Donne to Blakesley, 24 January 1839, *ibid.*

20 Henry Lushington to Milnes, 2 January 1837, Houghton MSS.

21 Monteith to Milnes, 31 December 1838, Houghton MSS; Venables to Milnes, 29 May 1837, *ibid.*; Monteith to Milnes, [?October 1839], *ibid.*

22 Spedding to Thompson, 17 November 1840, Thompson MSS; Blakesley to Thompson, 23 November 1840, Blakesley MSS.

23 Thompson to Blakesley, 5 November 1836, Blakesley MSS; Donne to Blakesley, 14 October [1839] and [1841], *ibid.*; H. V. Johnson to Donne, 20 August [1842], Johnson MSS; Venables to Milnes, 3 December [no year given], Houghton MSS; Henry Lushington to Milnes, 11 December 1843, *ibid.*

24 Spedding to Milnes, 22 June 1837, Houghton MSS; Blakesley to Milnes, 4 June 1841, *ibid.*; Donne to Trench, May 1851, Johnson MSS.

25 Donne to Blakesley, 19 November [1837], Blakesley MSS.

26 Donne to Blakesley, 18 May [1838], Blakesley MSS. Charles Buller was a prominent member and Arthur Buller a minor member of the Durham Commission.

27 Thompson to Blakesley, 1 October 1838, Blakesley MSS. Hare numbered three Apostles – Sterling, Tennant and Garden – among his curates in the thirties.

28 Henry Lushington to Milnes, 27 September 1839, Houghton MSS.

29 Henry Lushington to Milnes, 9–10 January 1842, Houghton MSS.

30 Kemble to Donne, [?8 May] 1842, Johnson MSS.

31 Henry Lushington to Milnes, 17 September [?1844], Houghton MSS.

32 Henry Lushington to Milnes, 3 December 1845, Houghton MSS.

Chapter 11 The Sterling Club

1 *Five Years in an English University*, I, 166–70. Cambridge University Library has a copy of the second edition of this work (one volume, 1852), with marginal notes that have been taken from a copy owned by F. W. Bowring (B.A. 1844) and that identify most of Bristed's pseudonyms and oblique references; the comment on Bristed's early reputation as a bore occurs on p. 120. The four University Scholars referred to by Bristed were Henry Maine, William Johnson, Franklin Lushington and Charles Evans.

2 See Sterling to Mill, 22 February 1838 and two further letters of August 1838, Keynes MSS.

3 Sterling to Hare, June 1838, in J. C. Hare, *The True Remedy for the Evils of the Age: A Charge to the Clergy of the Archdeaconry of Lewes, Delivered at the Ordinary Visitation in 1849, with Notes, Especially on the Educational, Matrimonial and Baptismal Questions,* reprinted in his *Charges to the Clergy of the Archdeaconry of Lewes, Delivered at the Ordinary Visitations from the Year 1840 to 1854, with Notes on the Principal Events Affecting the Church During that Period* (Cambridge, 1856), vol. III. The charge is separately paginated; the quotation occurs on p. 124.

4 Sterling to Mill, endorsed 14 July 1838, Keynes MSS; Spedding to Blakesley, 18 July 1838, Blakesley MSS.

5 Donne to Blakesley, 16 August 1838, Blakesley MSS.

6 Spedding to Donne, 25 July 1838, Johnson MSS. Further details about the founding of the club may be found in Blakesley to Milnes, 16 July 1838, Houghton MSS; Spedding to Blakesley, 18 July 1838 and 27 July 1838, Blakesley MSS. Mrs Brookfield's transcription of this letter is inaccurate (*The Cambridge 'Apostles'*, 301–3.)

7 Lyttelton to Blakesley, 20 March 1843, Blakesley MSS. For lists of Sterling Club members see *Life of Sterling*, part II, ch. 6; Pollock, *Personal Remembrances*, I, 113–14, 192, 239, 248; C. and F. Brookfield, *Mrs Brookfield and her Circle* (1905), I, 150, 156; A. R. Ashwell and R. G. Wilberforce, *Life of the Right Reverend Samuel Wilberforce, D.D., Lord Bishop of Oxford and Afterwards of Winchester, with Selections from his Diaries and Correspondence* (1880–2), I, 142, 153; *Record*, 8 and 15 March 1849.

8 Sterling to Hare, [?August] 1838, in Hare, *The True Remedy*, 124–5; *ibid.* 125.

9 Trench to Donne, 24 October 1838, Johnson MSS.

10 Hare, *The True Remedy*, 125–6.

11 Among the younger Apostles who joined the Sterling Club were W. F. Pollock, W. D. Christie, Charles Spring Rice, Horace Mansfield, H. F. Hallam and (apparently) Tom Taylor. Kenneth Macaulay was also a member. On the other hand the absence of certain Apostles may be noted, especially that of Kemble. The Blakesley MSS contain a somewhat mysterious letter of 3 May [1840] from Stephen Spring Rice to Blakesley: 'I am in the same mind that I was about Milnes – and being so, I am perfectly aware that I have no business to become a member of such a club as the Sterling.' But he may have changed his mind, for two Spring Rices were members by 1845 (C. and F. Brookfield, *Mrs Brookfield and her Circle*, I, 150).

12 Ashwell and Wilberforce, *Life of Samuel Wilberforce*, I, 142; Milnes to John Allen, 20 April 1849, in R. M. Grier, *John Allen, Vicar of Prees and Archdeacon of Salop: A Memoir* (1889) 132; *ibid.* 126–7.

13 Trench to his wife, 30 April 1840, in *Trench: Letters and Memorials*, I, 248. And see Ashwell and Wilberforce, *Life of Samuel Wilberforce*, I, 153.

14 Sterling to Emerson, 7 October 1843, in *A Correspondence between John Sterling and Ralph Waldo Emerson, with a Sketch of Sterling's Life*, ed. E. W. Emerson (Boston and New York, 1897), 71. Among the 'lads' who sympathized with Sterling was his young cousin William Coningham (see p. 161, above), who added his mite to the controversy over Sterling by anonymously publishing *Twelve Letters by John Sterling* (Brighton, 1851), a work that makes Sterling's rejection of Christianity quite plain and that Coningham published (as he admitted in the third edition, 1872) in the hope of 'dispersing the medieval darkness' of the time.

15 *Life of Sterling*, part I, ch. I; Hare to Whewell, 4 February 1848 and [?1848], Whewell MSS, Trinity College Library, Cambridge; *Memories of Old Friends*, ed. Pym, 279.

16 E. H. P[lumptre], 'Memoir', in *Guests at Truth, by Two Brothers* (1866), xxxviii; *Life of Sterling*, part I, ch. I.

17 *Politics for the People* (27 May 1848), 58. Such passages earned Kingsley the reputation of a radical in some circles, and brought Maurice a protest from his old friend J. C. Hare, but Kingsley was (as usual) only putting Maurice's ideas in his own words: Maurice had suggested that he write a series of articles 'about the right and wrong use of the Bible — I mean, protesting against the notion of turning it into a book for keeping the poor in order' (Maurice to Kingsley, 22 April 1848, *Life of Maurice*, I, 463).

18 For earlier reviews, see *English Review*, VII (March 1847), 163–70 and VII (June 1847), 440–3: the quotation is from p. 441. For the attack on Maurice, see X (September 1848), 213–14. For Palmer's article, see X (December 1848), 399–444.

19 *English Review*, X (December 1848), 401, 436–7.

20 *Thou Shalt Not Bear False Witness Against Thy Neighbour: A Letter to the Editor of the English Review, with a Letter from Professor Maurice to the Author*, reprinted in J. C. Hare, *Miscellaneous Pamphlets on Some of the Leading Questions Agitated in the Church During the Last Ten Years* (Cambridge, 1855); Maurice's statement is on p. 63 of the pamphlet, which is separately paginated. For a rebuttal of Hare's pamphlet, see *English Review*, XI (March 1849), 181–94. On the publication of a new edition of Coleridge's *Confessions of an Inquiring Spirit*, ed. H. N. Coleridge, the *English Review* took the opportunity to elaborate upon the thesis of Palmer's article; in their words (XII (December 1849), 251), to show 'that Coleridge, Blanco White, Sterling, and [J. A.] Froude agreed substantially in their view

of the authority of Holy Scripture; and thus to evince the insecurity of Coleridge's principle, and that of his disciples, from its results'.

21 The *Record* opened the subject on 1 March 1849 and returned to it at frequent intervals during March, April and May and less frequently for several months thereafter. The issues referred to and quoted are those of 1 March, 8 March, 15 March, 26 March, 29 March, 9 April, 19 April, and 26 April.

22 Manning to Wilberforce, 21 March 1849, Wilberforce Archive, West Sussex Record Office, County Hall, Chichester, MS 96, letter no. 65–made available to me through the kindness of Merrill Distad and quoted by permission of the West Sussex Record Office.

23 John Allen to the secretary of the Sterling Club (not identified), 30 March 1849, and the secretary's reply, in Grier, *John Allen: A Memoir*, 128–9; *Life of Sterling*, part II, ch. 6. The further history of the club, renamed the Tuesday Club, is not known to me.

24 Hare, *The True Remedy*, 123–4.

25 'Mr Brown's Letters to a Young Man About Town. Mr Brown The Elder Takes Mr Brown the Younger to a Club', *Punch*, XVII (1849), 187.

Chapter 12 The old order and the new

1 See Noel Annan, 'The Intellectual Aristocracy', in *Studies in Social History: A Tribute to G. M. Trevelyan*, ed. J. H. Plumb (1955), 243–87; the quotation occurs on p. 247. The term 'new intelligentsia' has also been taken from this article. Among the most valuable of recent writings on the new intelligentsia are Sheldon Rothblatt, *The Revolution of the Dons: Cambridge and Society in Victorian England* (1968) and Christopher Harvie, *The Lights of Liberalism: University Liberals and the Challenge of Democracy, 1860–86* (1976).

2 *Letters to the English Public on the Condition, Abuses, and Capabilities of the National Universities. No. I. By a Graduate of Cambridge* (1836), 14, 8–9.

3 Butler, *The Way of All Flesh*, ch. 47. It is an interesting fact that Patrick Brunty, who called himself Brontë to obscure his social origins, was one of the Johnian sizars in the early years of the century: one of the main reasons that his daughters turned to writing novels was that they knew of no other way of making themselves known to other people of taste and education. Charlotte Brontë established contacts with G. H. Lewes and Elizabeth Gaskell, who belonged to quite distinct and yet interestingly related social and intellectual circles. Mrs Gaskell had significant social links with F. D. Maurice and his circle, but Thackeray was the only major novelist of the period who can be said to

have belonged to the Apostles' milieu. The sociology of Victorian novel-writing would repay close study.

4 The friend of Thompson was W. H. Brookfield, and the story is recalled in Charles H. E. Brookfield, *Random Reminiscences* (1902), 51. Leslie Stephen's sarcastic comment is from *Some Early Impressions* (1924), 21. For an excellent treatment of the academic system at this time see Robert Robson, 'Trinity College in the Age of Peel', *Ideas and Institutions of Victorian Britain: Essays in Honour of George Kitson Clark*, ed. Robson (1967), 312–35.

5 Milnes to C. J. MacCarthy, *Life of Milnes*, I, 263. For a highly perceptive treatment of Thirlwall and the Apostles in their relation to the Broad Church movement, see J. C. Thirlwall, *Connop Thirlwall: Historian and Theologian* (1936).

6 Maurice to Hare, November 1843, in *Life of Maurice*, I, 358.

7 For fuller exposition of my views on Christian Socialism see 'F. D. Maurice and J. M. Ludlow: A Reassessment of the Leaders of Christian Socialism', *Victorian Studies*, XI (1968), 461–82, and 'Christian Socialism and the Broad Church Circle', *Dalhousie Review*, XLIX (1969), 58–68.

8 See *Life of Maurice*, II, 304–5.

9 The subject of this clipping is Charles William Stubbs (1845–1912), Dean of Ely 1894–1906, Bishop of Truro 1906–12, and a well-known advocate of Christian Socialism.

10 Sidgwick to A. C. Benson, [1897], in A. C. Benson, *The Life of Edward White Benson, Sometime Archbishop of Canterbury* (1899), I, 249–50.

11 Sidgwick to Oscar Browning, November 1865, in *Sidgwick: A Memoir* 133; *ibid.* 135, 137–8. For an excellent account of Sidgwick's attitude to the tradition of liberal Anglican moral thought at Cambridge, see J. B. Schneewind, 'Sidgwick and the Cambridge Moralists', *The Monist*, LVIII (1974), 371–404.

12 Maurice to Kingsley, 22 September 1829, in *Life of Maurice*, II, 591; *Sidgwick: A Memoir*, 205–6, 219.

13 See Blakesley to Thompson, 23 November 1840, Blakesley MSS; unsigned obituary of Blakesley, *Saturday Review*, 25 April 1885, 533–4; *DNB* (E. Venables).

14 Thirlwall to Milnes, 26 June 1851, in *Life of Milnes*, I, 448; G. S. Venables' biographical preface to *Some Writings and Speeches of Richard Monckton Milnes, Lord Houghton, in the Last Year of his Life* (1888). Milnes' relation to the younger members of the Society is evident from many letters in the Houghton MSS, chief among them Henry Lushington to Milnes, 2 January 1837; Vernon Lushington to Milnes, [17 November 1855]; H. M. Butler to Milnes, 9 July 1864 (one of several letters in which members of the Society reply to Milnes'

request at the dinner of 1864 that those present supply him with photographs of themselves; these photographs are, unfortunately, not with the Houghton MSS); William Everett to Milnes, [1865]; J. K. Stephen to Milnes, 27 March [1880]; J. J. Cowell to Milnes, [1863 or 1864] – quoted above, p. 229.

15 Donne to Blakesley, 18 April 1845, Blakesley MSS; Venables to Milnes, 23 December [1849], Houghton MSS. Smyth's successor was Sir James Stephen, father of J. F. and Leslie Stephen.

16 See Walter F. Cannon, 'Scientists and Broad Churchmen: An Early Victorian Intellectual Network', *Journal of British Studies*, IV (1964), 65–88.

17 J. F. Stephen to Venables, 1 August 1887, in Leslie Stephen, *The Life of Sir James FitzJames Stephen, Bart., K.C.S.I., A Judge of the High Court of Justice* (1895), 467 (and see 151–2); unsigned obituary of Venables, *Saturday Review*, 13 October 1888, 419–20.

18 The character of Venables' emotional life is evident from many sources, chief among them his personal journals for the years 1839–83, now at the National Library of Wales. For Venables' jealousy of Tennyson, see Venables to Emily Tennyson, 2 October [1855], Tennyson MSS.

19 *Autobiography of Taylor*, II, 208–9.

20 The anecdote about Seeley's lecture has several sources: mine was a clipping from *Pall Mall* (2 October 1886) in the J. W. Clark collection, Cambridge University Library; Merivale to Venables, 30 December 1886, Venables MSS, National Library of Wales.

21 Thompson to Blakesley, 5 June 1879, Blakesley MSS; Douglas Heath to Hallam Tennyson, 9 October 1894, Tennyson MSS.

22 This speech is enclosed in Donald MacAlister to William Everett, 24 June 1908, William Everett MSS, Massachusetts Historical Society, Boston, and is quoted with the kind permission of the Massachusetts Historical Society. The dinner of 1908 is also described in J. M. E. McTaggart to Nathaniel Wedd, 25 June 1908, Wedd MSS, King's College Library, Cambridge.

INDEX

WITHD